# INTEGRATIONS

Reading,
Thinking,
and Writing
for College Success

# INTEGRATIONS

## Reading, Thinking, and Writing for College Success

*William S. Robinson*
*Pam Altman*

THOMSON

HEINLE

Australia • Canada • Mexico • Singapore • Spain
United Kingdom • United States

# THOMSON

# HEINLE

English Editor: Stephen Dalphin
Development Editor: Amy McGaughey
Marketing Manager: Kenneth S. Kasee
Project Manager, Editorial Production: Barrett Lackey
Print/Media Buyer: Mary Beth Hennebury
Production Service: Impressions Book and Journal Services, Inc.
Copy Editor: Sarah Brown
Cover Image: Untitled by Kurt Schwitters. © Christie's Images/Corbis
Cover Printer: Webcom Limited
Compositor: Impressions Book and Journal Services, Inc.
Printer: Webcom Limited

Printed in Canada
1 2 3 4 5 6 7 05 04 03 02 01

For more information about our products, contact us at:
Thomson Learning Academic Resource Center
1-800-423-0563

For permission to use material from this text, contact us by:
Phone: 1-800-730-2214
Fax: 1-800-730-2215
Web: www.thomsonrights.com

ISBN: 0-15-50995-5
Library of Congress Catalog Card Number: 2002100333

Asia
Thomson Learning
60 Albert Street, #15-01
Albert Complex
Singapore 189969

Australia
Nelson Thomson Learning
102 Dodds Street
South Melbourne, Victoria 3205
Australia

Canada
Nelson Thomson Learning
1120 Birchmount Road
Toronto, Ontario M1K 5G4
Canada

Europe/Middle East/Africa
Thomson Learning
Berkshire House
168-173 High Holborn
London WC1 V7AA
United Kingdom

# Contents

# To the Student

We don't know how you feel about writing. You may not like it much. Or if you don't dislike it, you at least would rather do something else. That's not surprising.

Writing is not natural. Speaking is. All of us are born with a gene that tells us we have to talk, but we are not born with a gene that tells us we have to write. Still, we have learned that writing is essential to our development as human beings, so there we are. If we want to grow as individuals and as a society, we depend on the written word, and there's no getting around it. You know that as well as we do.

There is, however, an idea afloat that everyone should be able to write expertly. We don't understand why people think this way. No one thinks that everyone should be able to play baseball or the clarinet really well or that we should all be equally good scientists or philosophers. Why should we all be equally good writers? We aren't, and we never will be. At the same time, we don't need to be able to hit a curveball or play the Mozart Clarinet Quintet or discover the theory of relativity in order to make our way productively through life. And we don't need to be able to write expertly either. But if we aspire to a profession, if we want to live the life of an educated person, we pretty much need to write at least competently.

Some textbooks, adopting a cheerful tone, say or imply that writing is easy, if you only learn the rules. But that's not true. Writing is hard, and there are no rules. A famous British novelist once said, "There are three rules for writing well. Unfortunately, no one knows what they are." You may have heard that writing isn't as hard as you think, but that's incorrect too. It is as hard as you think. But even though it's not easy, it isn't impossible. Millions of people do it every day, and a lot of them earn their living doing it, so there must be a way. And there is.

Sometimes people who haven't had to do a lot of writing in their lives go about writing in the wrong way, and the process they use often makes writing more difficult for them than it has to be. One common problem is believing that writers sit down and write everything out fluently in one shot. This is by no means the case. In fact, nobody writes that way; it may interest you to know that what you are reading now is the fourth draft of this little essay. If you try to write what you have to write in one sitting, getting everything perfect the first time, your writing will be something a lot like a disaster.  So one of the main purposes of this book is to help you develop a better way of tackling your writing assignments, one that will help you write better than you have before.

Most people who feel that their writing isn't very good think that their "grammar" is bad, and in fact, they may even have been told this by teachers. But this is extremely unlikely. Children learn all of the grammar of a language at a very young age, usually around four. If they didn't, they wouldn't be able to understand anything said to them, and they wouldn't be able to talk to others. They wouldn't be able to understand what they hear on TV, not even *Sesame Street.* If you can hold a normal conversation, you know as much grammar as anyone else, including trained grammarians.

You may, however, be a little weak in what grammarians call "usage." "Usage" is mostly, although not entirely, those rules that affect only written English, not its spoken forms. Things like spelling, using apostrophes, knowing the difference between *its* and *it's,* punctuation, making subjects and verbs agree, and so on, are usage matters, and if you haven't done much reading and writing, you may not know as many of the rules for these things as you ought to. And so this book is also designed to help you with any usage problems you may have.

But writing well isn't just a matter of writing correct sentences. Writing well involves being able to organize a whole discourse, a paper if you like, and a big part of this book is designed to help you do that. In particular, it will help you organize the kinds of papers you will be called upon to write in college, which is probably a good idea since that's where you are. And you'll even learn to read better and think critically about what you read.

But then maybe you're wondering why you should bother making the effort to do all this. Certainly lots of people make a good living without writing, and not all of them are professional athletes. Perhaps if you're inventive enough and lucky enough and willing to work hard enough, you might be able to start your own business, hire a secretary to do your writing, and wind up with your own private jet. But for most people, that seems like kind of a long shot. Most of us have to make up resumes and write letters of application or fill out long forms in order to get a job, and some organizations even give writing tests to job applicants because they need people who can write clear, accurate reports and memos. And many of you will need to write essays for graduate school applications. If your writing is clear, organized, and error free, your chances of getting into graduate school or getting a good job are greatly increased.

Many people with poor writing skills do get hired to low-level jobs, of course, and if that's all right with you, then working on your writing may not be necessary. In fact, going to college may not be necessary.

If your written English is pretty weak, one class will probably not turn you into a fluent, skilled writer. As we said earlier, writing well is not easy. But if you put your share of work into your writing, you can make a major difference and build a solid foundation for further improvement. Like learning any difficult skill, it's a slow process, but it can be done, and it usually turns out to be worth it.

Good luck.

*—WSR/PA*

# To the Teacher

*Que sais-je?* What do I know? It was the question Michel de Montaigne asked himself, not in a spirit of self-congratulation but in a spirit of skeptical inquiry, the question that led him to create the essay (*essai* = attempt, exploration) and to write a series of the greatest essays in Western literature. It's the question more of us composition teachers, in the spirit of Montaigne, would do well to ask ourselves as we prepare our courses. And we might do even better by adding a second question: How do I know it?

In the composition program at San Francisco State, instructors are hired from among graduate students in English who have taken a minimum of four courses in the English language and the teaching of writing and who have passed competitive written and oral exams. They are expected to know their field, to be familiar with the best research, and to understand how to put it into practice.

Of course, other people show up periodically looking for work, as they do everywhere, and when I was running the composition program, I always gave them the courtesy of an interview. I always began with the same question and always got the same answer. The question was, "Tell me what you know about the teaching of writing," and the answer always began with the words, "Well, what I do is . . . " Montaigne didn't ask himself what he did. He asked himself what he knew.

But that always turned out to be a mystifying question, even when put in English rather than French. The idea that one should know something in order to teach writing, it turns out, seems for the most part an alien concept. In our imaginations, let us transform my interviews into similar ones conducted in the office of a department chair in, say, physics, or chemistry, or history, or psychology—in any academic field excepting the creative arts. Would a question like "what do you know?" be asked? Of course not. Knowledge of the field would be assumed and questions would be directed at specialized areas within the field. And no candidate would respond to a knowledge question by saying, "Well, what I do is . . . "

Is teaching composition, then, a creative art like painting or dance? Is it a field where the only thing that counts is individuality and imagination? In other words, is this a field where one approach is as good as another?

Or are there demonstrably better and worse ways? And if there are, how do we know which are the better and which the worse?

## Why This Rather than That?

As it happens, a lot of empirical research has been done in the area of teaching writing, and as it also happens, this research has pointed in very specific directions. Different approaches have been shown to work and others not to work. And the results of all this research are available. Some of it isn't easy to find, but most of it is, and the teacher's manual for this book will explore much of it. Interestingly, much of what has been learned is, to the person embarking on the teaching of writing, counterintuitive. Looking at a student's badly written text, the first thing one notices is errors. How to improve the writer? Get rid of the errors. Of course we want to rid our student papers of their errors, but designing a course to address that problem exclusively has been shown not to work. Another ready perception is that the weak student needs a good grammar course. Actually, no. Studies upon studies have shown that grammar programs have no effect whatever on writing ability.

What the grammar and error-elimination approaches have in common is that they define good writing in simply error-free sentences. Students quickly learn to produce good writing by this definition by dumbing down their sentences so that no error is possible. But, of course, that is only a facsimile of good writing. Good writing encompasses the ability to compose a logical, coherent discourse on an intellectually challenging subject that employs not only correct usages but also something like the full range of the syntactic resources of the English language. When the student who can produce a sequence of correct dumbed-down sentences in an essay with no intellectual content has to write on a reasonably challenging subject, as tends to happen in college, *everything* falls apart, including the carefully learned rules of usage. Everyone has heard the expression, "He can't even write a sentence—how can he write a paper?" We now know that this is exactly backward. He can't write a sentence *because* he can't write a paper.

## The Three Basics of Basic Writing

Research has shown that our basic writing courses should be informed by three ideas. The first is to improve reading comprehension. The most basic problem our weak student writers have is that they are poor readers. They have successfully mastered the task of decoding the words on the page—they can read in this sense—but their comprehension of what they have decoded is very poor. Meaning comes in contexts, not in individual words or even sentences, but students who end up in basic writing classes don't understand this. Here is an example. Following are the first two paragraphs of a short item from a newspaper:

> A North Hollywood man, victimized by burglars two months ago, shot and killed his 3-year-old son early yesterday when he mistook the boy's shadow for that of an intruder, police said. Manuel Sesmas, 30, told police that he and his wife, Nely, were awakened by the opening and closing of their bedroom door at 3:45 a.m. . . .

In a class I taught, the five weakest students thought that "a North Hollywood man" and "Manuel Sesmas" were two different people, even though that made no sense whatever. But this didn't alert them to a problem. Their readings *never* made any sense to them. It was normal. When basic writing students read an essay in which an author explains a position in order to refute it, they see both the position and the rebuttal as expressing the author's point of view. They work out meaning sentence by sentence, not in terms of sentences (or paragraphs) in larger contexts, and so they don't notice that the meaning they find makes no sense in the overall context. Because they don't understand how texts work, they can't produce them. If the text comprehension problem is not addressed in the basic writing course, there will be no improvement in the students' ability to write—that is, to create mature coherent texts.

The second idea is to make sure we understand the difference between "declarative" and "procedural" knowledge and not to confuse them in what and how we teach. In short form, declarative knowledge is knowledge of *what*, and procedural knowledge is knowledge of *how*. In writing, obviously, there is a certain amount of declarative knowledge one needs—knowledge of the rules of usage, knowledge of how texts are put together—but simply acquiring this knowledge won't do the trick. If it would, we could teach our writing classes in large lecture halls. But learning to write, like learning to make a cabinet or ride a bicycle, involves procedural knowledge, which means assignments and teacher help that address not *what* but *how*. Athletic teams understand this distinction; that's why they have coaches rather than manuals of rules.

Finally, we must forget the trite maxim, "I want to start my course with where the students are at." That is exactly what we do not want to do. There is no point in addressing what students can already do. Learning takes place at what Lev Vygotsky, in *Thought and Language*, calls the "zone of proximal development"—that is, the place where students can learn with help.

So our basic writing classes should be informed by these three ideas. Since our students are poor readers who do not know how to construct the kinds of texts valued in the academic and professional worlds, they must be set to work improving both their reading and writing abilities simultaneously. They must further begin learning these procedural tasks immediately, not wasting time on tasks they can already accomplish. And finally we must provide them with the right kind of procedural help to enable them to achieve these skills.

## Something Completely Different

We have learned from several important studies that the single most effective way to improve student writing is to use what one researcher has called "inquiry" writing assignments. Many teachers, perhaps most, believe that students write best about what they already know and that, in consequence, they should be given topics that will enable them to draw on their experience. But, again, what seems intuitively correct turns out to be wrong. Inquiry topics produce longer, better papers, papers that demonstrate a greater commitment by the student writer to the task, than papers based on personal experience.

In inquiry assignments, the teacher sets up a specific problem to be solved or discussed in a particular way and, in most cases, provides the data with which to address the problem. Inquiry topics thus mimic the kinds of writing assignments students are usually given in their other classes, and so are particularly relevant to the freshman composition enterprise. The student does not have to wrack her brains to find a topic, does not have to find (or invent) "specifics" with which to develop the topic, and does not have to learn invention heuristics, an enterprise for which there is no perceptible market outside traditional English classes.

Because inquiry topics, properly used, require the whole class to work on the same assignment, using the same data, they offer a number of very powerful advantages. For one thing, it becomes easy for the teacher to critique papers that do not adequately deal with the data or that present unreasonable inferences, so that critical thinking becomes an integral part of the writing class. It is a truism that basic writers tend also to be students whose inferencing skills are poor. Well-designed inquiry topics address this issue by requiring the students to make sensible inferences. When they do not, the teacher will know it, whether during class discussion, at the planning or drafting stage, or in the final version. At the same time, such topics obviously enable the teacher to help students develop their reading skills as well. Separate lessons or exercises in reading and inferencing are not necessary. Skills in these areas develop as students and teacher work together on the writing assignments. Inquiry topics also enable the teacher to bring much of the writing process into the classroom, a difficult thing to do when everyone is working on a separate project.

The most traditional way of teaching composition has been to provide the students with sets of rules for composing texts and then send them home to apply those rules. In this approach, students are given rules for writing introductions and conclusions, for forming thesis and topic sentences, for developing paragraphs, even for organizing the whole essay, regardless of subject. The teacher then reads the finished products and assigns grades based primarily not on content, which has been rendered essentially irrelevant, but on how well the rules have been followed. If students review each other's rough drafts, they are looking not at content but at how well or poorly the rules for composing have been followed. There will be no serious discussion of an issue because there is no issue to discuss. No thinking will take place, because none is expected. This is not the way writers write, and to the student victim it is sterile and boring.

The creation of a text, a procedural process, cannot be taught through declarative means, not to mention the fact that the rules for introductions and all the rest have no basis in reality. The ultimate travesty of this approach is the five-paragraph essay formula, which is to be found nowhere in the world of real discourse and which does not teach the student how to organize an effective paper when presented with an assignment requiring real discussion of a real issue.

## Collaborative Learning

Collaborative approaches to composition have had a rocky history. Praised in theory, they have usually proven difficult and frustrating in fact. Much of the problem comes back to the personal essay, the basis for most assignments. How can you tell whether a rough draft is well organized when you don't know the material it's based on? How can you tell whether the development is really appropriate? And how many students want to critique the personal writing of a peer? But when they're all involved in the same enterprise and that enterprise involves a shared problem, they can discuss issues facing them intelligently, learning from each other. They can talk about the crucial issues of content and organization in meaningful ways, and they can pool their weak editing skills.

Just as importantly, collaboration in planning and drafting has a strikingly positive effect on class morale. Lacking confidence in an endeavor at which they know they are unskilled, basic writers naturally assume that everyone else can do the task better than they can. Moreover, working alone, they tend to procrastinate, to stall, to try not to start something they know will turn out badly. When they can work together, they encourage each other and see that others are in the same boat they are. Working in pairs or threes in class, they can call on the teacher for help and get it, instead of getting red marks on the product and a low grade. Perhaps even more important, when students work together, they get to know each other, and the classroom becomes a valued social setting, one to look forward to. In the teacher's manual, you will find suggestions for making collaboration work with the material of this book.

## How to Use This Book

The assignments in this book are not organized rhetorically in traditional ways. There is an excellent argument to be made for using at least some elements of a rhetorical approach. Studies have shown that there is no market in the academy or the professional world for extended descriptions, narratives, or process analyses, but a case can be made for classifying, comparing, analyzing, and arguing. But there is also evidence that very few texts turn out to be classification or comparison essays. Generally, these are tools used for wider ends. The ability to classify, to compare, to analyze is a skill that goes into the production of most kinds of academic/professional texts, but these modes seldom govern those texts. Accordingly, while the assignments in this book cannot easily be put into the traditional rhetorical modes, they involve developing the same skills.

The chapters are sequenced according to degree of difficulty. The first four chapters contain made-up problems designed to develop students' skills without defeating them. The assignments in Chapter 5 contain published readings about real-life issues, and those in Chapter 6 are historically based, topics in which students evaluate real events in the past that bear on the present or have some greater than usual intrinsic interest. Chapter 7 involves students in more extensive reading and writing about problems we face today, and Chapter 8, while also providing readings on a current topic, guides students to conduct further research using primary sources. When there is a difference between the assignments in a chapter, the last assignment is the more difficult. Beginning in Chapter 5, words most likely unfamiliar to students are preceded by numbers in parentheses; their definitions are listed by number in a glossary at the end of each chapter.

*The instructor should choose one writing assignment from each chapter unless he or she finds that the students need more practice in a chapter.* It would be a very good idea for the instructor to read each set of assignments in a chapter before deciding which to use. There are about three or four times as many writing assignments here than one could expect to handle in a semester-long basic writing course, so instructors should decide which ones they feel most comfortable with.

The sentence-level issues covered in the Getting Your Writing Right sections of the seven main chapters fall into two categories—error-elimination material and sentence-building material. *It is crucial that the class complete these exercises well before they write their final drafts so that they can benefit from this work when they write.* In addition, there is a workbook section at the end of the text in which many common errors are covered.

## Using the Workbook

The mechanical issues covered in Chapters 1 through 7 are the most likely to benefit every member of the average American basic writing class, if there can be said to be such a thing. Problems most likely to crop up among individual students are covered in the Workbook.

Since the lessons in the Workbook are self-teaching, each student should be assigned, one or two at a time, lessons that address mechanical issues that show up in their writing. These assignments should be done over the course of the term, and the instructor should keep track of them.

When grading papers, one should not mark down for errors in matters that the class or individual students have not yet studied. On the other hand, one should insist upon correctness in the ones they have. At the same time, one must remember that doing exercises does not necessarily enable students to master an issue immediately. There can be, and often is, a gap between the successful completion of exercises and the student's ability to incorporate new knowledge into his or her text production. In such cases, a checkmark should be made in the margin alongside the line where the error appears, and the student's grade withheld until he or she finds and corrects the error(s).

## The Easy Way and the Hard Way

The easy way to teach basic writing is to order a grammar workbook and have one's students do the exercises day in and day out. It's a lot easier to correct exercises than it is to read whole papers, and it gets easier all the time since students get bored with doing them, don't see the point (because there isn't any), and start dropping out. But this is the hard way to teach them to write because it doesn't work.

The hard way to teach basic writing is to use a textbook like this one and actually have the students dealing with all the real-life issues of composing mature texts. It's hard because they do so badly at first, and it's hard because they present so many problems that have to be addressed. But it's the easy to teach them to write because it works.

For the teacher who uses this approach, there is also (naturally) a hard way and an easy, or at least easier, way. The hard way is to shortcut the process of making each essay, to rely on lecturing (declarative teaching) rather than having students work together (procedural). Another part of the hard way is to mark every single error each student makes on each paper. This takes a great deal of time, and it defeats the student. It is easier and more effective to see error elimination as a long-term project, with each student working gradually to get rid of his or her own errors, and no one held accountable for ones they haven't yet worked on. For more on error analysis and approaching error productively, see the teacher's manual.

The good thing about this way of teaching basic writing is that students find it interesting and motivating, and both students and teachers will be surprised, by the end of the term, at how much they've been able to accomplish. For the first time in their lives, probably, most of the students will have written papers they can genuinely be proud of.

—*WSR*

# A Note

This book has been designed for use in a beginning-level basic writing course, and most of the book's material has been class tested at that level at both San Francisco State University and City College of San Francisco. We would like to thank our colleagues at both colleges, particularly Susan Zimmerman and Linda Legaspi of CCSF. We also want to thank the reviewers of *Integrations*, Nancy Anter, Wayne State University; Caren Kessler, Blue Ridge Community College; Robin Ramsey, Albuquerque Technical Vocational Institute; Linda Ranucci, Kent State University; Brian Richards, Shawnee State University; and Karen Standridge, Pikes Peak Community College, for their careful consideration of this text and their valuable suggestions. Much gratitude goes to our editor at Heinle and Heinle, Steve Dalphin, and Editorial Assistant Amy McGaughey for their expertise and patient support throughout the publication process.

For those interested in looking further into composition research and theory, there is a more thorough essay on the subject in the teacher's manual along with a bibliography. We further strongly recommend the teacher's manual for discussions of encouraging collaborative learning in the basic writing course, approaching the writing topics, teaching organization, presenting the Getting Your Writing Right sections, and responding to student papers.

# CHAPTER ONE
## Choosing Options

### In This Course You Will Write Essays

An essay is a piece of writing shorter than book length that isn't a story. It explains something to you or informs you about something or argues a point. It might appear as a newspaper or magazine article, or as an article in a professional journal—say, an engineering or psychology journal—or it might be a paper you have to write for a course you are taking. All of those things are essays. If you have a typical college career, you will have to write a lot of essays. If you go on to a professional career after college, you may well have to write a lot more essays. In both of these cases, the quality of your essays will have much to do with your success.

### How Do You Write an Essay?

The obvious answer is the wrong answer. You don't just sit down and start writing.

In most of the instances in which you have to write an essay, you will have little or no choice about your subject. You won't have to sit and think up something to write about. Rather, your teacher or your boss will have a definite idea about what he or she wants you to produce, and you'll have to produce that. Nobody will care whether you like the subject or not. Nobody will care whether you think the assignment is fun. All they'll want is good results.

If you decide to get your kitchen remodeled, you hire a cabinetmaker, tell him or her exactly what you want, and expect good results. The same is true for papers in school and reports in the professional world. You are the cabinetmaker, and whoever tells you what to produce will expect good results.

Most writing assignments will require you either to report on information you have acquired or solve a problem and report your solution. Most of the time, you will have to do quite a bit of reading as the basis for your paper.

## THE WRITING PROCESS

Normally, you'll go through something like the following process:

   a. Acquire the information you need.
   b. Think about what it means and how you need to use it.
   c. Make a plan for how you'll organize your paper.
   d. Write a rough draft of your paper.
   e. Revise the rough draft.
   f. Write the final version of the paper.
   g. Proofread the paper.

In most professional situations, collaboration—working with others—is very common. In this course, you will work with other members of the class and with the teacher in many steps in the process of writing your papers.

- Each chapter in this book contains case studies that are the basis for writing assignments. You will find the information you will need for each writing assignment in each **Case Study,** specific instructions for each assignment under **Assignment,** and guidance for approaching the writing task under **Discussion.**
- With classmates, as you follow **steps** given in each assignment, you will think about what the information in the case means, how you will need to use it, and how you can organize your essay, following **organization guidelines** for each case.

- A **Checklist for Evaluating Rough Drafts** will help you evaluate your own rough draft as well as the drafts of other members of your writing group.
- While you are going through the steps in the writing process, you will also be working on the **Getting Your Writing Right** section in each chapter to develop your writing skills and proofreading strategies.

The following are general guidelines for building a paper, and you will be given specific guidelines with each writing assignment in this book.

## Building a Paper

### Introductions and Thesis Statements

As you know, essays of whatever kind need introductions. Introductions come in two basic varieties. One kind is the "grabber" introduction you usually find in magazine articles. This introduction is designed to startle or intrigue readers so that they will want to read what follows. Here's a fairly typical grabber introduction from a popular magazine:

> My blind date is trudging up the four flights to my New York apartment. I'm waiting, in suspense. Will he be a little like William Hurt? Have a touch of Tom Hanks' winsomeness? When there's one flight to go, I can't wait any longer. I poke my head out the door and over the banister to check him out. Not bad—except that he looks like his best friend just died.
>
> Until he glances up and sees me. In a second his brow relaxes, his eyes brighten, a wave of visible relief sweeps across his face. He grins and bounds up the last few steps. Why is this man suddenly so cheerful? I already know the reason: it's because I'm pretty. And does this little scene make me feel great? Well, yes. But I'm used to it.
>
> Ellen Paige,
> "Born Beautiful: Confessions of a Naturally Gorgeous Girl"

Feel like reading the rest of that article? Probably you do. It's a terrific introduction. Grabber introductions can be fun, and high school students are often encouraged to write them, but in the academic and professional worlds, there is little market for them.

Professors and businesspeople don't want to be held in suspense about what they're going to be reading. They want to know right up front. What they want to know in the first paragraph is simply what you are going to be writing about and why. What's the issue and why is it an issue? Here's a fairly typical example of the sort of thing they're looking for:

> When it comes to conversation, husbands and wives often have problems that close friends of the same sex don't have. First, they may not have much to talk about, and second, when they do talk, misunderstandings often develop that lead to major fights. Our research concludes that these problems are particularly resistant to solution. Not only do men and women like to talk about different topics, spoken language serves different functions for the sexes.
>
> Mark A. Sherman and Adelaide Haas,
> "Man to Man, Woman to Woman"

This introduction not only tells what the subject of the article will be—the differences between female and male conversations—but even spells out in a thesis statement the main categories of the discussion—that they like to talk about different things, that they often misunderstand each other, and that conversation serves different functions for them. Academic or professional introductions need not be this specific about the content of the body of the essays following them, but they do need to be absolutely specific about the subject to be covered.

In your previous writing classes, you might have been given formulas or lists of guidelines for creating effective thesis statements, but writing thesis statements is a skill student writers learn with practice, by writing essays in composition classes, not by following "rules." A thesis statement is a sentence or two that tells what the essay is about, and the purpose of your essay determines the kind of thesis statement you will write; thus, if you are writing an informative essay, your thesis will name the subject of the essay, and if you are writing an argument or position paper, your thesis will state your opinion or position. In each essay assignment in this book, you will be making a recommendation or explaining your opinion; by giving your recommendation or opinion in a thesis statement, in a sentence or two, you will make your point of view—and the subject of your essay—clear for your reader.

## Organization and Body Paragraphs

A glance at any newspaper or magazine article or any book will reveal that writers divide their texts into body paragraphs, and there are some general guidelines for organizing the body of the essay as well as for organizing the information within paragraphs. Mostly, paragraph indentations are like punctuation marks. In fact, the word *paragraph*, which means "alongside writing," originally referred to a written mark just as the words *comma* and *period* do. The paragraph looked like this: ¶. And true to its name, it was put alongside the main text to show where a new point was starting. Now we indent lines to tell the reader when one main point has ended and another one is beginning.

Body paragraphs usually contain one major point in an essay. The first sentence of the body paragraph, which is called the *topic sentence*, tells what that point is, and the rest of the paragraph examines it or supports it or argues for it. Here is a body paragraph from an essay entitled "Management Women and the New Facts of Life," about women in the business world. In her first sentence, the writer, Felice N. Schwartz, tells us what the body paragraph will be about:

> **Like many men, some women put their careers first.** They are ready to make the same trade-offs traditionally made by the men who seek leadership positions. They make a career decision to put in extra hours, to make sacrifices in their personal lives, to make the most of every opportunity for professional development. For women, of course, this decision also requires that they remain single or at least childless or, if they do have children, that they be satisfied to have others raise them.

In another essay entitled "The Origin of the Family," Kathleen Gough, an anthropologist, explains the basic nature of primitive hunting societies. Note that the first sentence in this body paragraph makes her point:

> **In spite of their varied environments, hunters share certain features of social life.** They live in bands of about 20 to 200 people, the majority of bands having fewer than 50. Bands are divided into families, which may forage [search for food] alone in some seasons. Hunters have simple but ingenious technologies. Bows and arrows, spears, needles, skin clothing, and temporary leaf or wood shelters are common. Most hunters do some fishing. The band forages and hunts in a large territory and usually moves camp often.

In still another essay, a writer begins one body paragraph with this topic sentence:

> **Apart from considerations of winning and losing, playing chess may reflect many other human motives.**

The paragraph then outlines what those motives could be; the next body paragraph will analyze the motives, so it begins with this topic sentence:

**Every sort of human behavior and thought is open to this type of analysis.**

As you can see, it is often (although not always) possible to follow the main outlines of a writer's argument just through the topic sentences—the first sentences of his or her body paragraphs. Following are the thesis statement in the introduction and the topic sentences for the body paragraphs in an essay about male and female communication written by a college freshman:

**THESIS:**
After reading "Man to Man, Woman to Woman," by Mark Sherman and Adelaide Haas, and excerpts from Deborah Tannen's books, **I've discovered that males' and females' differences in topic choices, styles, and functions of communication can lead to several relationship problems.**

**TOPIC SENTENCES:**
Establishing good communication with the opposite sex can be difficult, especially if the people prefer different topics.

With so many different things to talk about, males and females are bound to have conflicts with each other.

In addition to having varied topics of discussion, men and women also have different styles of listening and responding.

I would have to agree with Sherman and Haas that these differences in styles of communication can cause serious relationship problems.

Different conversational purposes are also important to keep in mind when communicating, just as the differences in styles and topics are important.

But there is also a danger side to the different purposes of communication.

Carolyn Nguyen

This student's thesis makes the subject of the essay clear, and all of the topic sentences make the subjects of their body paragraphs clear.

A body paragraph that begins with a topic sentence like "There are many reasons why men and women have communication problems with the opposite sex" obviously does not make one main point, since its topic sentence covers an entire range of points. That's almost half of the total essay to be written, way too much for one body paragraph.

Body paragraphs like this are often called "sack" or "shopping bag" paragraphs since they are like shopping bags that you just throw all your purchases into without regard for order. Such body paragraphs are irritating for readers to read; it's hard to remember what they've read when they've finished one of them because nothing is connected to anything else.

Since the whole point of writing is to communicate your ideas, you need to do everything you can to help your reader follow them. If you put all the arguments for or against something in one body paragraph, then you are saying to your reader, "Remember all this stuff so you can compare it with the opposing arguments when I present them next." Readers can't and won't do that. You need to organize your discussion point by point, giving the matching pros and cons for each main point together in the same body paragraph. If you make a list of the main arguments for and against something and match related arguments, all you have to do is decide what order you will present these arguments in. That will be the outline for most of your papers.

## Conclusions

Most writers conclude whatever they're writing by stopping when they've said what they have to say, and that's good advice. As you work on each writing assignment in this book, you'll discover that your essay has a purpose—to recommend a course of action and to explain why you are recommending it or to take a position and explain why you have taken it. Your conclusion is a good place to explain your recommendation or position.

## Proofreading

Proofreading involves going back over one's finished paper looking for errors—typos, misspellings, common errors like missing plural -s endings, or sentences that for some reason or other don't work. Most people hate to proofread. But not proofreading one's work is a *BIG* mistake.

It is guaranteed that when you don't find an error in your work, your reader will.

It is guaranteed that every error your reader finds will make him or her think you are careless and sloppy.

It is guaranteed that every error your teachers find will make them think you are careless and sloppy.

It is guaranteed that when people think you are careless and sloppy, they will also think that you aren't too bright.

Teachers are not going to give high grades to students they think are careless and sloppy, and employers are not going to hire or promote someone they think is careless and sloppy.

So don't be careless and sloppy. Proofread carefully.

### Tips for Proofreading

- Never, ever try to proofread on a computer screen. For some reason, even the very best writers cannot find all their mistakes on a screen. We can find some of our mistakes on the screen (and if you find any, you might as well fix them), but we can't find them all. You have to proofread a printed copy.
- Never rely on a grammar checker. No matter how many wonderful claims the publishers of these devices make, they don't work. They will simply confuse you.
- Never rely on a spellcheck. Go ahead and use one if you've got one, but you'll still have to proofread on your own anyway. The trouble with spellchecks is that they only know whether a word exists. They don't know whether it's the right one for the place it's in. For example, a spellcheck would think the following sentence is just fine:

  > Their was a pretty ladle gull whom lived with her mutter in there small mouse on the itch of town.

  All of those words are real words, and that's all a spellcheck cares about.
- Whenever possible, try to put your paper aside for a time after you've finished composing—a day if possible, a couple of hours at least—before you proofread it. That will help you see it more objectively.
- Go somewhere private and read your paper out loud to yourself; you will be more likely to find mistakes you otherwise won't notice.
- Make a list of the mistakes you know you commonly make and when you proofread, look in particular for those. Nobody makes every kind of error, but we are all prone to make a few of them. As this course goes

along, you will learn that you are prone to make certain errors. Put them on your list and look for them.

## Special Proofreading

As you go through the steps of the essay assignments in this book, you will also be working on sentence-building and proofreading skills in the **Getting Your Writing Right** sections at the ends of the chapters. Follow the guidelines in the **Special Proofreading** section at the end of each case study.

---

### CASE STUDY ONE: MARTHA JOHNSON'S INHERITANCE

Following is an explanation of a problem a fictional person named Martha Johnson is facing. It will be your job to write a paper recommending a solution to Martha's problem. To do this well, you must do two things before you even think about writing. You must:

a. fairly quickly read Martha's case,
b. carefully read the assignment following the case to see exactly what you are being asked to do, and
c. read the short discussion of the case.

---

When you have done those three things, read the case again, this time carefully, underlining or highlighting the most important aspects. Don't try to highlight on first reading, or you'll wind up highlighting a lot of irrelevant material and make your writing job more difficult later on.

## Martha Johnson's Inheritance

Martha Johnson comes from an average working-class family living in a medium-size city. None of her family members went to college, and while her high school is not considered one of the better ones, at least she was an excellent student there. She aspires to become a businesswoman, although she has only a hazy idea of what businesswomen do. She hopes to go to the state university in her hometown and major in business.

Martha has been working at fast food places for the past three years to earn spending money. She has accumulated a little savings and has been living the normal life of a teenager. Her work has enabled her to save enough to finance the beginnings of an education if she can get additional help through the Educational Opportunity Program.

Martha's father has worked for the past 26 years as a warehouseman and has been successfully paying off the mortgage on the family house. Martha's mother has suffered from poor health most of her life, and her illnesses have been an increasing drain on the family income. Ballet lessons for Martha's older sister, a talented dancer, are also costly. Partly because of the children and partly because of her mother's illnesses, the family has rarely gone on vacations. Martha and her sister have, however, gone to Texas several times to visit Martha's grandparents and some other relatives, and Martha has developed a close friendship with one of her aunts.

Suddenly, near the end of her last term in high school, Martha has received a small inheritance from the aunt in Texas, who has just died. The sum is modest, but it is enough that she can seriously consider making some new plans. Her father and mother hope that she will spend the money wisely or else save it, but they have told her that they will not give her advice unless she asks for it. They say that she is old enough to make her own decisions about matters like that. Here is what she is considering.

She could buy a pretty good used car. The money might not cover license and repairs, and gas would represent an additional burden on her tight budget, but she would be able to drive to and from school and work rather than taking public transit, a major saving in commute time and thus a major addition to study time. She would love to have the freedom of being able to get out into the country sometimes, visit friends, or go to a club by herself.

A second option would be to move into her own apartment near school. Again, she could avoid wasting time commuting once school begins. Her inheritance would probably cover about a semester's worth of rent for a small studio or a year's rent for an apartment if she could find a roommate. Having a quiet place of her own near school would be a huge benefit during her freshman year, and as much as she loves her parents, she would like to get out of their rather small house.

Or she could live at home and go to school for a full year without working. She has heard—correctly—that the workload of college classes is much greater than that in high school, and she has already learned that she has deficiencies to

*needs to take non-transfer courses at first*

make up in both English and mathematics, both very important subjects in a business career.

 She could take a vacation to Hawaii for three weeks. She has fantasized about such a trip a thousand times, and now she actually has the money to make it possible. Her best friend is already planning such a trip, and for Martha it seems like a once-in-a-lifetime opportunity.

Finally, she could save the money for the future. Her current savings will not last long, even if she does get financial assistance, and she faces a minimum of four years of undergraduate work and maybe even graduate work for a master's degree in business administration. Perhaps the best thing to do would be to put the money in a high-interest money-market fund and try not to touch it for the time being.

---

**ASSIGNMENT**

Discuss which course of action Martha should take and explain why it is better than the other options. Be sure to consider the advantages and disadvantages of all of her options.

---

### Discussion: Questions to Consider

As you evaluate each of Martha's choices, you will need to consider what you know about Martha's life—her financial situation, her family concerns, her potential performance in college, her career interests, and anything else that you think is relevant to her decision. Consider how each of the options could affect these aspects of both her present life and her future. Answer the following questions about each of her options, and be sure to consider both negative and positive effects:

How will each option affect Martha's financial situation in the present and in the future?

How will each option affect her responsibilities to her family?

How will each option affect her school performance?

How will each option affect her ability to pursue her career interests?

### *Step One: Make Notes and Compare Them with Others*

After you have underlined or highlighted the most important points in this case, write these points down on paper. Then answer the questions to consider. Your notes and answers will be the basis for the next step in the process of writing this essay.

In class, work with two other students, comparing your notes and answers to the questions to consider. If you find some disagreements, as you should, discuss them with each other. Try to see whether you can come to a group agreement—a consensus—on which points are most important. If you can't entirely agree, don't worry about it. You don't all have to agree on everything, but it's usually helpful to hear other people's points of view. Sometimes they will have good ideas you hadn't thought of.

Each group should now report on the points the group members consider most important and on the answers to the questions to consider, so that the teacher can write them on the board for class discussion. Now the class as a whole can come to a consensus on the most important points. Write these points down since your notes will form the basis for the next step in the assignment. Note that even though your classmates may pretty much agree on the most important points, they do not have to agree on the best solution. Your solution is your solution.

### *Step Two: Make an Outline and Compare It with Others*

Read the following guidelines for organizing "Martha Johnson's Inheritance." At home, go over your notes and decide how you think you might organize them into an essay. On paper, make a rough outline just listing your main points in the order you think would be best for writing them. Bring this list to class.

In class, compare your list outlines with those of the other members of your writing group so that you can make any changes that seem like a good idea. Then your teacher will call on four or five students to read out their list outlines, and he or she will put them on the board for discussion of good ways to organize this paper. Remember that there is not necessarily one best way to organize any paper; there may be many good ways of doing it. Be sure to take notes during this discussion because a good plan is the basis for all good writing.

## Organizing "Martha Johnson's Inheritance"

In your essay about Martha Johnson, the issue is the choice that Martha Johnson has to make, and the importance of her making the right choice, so your introduction should briefly introduce Martha Johnson and inform your reader about what her choices are. You can announce in a thesis statement which of her options you think is best, or you can save your recommendation for your conclusion.

As you plan the organization of the body of your essay, consider the best way to help your reader compare Martha's options. You can write a body paragraph about the advantages and disadvantages of each option—one body paragraph about buying a car, one about getting her own apartment, another about funding a full year of school without working, one about taking a three-week vacation to Hawaii, and one about saving her money. If you choose this organization plan, you will still need to write a paragraph or two comparing Martha's options so that your reader will be able to see how you evaluated them and arrived at your recommendation.

You can instead base your organization plan on the parts of her life that will be affected by her choice, devoting, for example, one body paragraph to her education and the ways each choice could affect her education. The rest of your body paragraphs would each focus on a part of Martha's life and the ways each choice could affect it in positive and in negative ways. This point-by-point plan gives you the opportunity to compare her choices in each body paragraph, and your reader can easily see the comparisons.

Whichever organization plan you choose, be sure to start each body paragraph with a topic sentence that says what the paragraph will cover. Then your reader can easily follow your discussion and you will find it easier to stay on track and not wander off into unrelated ideas.

Your conclusion is your chance to explain your recommendation so that your reader can see what conclusions you have made from the information in the body paragraphs.

### Step Three: Write a Rough Draft

At home, using your list outline as your basis, write a rough draft of your essay on Martha's problem. In doing a rough draft, it is important that you *not* worry about such things as spelling and other kinds of mechanics. Your only concern should be to get your ideas on paper in a logical order. Go over the following Checklist for Evaluating Rough Drafts to make sure that you have met the assignment requirements, and use it in class during peer review when you evaluate the rough drafts of the members of your writing group.

Make two copies of your draft so that you have three copies to bring to class.

## CHECKLIST FOR EVALUATING ROUGH DRAFTS

1. Does the introduction tell what the essay will be about and why the subject is important?
2. Is the essay divided into body paragraphs that cover single subjects?
3. Does each body paragraph start with a topic sentence, a sentence that tells what the paragraph will discuss?
4. Are all the sentences in each body paragraph related to the point expressed in the topic sentence? Are there any places where unrelated ideas seem to come into any body paragraphs?
5. Are the advantages and disadvantages of all of Martha's options covered?
6. Does the order of the points covered seem logical, or does anything seem out of place?
7. Is there a conclusion explaining what Martha should do and why?

### Step Four: Peer Review

In class, in groups of three, give copies of your rough draft to your group members and take turns reading your own drafts aloud. Although you did not worry about making mistakes in writing your rough draft, if you spot any when you are reading it aloud, correct them. Using the Checklist for Evaluating Rough Drafts, go over each draft question by question and discuss with your partners the strengths and weaknesses you notice in the drafts. Call in the teacher if you need help or advice. Here you are working together to help each other do the best possible final paper, and your teacher is a resource, like a good dictionary or encyclopedia.

### Step Five: Write a Final Draft

At home, write the final version of your paper, using your peers' and teacher's advice for guidance. Then, after reviewing the following Special Proofreading section and the proofreading tips on pages 8–9, proofread your paper—a printed copy, not the text on the computer screen.

## Special Proofreading

- Once you've completed this chapter, you will know how to identify subjects and verbs in your sentences, and you will know the rules for subject-verb agreement. Proofread each of your sentences, especially for subject-verb agreement. This final step will help not only on this paper but on future ones as well, since the more you practice getting your subjects and verbs right, the easier and more automatic it will become later on.

## Getting Your Writing Right

### Identifying Verbs

You may have learned that verbs are action words. Some of them are, but some of them aren't, and besides that, English is full of action words that aren't verbs (including the word *action*). Look at this sentence:

> Acting in plays is my favorite activity.

What are the action words? Obviously, *acting* is an action word, and *activity* is too. But neither one is the verb. Compare the following sentences. They are identical *except for one word*.

> Acting in plays is my favorite activity.
> Acting in plays was my favorite activity.
> Acting in plays will be my favorite activity.

The word that changes is the verb. Since English verbs change form when the time of the sentence changes, it's easy to find them. You will have noticed that in the third sentence above, the verb became two words: *will be*. English verbs are often more than one word:

> She *is writing* her life story.
> She *has been writing* her life story.
> She *will write* her life story.

### Exercise 1A

The sentences below are all in the present time, or tense. You are to rewrite them in the past tense. Follow these steps:

a. Imagine that your new sentence is going to begin with the word *Yesterday*, and identify the word that will change its form.

b.   When you have identified that word, the verb, write it in the parentheses after the original sentence.

c.   Starting with the word *Yesterday*, write the complete new sentence.

EXAMPLE:   Arthur sings in the church choir. (*sings*)
            Yesterday Arthur *sang* in the church choir.

1.  Juwon wants to go to the football game. (_____)

_____

2.  Alfredo prefers to watch a soccer game on television. (_____)

_____

3.  Kwok disapproves of their laziness. (_____)

_____

4.  He tries to get them to do something active. (_____)

_____

5.  He suggests lessons at the Karate Academy. (_____)

_____

6.  Juwon likes boxing better than karate. (_____)

_____

7.  Alfredo admires dancing more than fighting. (_____)

_____

8.  Kwok decides to work on his karate. (_____)

_____

9.  Juwon goes to the football game. (_____)

_____

10.  Alfredo's TV dies, so he goes dancing with Melitta. (_____) (_____)

_____

## Exercise 1B

The sentences below are all in the present time, or tense. You are to rewrite them in the past tense. Follow the same steps that you followed in Exercise 1A.

1.  Cathy has an excellent job. (_____)
_____had_____

2.  She specializes in making maps and charts. (_____)
_____specialized_____

3. Maps and charts of every kind <u>are</u> widely <u>used</u> by the media and large corporations. (_____)

_____ *were widely used* _____

4. In some cases, they <u>illustrate</u> very abstract information. (_____)

_____ *illustrated* _____

5. A famous chart <u>shows</u> the destruction of Napoleon's army in its invasion of Russia in 1812. (_____)

_____ *showed* _____

6. The chart <u>depicts</u> an army of 422,000 men invading Russia at the beginning of the war. (_____)

_____ *depicted* _____

7. It also <u>shows</u> an army reduced to 100,000 men reaching Moscow, the capital of Russia. (_____)

_____ *showed* _____

8. It finally <u>allows</u> us to see an army of only 10,000 men returning to Poland at the end of the campaign. (_____)

_____ *allowed* _____

9. We <u>can</u> almost <u>see</u> the deaths of over 400,000 men in the Russian winter. (_____)

_____ *could almost see* _____

10. Because of this kind of power, Cathy's specialization <u>is</u> in great demand. (_____)

_____ *was* _____

## Exercise 1C

The following passage is written in the present tense. On a separate sheet, rewrite it so that it is in the future. Underline every verb you change.

EXAMPLE:  Henry graduates from high school in June.
Henry *will graduate* from high school in June.

Henry <u>attends</u> the local state university in the fall. He <u>works</u> hard, but he also <u>joins</u> a movie club. He <u>gets</u> all his work in on time, and he <u>learns</u> a lot. He <u>gets</u> excellent grades in math, English, chemistry, and political science. He <u>thinks</u> of possibly majoring in chemistry. In the movie club, he <u>gets</u> to see many classic movies for the first time. He <u>sees</u> *Citizen Kane, La*

*Grande Illusion*, and *Potemkin*. He wonders whether it is possible to minor in film, but he decides to keep movie watching as just a hobby.

## Identifying Subjects

In English the subject normally comes in front of the verb. It is usually the first noun in the sentence. Nouns are words that you can put the word *the* in front of:

    (the) cat
    (the) club
    (the) computer
    (the) thing
    (the) idea

Sometimes there is only one noun before the verb, but sometimes there are several of them. In the following examples, all the nouns preceding the verbs are underlined:

    The cat in the hat ate my goldfish.
    The old green thing in the corner looks like your dog.
    The latest technology for editing manuscripts doesn't work very well.

In each of these cases, the first noun, not the second, is the subject:

    cat . . . ate
    thing . . . looks like
    technology . . . doesn't work

## Exercise 1D

In the following sentences, find the verb in each sentence by changing the time of the sentence.

    a.   If the sentence is in the present, change the time to past or future.

    b.   If the sentence is in the past, change the time to present or future.

    c.   Underline the verb.

    d.   After you have underlined the verb, find the subject. Remember that it is the first noun in the sentence.

    e.   Underline the subject twice.

EXAMPLE:   The books in my backpack are too heavy.
                 The <u>books</u> in my backpack <u>were</u> too heavy.

1.  The cover of your book is very attractive.

    _____

2.  The work on my desk is very unattractive.

    _____

3.  The hole in the corner of my roof needs to be fixed.

    _____

4.  The music on that disc sounds like an alligator belching.

    _____

5.  The clouds in the western sky looked threatening yesterday.

    _____

6.  My efforts to improve my grades failed.

    _____

7.  Her appetite for desserts never failed her.

    _____

8.  My cousin's secretary had a police record.

    _____

9.  Her dirty old scruffy dog liked liver.

    _____

10. The picture window in the front of their house needed repairs.

    _____

**-Ing Words as Subjects**    Besides regular nouns, another group of words can also be subjects—words ending in *-ing*. Although these words are usually parts of verbs, they may also serve as nouns:

She is *watching* her cat play. (verb)
*Watching* her cat play gives her pleasure. (noun subject)

Notice that like regular nouns, these *-ing* words come at the beginning of the sentence.

## Exercise 1E

Rewrite the following sentences in the past tense. When you have finished, underline all *-ing* subjects twice. Do not underline *-ing* verbs.

EXAMPLE: Imagining an exciting future is fun to do.

<u>Imagining</u> an exciting future <u>was</u> fun to do.

1. Thinking about her future is Jenny's favorite pastime.

   _____

2. She isn't watching out for her present life.

   _____

3. Dreaming about a better life is taking up too much time.

   _____

4. Hoping to get rich somehow is replacing the effort necessary to actually do it.

   _____

5. Fantasizing is fun but not productive.

   _____

## Subjects in *There* Sentences

There is a special kind of sentence that does not begin with a noun or an *-ing* word, and you have just read one of them. It is the *there* sentence. In *there* sentences, there is a special word order:

$$There + verb + subject$$

Just as the first noun in regular sentences is the subject, so the first noun *following the verb* in *there* sentences is the subject. In the following sentences, the subjects are underlined twice:

There are three <u>people</u> in the elevator.
There is a big <u>problem</u> with my car.

## Exercise 1F

Find the verbs in the following sentences by changing the tense of the sentence. Underline the verbs once. Find the subjects following the verbs and underline them twice.

EXAMPLE: There are many cats in my neighborhood.

There <u>were</u> many <u>cats</u> in my neighborhood.

1. There are problems with my computer.

2. There are bats in my basement.

3. There were 20 or 30 green bugs in the closet.

4. There were many colorful and artistic pictures on the wall.

5. There is one major difficulty facing us.

6. There will be a new president next year.

7. There is no reason to get upset.

8. There will be a new math teacher in the fall.

9. There are some things better left unsaid.

10. There is a huge debt to pay.

## Agreement between Subjects and Verbs

Compared with other European languages, English has a very simple verb system. In the past tense, with two small exceptions, the verb forms stay the same regardless of whether you are talking about yourself or someone or something else.

But there is one important and troublesome change in the present tense. Here is how our verbs work in the present:

I walk
you walk
he/she/it walks
we walk
they walk

Which verb form is different?
How is it different from all the others?

If you wrote the following two sentences, would they both be correct?

> My mother work as a sales manager.
> She often complains about her boss.

Which sentence has the incorrect verb?
Why is the verb incorrect?
How should it be written?

In the regular past tense, all English verbs take the same form except the verb *be* (common forms of the verb *be* are *am, are, is, was,* and *were*):

> I *was taking* two classes.        You *were taking* two classes.
> He/she/it *was taking* two classes.    We *were taking* two classes.
>                                      They *were taking* two classes.

We use *were* in the past tense with all subjects except which ones?

### Exercise 1G

Rewrite each sentence, writing the correct form of the verb. The verb or verbs to use are in parentheses in the sentences. In the first six sentences, use the present-tense form of the verbs. In the last four sentences, use the past-tense form of the verbs. Sometimes the verb *be* is called for. Remember that this verb takes the following forms: *am, is, are* (present), *was, were* (past).

#### Present Tense

EXAMPLE: John (*think*) he (*be*) a great boyfriend. (present)
              John *thinks* he *is* a great boyfriend.

1. John (*make*) me crazy sometimes. (present)

   _____

2. He never (*want*) to do anything I (*want*) to do. (present)

   _____

3. When I (*decide*) to go to a ballgame, he (*say*) that he (*want*) to go on a hike. (present)

   _____

4. But if he (*want*) to do a particular thing, he (*expect*) everyone to go along with him. (present)

   _____

5. In most cases, this habit of his (*do*) not matter. (present)

_____

6. We are not chained together at the leg, so we (*do*) most things separately anyway. (present)

_____

### Past Tense

EXAMPLE:  When John (*be*) a little boy, he (*be*) just as difficult. (past)
            When John *was* a little boy, he *was* just as difficult.

7. When he (*be*) small, his mother (*be*) concerned about this problem. (past)

_____

8. She (*be*) worried that he (*be*) growing up with the wrong values. (past)

_____

9. His playmates hit him with their toys when they (*be*) irritated by him. (past)

_____

10. Even as kids, we all (*be*) fond of him, even though he (*be*) irritating even then. (past)

_____

### Exercise 1H

Rewrite each sentence, writing the correct form of the verb. The verb or verbs to use are in parentheses in the sentences. Use present or past tense as indicated after each sentence. Sometimes the verb *be* is called for. Remember that this verb takes the following forms: *am, is, are* (present), *was, were* (past).

1. Eduardo (*love*) Marcella, but Marcella (*do not*) know that Eduardo (*exist*). (present)

_____

2. Their friends (*understand*) this problem. (present)

_____

3. Eduardo (*do not*) understand this problem, and out of frustration he (*act*) crazy. (present)

_____

4. When he (*call*) Marcella, she (*think*) it is a crank call. (present)

_____

5. When he (*write*) her, she (*believe*) someone has gotten the wrong address. (present)

   _____ writes _____ believes _____

6. When Marcella (*be*) a little girl, she (*be*) isolated from other children. (past)

   _____ was _____ was _____

7. She (*be*) raised in a remote part of the country where her family members (*be*) out of contact with other people most of the time. (past)

   _____

8. They (*be*) only accustomed to each other's company, and the children (*be*) uncomfortable with strangers. (past)

   _____ were _____ were _____

9. As a result, Marcella (*be*) not used to getting attention from others, and to her, Eduardo (*seem*) a lot like some kind of visitor from another planet. (present)

   _____

10. Actually, though their friends (*do not*) know this, Eduardo (*be*) a visitor from another planet. (present)

    _____ do not _____ is _____

**Subject-Verb Agreement with *Has* and *Have***     There is another past tense we often use in which you have to watch out for the verb in the *he/she/it* form. That's the tense in which we use *have* or *has:*

> I *have* always *done* it this way.
> You *have* never *done* it my way.
> She *has complained* about my way.
> He *has* never *complained* about anything.
> It *has been* a rainy day.
> They *have been* wasting their time.

Remember that in the present tense, the verb that goes with *he/she/it* ends in *-s*. Which form of the verb *have* ends in *-s?*

## Exercise 1I

Complete each sentence, writing the correct form of the verb *have:* either *has* or *have.*

EXAMPLE:  Americans (_____) an idealized view of themselves.
Americans *have* an idealized view of themselves.

1. The United States (_____) always thought of itself as the "land of opportunity."
2. We Americans (_____) traditionally believed that the future was always open to us.
3. Of course, this was only true to a limited extent, but it (_____) been part of the national myth.
4. Since World War II, however, this myth (_____) gradually been losing its force for most people.
5. While some parts of society (_____) continued to prosper, other parts (_____) found themselves growing poorer.
6. Immigrants (_____) continued to find opportunities, but these (_____) been good mainly in comparison with the opportunities in their former lands.
7. The average American working person (_____) learned that he or she can be laid off at any time.
8. This person (_____) found that even as the country grows richer, he or she (_____) grown poorer.
9. The millionaire, meanwhile, (_____) become a multimillionaire or even a billionaire.
10. The disparity between the very rich and the rest of us (_____) grown greater every year.

## Exercise 1J

Write the subject and the correct *have* form of the verb—*have* or *has*—below each one of the following sentences.

EXAMPLE:  A friend from high school (_____) called me every day.
friend *has* called

1. The man in the house next door (_____) made too much noise with his stereo.

   _____

2. He (_____) played it so loudly it (_____) drowned out our own music.

   _____

3. The neighbors (____) complained to the police several times.

_____

4. Maria and Jaime across the street (____) tried to reason with him.

_____

5. But he and his wife (____) not listened to anyone.

_____

6. The noise (____) made everyone crazy.

_____

7. The loud sounds and the thumping of the bass (____) knocked plaster off our walls.

_____

8. The discordant noise (____) driven our cats mad.

_____

9. One of the neighbors (____) started a petition to protest this nuisance.

_____

10. But the nuisance (____) continued anyway.

_____

## Exercise 1K

For each sentence, write both the subject and the correct form of the verb *have* or the verb *be*. Remember that the verb *be* takes the following forms: *am, is, are, was, were.*

> EXAMPLE:  Most people (*be*) unaware of their prejudices.
>           most people *are*

1. Prejudice against foreigners and those who look different (*be*) not a national trait but a human trait.

_____

2. Many Chinese (*have*) emigrated from China to other countries, where they (*have*) found themselves discriminated against.

_____

3. But China itself (*be*) famous for its extreme xenophobia—fear and dislike of foreigners—and one characteristic of many Chinese immigrant communities (*be*) their unwillingness to intermarry with those around them.

_____

4. Japan also (*carry*) dislike of foreigners to extremes, for a non-Japanese person (*be*) not permitted to become a citizen of Japan.

   _____

5. A word that used to be used a lot to mean disliking foreigners (*be*) "jingoism."

   _____

6. This word (*be*) from an old antiforeigner English music hall song that (*have*) the refrain "by jingo" after every verse.

   _____

7. Another word indicating extreme and unthinking patriotism (*be*) "chauvinism."

   _____

8. The French (*have*) given us this word, which comes from the name of a super-patriot sergeant in Napoleon's army, Nicholas Chauvin.

   _____

9. In the nineteenth century in the United States, the Irish, as well as the Chinese, the former slaves, and Native Americans, (*be*) all victims of extreme prejudice.

   _____

10. At this time, notices of available jobs often (*be*) written with this last sentence: "No Irish need apply."

   _____

### Agreement of Subjects and Verbs in *There* Sentences

As you have learned, the subject of a *there* sentence is the first noun following the verb. So the verb has to agree with the noun following it. If the noun following the verb is a *he/she/it* word, the verb will have an -*s* ending, usually *is* or *was*.

> There *are* several problems with your analysis.
> There *is* one problem with this car.
> There *were* quite a few signs of trouble.
> There *was* one in particular.

### Exercise 1L

Rewrite each sentence, writing the correct form of the verb in the blank following the word *there*. Use present tense in the first five sentences and past tense in the last five. Use *is* or *are* for present-tense sentences and *was* or *were* for past-tense sentences.

### Present Tense

EXAMPLE:  There _____several problems in our environment.
There *are* several problems in our environment.

1. There _____ several things we can do about smog and traffic congestion.
2. There _____ no reason why we have to live with these evils.
3. There _____ not enough incentives to make high-income people drive to work.
4. There _____ some cause for alarm.
5. There _____ two or three problems, but there _____ only one solution.

### Past Tense

EXAMPLE:  There _____ many problems in our society.
There *were* many problems in our society.

6. There _____ some advantages and some disadvantages to our former ways of doing things.
7. There _____ good points and bad points.
8. There _____ reason to feel that everything would eventually improve.
9. There _____ optimism about the future.
10. There _____ many people who saw only good times ahead.

## Summary and Review of Chapter 1

### Introductions

Introductions should tell the reader what your essay will be about and why the subject is important. You can state your main point, or your recommendation, in a thesis statement in your introduction, or you can state your recommendation in your conclusion.

### Body Paragraphs

A body paragraph should focus on one main point, expressed in a topic sentence. Plan the outlines of your essays so that each body paragraph focuses on a point. Avoid "shopping bag" or "sack" paragraphs in which you write all of the reasons for something in one body paragraph, and all the reasons against it in another.

### Conclusions

Conclusions differ, depending on the purpose of the essay you are writing. When you are writing about a problem and recommending a solution, your conclusion is a good place to explain your recommendation.

### Proofreading

- Never proofread solely on a computer screen; always do your final proofreading on a paper copy of your essay.
- Never rely on a "grammar" or "style" checker.
- Do not rely solely on a spellcheck.
- Try to leave time between completing your final draft and proofreading it, the more time the better.
- Read your paper aloud to yourself as you proofread.
- Keep a list of your most frequent mistakes and look for those particular problems when you proofread.

### Identifying Verbs

Verbs are the words that change form when you change the time or tense of a sentence.

### Identifying Subjects

In normal sentences, the subject is the first noun in the sentence, the one farthest away from, not closest to, the verb.

In *there* sentences, the subject is the first noun after the verb, the one closest to it.

**Subject-Verb Agreement**

In the *present tense*, verbs have the same spelling with all subjects except one. A verb that has a word equal to *he, she,* or *it* as subject must end in *-s.*

In the *past tense*, verb forms are spelled the same with all subjects except for the verb *be.* With this verb:

- The verb that follows *I* ends in *-s (was).*
- The verb that follows a word equal to *he, she,* or *it* ends in *-s (was).*
- The verb that follows a word equal to *you, we,* or *they* is *were.*

# **TWO** Evaluating Information

## CASE STUDY ONE: GEORGE MAXWELL'S DECISION

Following is a case involving a workplace decision. Your job is to evaluate the information having to do with this case and make a recommendation. To do so, you must do three things:

a. read the case
b. read the assignment carefully to see exactly what you are being asked to do, and
c. read the short discussion of the case.

When you have done these three things, go back over the case and read it carefully, underlining or highlighting the most important points, the ones you will want to consider in your essay. Don't try to find this information on your first reading.

## George Maxwell's Decision

George Maxwell started his business, Maxwell's Plumbing Supply, 20 years ago, and through hard work, knowledge of his trade, and good connections with the community, has built it up to be the leading supplier of plumbers and small plumbing contractors in the city. His clients rarely work on large jobs, such as new office buildings. Mostly they are plumbing companies and plumbers who do household work and repairs for smaller businesses. George, himself African-American, has always been sensitive to issues of racial diversity and minority hiring, and among his 19 employees, 7 are African-American, 6 white, 4 Filipino, and 2 other Asian.

Now George has a problem. He has to replace his supervisor, the man most responsible for the day-to-day working of the business, who is about to retire. While George works as chief executive and chief salesman for the company, his supervisor, with his own secretary, is in charge of the other employees, solves special problems customers bring in, and makes sure that the large and diverse inventory of the company is always up to date. It is a big job, and it requires someone who is intelligent, dedicated, and good with people.

George is loyal to his workers, and he would prefer to promote one of them to the position of supervisor. He even has one person in mind. Hector Miranda, one of the Filipinos with the firm, has been with the company for 12 years (although others have been there longer) and has, George believes, all the qualities the job calls for. He is hard working and reliable—though just about all George's employees are—and he has made numerous suggestions in the past that have increased the efficiency of the company. George considers Hector to be his best employee. In fact, much as George likes and respects the rest of his workers, he feels that only Hector has the qualities necessary to run the company the way the supervisor must.

But Hector brings with him some problems. For one thing, since five other employees have been with the firm longer than Hector has, George is worried that they will feel slighted if one of them is not given the job. In the workplace, seniority is important. Another problem is that Hector's English is not as good as George would like. He speaks English fluently but not always very well, and with his accent, he can sometimes be hard to understand, especially on the telephone. But he will have a secretary to deal with his written communications. Finally, alongside the seniority problem, there is another possible morale issue that might arise if he makes Hector supervisor.

About 18 months ago, a controversy arose among George's employees that resulted in several of them threatening to quit and in the possibility of others dragging his company into court. Although there are two small local restaurants that serve work people in the area, and some of George's employees go to them at lunchtime, George has provided a lounge for his workers, a place where they can take their coffee breaks and where, if they wish, they can bring their lunches and eat. All of the employees, regardless of race or ethnicity, mingle together there during the noon hour, except for three female Filipino employees, who regularly get together in a corner of the room and spend the hour talking in their native language, Tagalog. After several months of this, some of the other employees—George is not sure how many—began to resent this group. They didn't like these people closing themselves off from everyone else by speaking a foreign language, and from the expressions on the three women's faces, the other employees were sure that the women were talking about them right in their presence. Two of them came to George to complain. Unsure what to do, George called the women in and explained the problem. They were not cooperative. In fact, they enlisted Hector as their leader and demanded that he see a lawyer. They argued that the freedom of speech entitled them to talk in Tagalog instead of English in their private conversation if they wanted, and Hector stood up for them. The lawyer they hired made it clear that if they were forced to speak English at lunchtime, he would take George to court.

George had not intended to force them to do anything; he had merely hoped that they would understand the feelings of the others. People do not like to sit listening to a conversation in a language they don't understand when the people having the conversation are capable of speaking the common language and appear to be talking about the other workers. The workers were polarized, and Hector had allowed himself to be made a part of the group the others saw as the enemy.

George does not believe any one of the other employees is as qualified as Hector to be supervisor, but he is afraid that if he promotes him, resentments will boil over and good people will either quit or start working poorly. Another alternative might be to hire someone from outside the firm, but you never really know what you're getting when you hire an unknown, no matter what kind of references he or she might have, and again his long-time employees might resent a person being brought in over their heads. Before making a decision, George decided to talk to a few of his oldest employees to see how they felt. Following are brief summaries of what each of them told George.

### Myron Johnson (African-American)

I think Hector would make a good supervisor. The work he did on fixing our inventory control system—that was fantastic. I know I've got more seniority than he does, but you have to give the man credit. He's really got more brains than the rest of us, and he's a good man. I like him. We get along well. I was surprised when he joined up with those women who want to speak that Filipino language at lunchtime. You know, whenever they'd talk to him in that language, he'd always answer them in English. He knew how the rest of us felt. But then he went and joined them with that lawyer. I never understood that. We had a family in this company until all that stuff came along. Now it's hard to think of him as one of the family in the same way.

### Cynthia Pressman (white)

I can't imagine what Hector was thinking to let himself get caught up in that stupid Tagalog issue. I always gave him credit for more brains than that. I don't know whether you've noticed or not, but nobody will talk to those three women anymore unless they have to for work reasons, but everyone still speaks to Hector. Still, you can tell they don't have the same feeling about him as before. The question is, will this change in time? Hector is really a great guy and very bright, so I expect it probably will. People get over things. But a lot of people have the feeling that, well, he's more involved with racial stuff than we thought.

### Patricia Nguyen (Vietnamese)

This is a hard one for me. After all, I'll be his secretary if you promote him, so we'll have to get along. I hate to say this because I come from a family where my parents and relatives don't speak very good English, but if you want Hector to be supervisor, you ought to get him to take some classes. Customers have told me they have a hard time understanding him on the phone. Except for that, though, he seems like a good choice to me. But I don't know. A lot of people here were really bothered by that lawsuit deal, and we were surprised that he was involved in it. We've never thought like that or behaved like that in this company. What I think is that he let the women talk him into it. They probably twisted his arm and said, "Hey, you're a Filipino too. How come you're not with us?" And then he felt guilty and went along with them. I don't know, but I'd think he's ashamed of what he did. You know, everybody liked him before and I think they still do. This is a tough problem.

## Discussion

As George Maxwell makes his decision, he needs to think about his and his company's needs, specifically the requirements for the supervisor job and the qualifications of anyone who fills the position. In this case study, you do not have a list of qualifications for the supervisor position, as you might in a job description or a help-wanted ad in a newspaper. But the qualifications a supervisor needs all appear in the case. It's important that you underline or highlight these qualifications as well as any information that suggests whether Hector does, or does not, meet these qualifications.

### Step One: Make Notes and Compare Them with Others

At home, after you have underlined or highlighted the requirements of the supervisor's job and any information showing whether Hector does or doesn't meet the requirements, list the job requirements and Hector's strengths and weaknesses in two columns. In one column, write down all the main job requirements. In another column, write down how Hector matches or does not match each requirement.

In class, work with two other students to compare your notes. If you find disagreements or omissions, try to come to a consensus on each point. If you find that you continue to disagree, that's all right; the important thing is to listen to other points of view and at least consider them.

Each group should now report to the teacher on the points the group members have listed so that the teacher can write them on the board for class discussion. The class as a whole can try to come to a consensus on these points. Take notes on this discussion so that you won't forget any good ideas you hear from other students.

### Step Two: Make an Outline and Compare It with Others

Read the following guidelines for organizing "George Maxwell's Decision." At home, go over your notes and decide how you think you might organize them into an essay. Make a rough list outline just as you did for your previous essay assignment, and bring the list to class for discussion of ways to organize the paper.

### Organizing "George Maxwell's Decision"

Your introduction should explain briefly what decision George Maxwell has to make and why it is a difficult one; you can state your recommendation in a thesis in your introduction, or you can save your recommendation for your conclusion.

Since the whole point of writing is to communicate your ideas, you need to do everything you can to help your reader follow them. If you write "sack" paragraphs, putting all of the arguments for promoting Hector in one body paragraph or section of your essay, and all of the arguments against promoting him in another, then you'll be asking your reader to remember all the reasons for promoting him and compare them to the reasons against promoting him. "Sack" paragraphs do not give you the chance to show your reader how you have related Hector's strengths and weaknesses to the qualifications for the supervisor position.

In this assignment, you have a basic list to work from—your list of the qualities a supervisor should have. You can base your organization on this list, focusing each body paragraph on one category of job performance, explaining what it is, and discussing whether or not you think Hector has the necessary quality. If you find that in some ways Hector has both strengths and weaknesses in each category, that is natural. You will want to compare his strengths and weaknesses in each category.

Or you can base your outline on Hector's qualities, focusing each body paragraph on a quality, and show how it matches or doesn't match the job requirements.

Be sure to avoid "sack" paragraphs in which you discuss all of Hector's strengths in one paragraph or section of your essay, and all of his weaknesses in another.

Start each body paragraph with a topic sentence, a sentence that tells what the paragraph will cover. Topic sentences not only help your readers but also help you stick to your point in the paragraph.

### *Step Three: Write a Rough Draft*

At home, using your outline as your basis, write a rough draft of your essay. At this point, as you are trying to get all of your ideas on paper in a logical order, do not worry about spelling or grammar. Use the following Checklist for Evaluating Rough Drafts to see whether your draft meets the requirements for the assignment, and use it in class during peer review, when you are reading the rough drafts of the other members of your writing group.

Make two copies of your draft so that you have three copies to bring to class.

**CHECKLIST FOR EVALUATING ROUGH DRAFTS**

1. Does the introduction indicate what the essay will be about and why the subject is important?
2. Is the essay divided into body paragraphs that cover single subjects?
3. Does each body paragraph start with a topic sentence, a sentence that tells what the body paragraph will discuss?
4. Are all the sentences in each body paragraph related to the point expressed in the topic sentence? Are there any places where unrelated ideas come into any paragraphs?
5. Are all of the important issues covered?
6. Does the order of the points covered seem logical, or does anything seem out of place?
7. Is there a conclusion explaining what George Maxwell should do and why?

### Step Four: Peer Review

In class, in groups of three, exchange your rough drafts and take turns reading your own drafts aloud. If you spot any errors as you read, correct them. Using the Checklist for Evaluating Rough Drafts, go over each paper question by question to identify both strengths and weaknesses. It is just as important to tell when something works really well as when it doesn't work. Ask your teacher if you need help or advice.

### Step Five: Write a Final Draft

At home, write the final version of your paper, using your peers' and teacher's advice for guidance. Then, after reviewing the proofreading tips in Chapter 1 and the following Special Proofreading guidelines, proofread a printed copy of your paper.

### Special Proofreading

- As you did on your last paper, proofread for subject-verb agreement.
- Now that you have completed the Getting Your Writing Right section in this chapter, you understand the function and importance of -*ed* endings on verbs. In much of your paper you will be writing about things that happened or were said in the past, so be sure that all verbs naming past events are in the past tense. Check your verbs for past-tense -*ed* endings. Also check for -*ed* endings on verb forms following forms of the verbs *be*, *have*, *get*, and *become*.
- You have also completed work on -*s* endings on plural nouns; proofread your paper for these features also.

### CASE STUDY TWO: SHOULD DENISE LIU BE WORKING?

Following is a problem typical of ones that come up in many families with young teenagers. It will be your job to evaluate the evidence having to do with this case and recommend a solution. To do this well, you must do three things:

   a. read the case,
   b. read the assignment carefully to see exactly what you are being asked to do, and
   c. read the short discussion of the case.

When you have done these three things, go back over the case and read it carefully, underlining or highlighting the most important points, the ones you will want to consider in your essay. Don't try to identify these points on your first reading.

### Should Denise Liu Be Working?

Your best friend's family is having a major crisis. The school year has just started and Denise Liu, the second-oldest child, has just started her first year in high school, where she has made friends with a small group of freshman girls, all of whom have jobs while Denise doesn't. Of course, Denise now insists that she must have a job too. Mr. Liu is absolutely opposed to Denise's working because he believes that a daughter's place is in the family, and that she should use her free time to help her mother with the cooking and housekeeping. Denise's mother is not happy about the thought of her working either, although she is more sympathetic. She is not so insistent that Denise do housework, but she does believe that Denise's first obligation is to her schoolwork, and that a job will take away from it. She realizes that as the American economy is developing, a person leaving school with only average or below-average skills will be virtually unemployable, and she is anxious for her children to be successful. Her oldest child, your friend, did not work while in high school and is now majoring in computer science at a good college and seems to have a bright future ahead, and Denise's mother is holding this example before Denise.

Because the atmosphere is getting quite tense in your friend's house, the two of you decide to do a little research on the question of whether high school students should work. You have read a couple of articles on the subject that you found in the library, and you have interviewed some of your fellow college students who worked when they were in high school. Here are your findings.

The article that supports students' working gives examples of individuals who started work at places like McDonald's and went on to become successful in the fast food industry, but the writer of this article admits that these cases are rare. He does argue, however, that the skills learned in such jobs are important—such things as being on time, being dependable, and being honest.

The article that opposes students' working argues that such jobs require no skills or creativity, that they are "breeding grounds for robots." The author of this article says that such jobs take away time not just from schoolwork but from the opportunity to socialize and develop character, to live a normal teenage life.

You have gotten the following information from interviewing classmates of yours at college.

### Glenisha Marks

I didn't work until the last two years of high school, and I think that was a good thing. I started working because I wanted to buy a lot of stuff—clothes mainly—that my parents couldn't afford, so I was putting in about 25 or 30 hours a week. I kept my grades up but just barely, and I didn't have much time to go out or do anything except work and keep up with my classes. So I bought a lot of junk I thought was really cool at the time, and now I don't have any of that stuff or any of the money either.

### Suzie Pangilinan

My parents were totally against my working, but they finally let me do it when I was a junior. I could work 12 hours a week but only as long as I kept my grades up. I wanted the job so much I actually studied harder and my grades improved. But it was a pretty boring job. I worked weekends as a cashier in the restaurant of some friends of my parents, and it was incredibly monotonous just sitting there making change over and over again and smiling and being polite to everyone. I hated it, and I finally stopped after a couple of months. It wasn't worth it. But I learned that I'd better do well in school so that I wouldn't end up stuck in this kind of job in the future.

### Franco Montoya

My uncle owns a nightclub, and when I was a sophomore, he gave me a job cleaning up the place on Saturday and Sunday mornings. Man, it was a mess. Really disgusting. But I'd get there at 8:00 and have the place ready to go by noon. Two other kids worked there too, and we worked together. I think I got some valuable experiences out of that job. I always wanted to lie around in bed until noon, but when I had the job I had to get up early even if I didn't feel like it, and I learned that it wasn't so bad. I felt more like an adult. I also learned that when you have a job, someone is counting on you to do it, and so you have to do it even when you don't feel like it. If I didn't go in, the job wouldn't get done on time, or if it did, it would be because my partners had to do my work too. So if I indulged myself, I'd be letting them or my uncle down. I really learned responsibility on that job. Also, some parts of the job were worse than others, so the three of us had to work out a fair way to share the dirtiest parts, and that helped me learn not to be so self-centered and to be part of a team. I'd say that job was really a great experience for me, and I made two good friends from having it.

### Alice Martin

I started working when I was too young. I had my first job when I was 14 at an ice cream shop. I started during the summer, and that was okay, but when school started, I wasn't ready to do both things. When my parents saw my first report card, they made me quit working, and we had a huge fight over it. Then I told them that if I couldn't work, I wouldn't study either, and my grades really went downhill. We finally worked out a compromise where I got to work three afternoons a week. I wasn't making enough money to buy the stuff I wanted, but my parents chipped in a little bit extra and it worked out okay. I think that it can be good for kids to work. They can get a sense of what holding a job is really like, and there's a nice feeling when you get your paychecks, but really, the only kinds of jobs you can get as a teenager are pretty stupid and boring. I think from my experience it's probably okay as long as you don't overdo it.

Having done this research, you and your friend are thinking about what it might mean, if anything, when you happen to mention it to your English teacher. She asks a few questions about what you've done and then makes a suggestion: "Sometimes," she says, "the best way to work out your ideas is to try to write them down in some organized way because you often find out what you really think." She then goes on to make an offer: "If you write out your recommendation in organized form, using all the evidence you've collected, you can hand that in for your next assignment instead of doing the regular classwork." Since (naturally) you hate the next assigned topic, you take her up on this deal.

### ASSIGNMENT

Write an essay in which you evaluate the information from the two articles and the experiences and opinions of your four classmates and conclude with a decision about whether you think your friend's sister should be allowed to work.

### Discussion

Notice that although this situation, like many in real life, seems at first to be an either-or problem, it really isn't. The question of working can be seen not so much as *whether* the young student should or should not work, but as *how much* she should be allowed to work and/or *when* she might be allowed to work—that is, how old she should be before working might be a consideration. After all, if a 14-year-old demands to be allowed to drive, we don't say, "No, you can't drive." We say, "No, you can't drive now, but you can drive next year" (or whenever it's legal in your state). Another matter to consider is the kind of job the student might be allowed to work at. Not all jobs are equally good or equally bad and not all make the same kinds of demands on the worker. If you think that the student should be allowed to work, you may want to specify the kinds of work she should be allowed to do.

But before leaping to any conclusions about this problem, you should out-line it for yourself—put down on paper all the arguments for working and all those against working, as well as any points you will want to keep in mind about hours, kinds of work, and so on. Keep in mind here that many states have laws that prohibit young teens from working after 7:00 P.M. on school days.

### *Step One: Make Notes and Compare Them with Others*

After you have made lists of the arguments for and against the young teenager's working, along with any other considerations you think should affect the decision, compare your notes in class with those of two other students and try to come to a consensus on what the most important points are. If you find that you disagree even after discussion, that's all right. The point here is to listen to other points of view and at least consider them.

Each group should now report on the points the group members have listed so that the teacher can write them on the board for class discussion. Now the class as a whole can attempt to come to a consensus on these points. Take notes on this discussion so that if you hear good ideas from other students, you won't forget them. (You may think you'll remember them, but if you don't write them down, you won't.) Remember that you don't have to agree with anyone else on what your recommendation will be.

### *Step Two: Make an Outline and Compare It with Others*

Read the following guidelines for organizing "Should Denise Liu Be Work-ing?" At home, go over your notes and decide how you think you might orga-nize them into an essay. Make a rough list outline just as you did for your first assignment, and bring your outline to class for discussion of ways to organize the paper.

### Organizing "Should Denise Liu Be Working?"

In your introduction, you should briefly describe the problem the Liu family is facing. You can state your recommendation in a thesis statement in your intro-duction, or you can do so in your conclusion.

Since the whole point of writing is to communicate your ideas, you need to do everything you can to help your reader follow them. If you write "sack" paragraphs, putting all the arguments for working in one body paragraph or section of your essay and all the arguments against working in another, then you are saying to your reader, "Remember all the reasons for Denise to work so you can compare them with the reasons she shouldn't work when I present them next." Your readers want to be able to compare related points together and think about them, not waste time trying to figure out how your points relate.

You should organize your discussion in a point-by-point plan so that you give related pro and con arguments for each main point at the same time. For example, you know that a major reason people work is to earn money, so an obvious benefit to working is the financial one. But your readings also point out some disadvantages to teens having money. You can consider the financial issue—the benefits and the problems of teens having money—in one body paragraph. Then your readers will be able to see contrasting related points together. What other issues, besides money, should you consider as you recommend whether she should work or not?

You need to keep in mind that you have to cover several possible recommendations—whether she should work at all or not, how much time she might be allowed to work, at what age she might be allowed to work, and what kinds of jobs, in general, she might be allowed to work at. The order in which these points are listed here is probably not the best one for an essay, so think about which recommendation you want to make and plan your organization from there.

Be sure to write topic sentences for your body paragraphs so that their main points are clear.

In your conclusion, you should explain why you have made the recommendation you've chosen.

### Step Three: Write a Rough Draft

At home, using your outline as a basis, write a rough draft of your essay. Try to get all of your information on paper in a logical order, without worrying about spelling and other mechanics. Use the following Checklist for Evaluating Rough Drafts to see whether your own rough draft meets the requirements for this assignment, and use it in class in peer review when you are reading the rough drafts of the members of your writing group.

Make two copies of your draft so that you have three copies to bring to class.

## CHECKLIST FOR EVALUATING ROUGH DRAFTS

1. Does the introduction indicate what the essay will be about and why the subject is important?
2. Is the essay divided into body paragraphs that cover single subjects?
3. Does each body paragraph start with a topic sentence, a sentence that tells what the paragraph will discuss?
4. Are all the sentences in each body paragraph related to the point expressed in the topic sentence? Are there any places where unrelated ideas seem to come into any paragraphs?
5. Are all of the important issues covered?
6. Does the order of the points covered seem logical, or does anything seem out of place?
7. Is there a conclusion explaining what Denise should do and why?

### Step Four: Peer Review

In class, in groups of three, exchange your rough drafts and take turns reading your own drafts aloud. If you spot any errors as you read, correct them. Using the Checklist for Evaluating Rough Drafts, go over each paper question by question to identify both strengths and weaknesses. Call in your teacher if you need help or advice.

### Step Five: Write a Final Draft

At home, write the final version of your paper, using your peers' and teacher's suggestions for guidance. Then review the proofreading tips in Chapter 1 and the following Special Proofreading section, and proofread a printed copy of your paper.

### Special Proofreading

- As you did in your last paper, proofread for subject-verb agreement.
- Now that you have completed the Getting Your Writing Right section in this chapter, you understand the function and importance of -ed endings on past-tense verbs. Since you will be telling about past events in

this paper, be sure that all sentences about those past events are in the past tense. Check your verbs for past-tense *-ed* endings.

- You have also worked on *-s* endings on plural nouns. Check your writing for these features also.

---

**CASE STUDY THREE: CHOOSING A TREASURER**

Read the following case, which concerns choosing the most qualified applicant for a difficult and sensitive job in student government. It will be your job to rank the applicants in the order you think is best. To do this well, you must do three things before you start writing. You must:

a. read the case,

b. read the assignment carefully to see exactly what you are being asked to do, and

c. read the discussion following the assignment.

When you have done these things, go back over the case, reading carefully and underlining or highlighting the most important information. Don't try to identify this information on your first reading.

---

## Choosing a Treasurer

United Students, the student government at your university, appoints rather than elects its treasurer, and you are a member of the committee assigned to make this appointment. The treasurer is a student who gets paid $1,850 a month and has the following duties:

- The treasurer works with an accountant assigned by the university to keep an accurate account of all money received and spent by the United Students. Money received comes from student fees and from various United Students activities, such as dances, movies, concerts, student art shows, and so on. Money spent by the United Students goes toward the salaries of officers, grants made to student organizations, and setting up and promoting activities. Many thousands of dollars are involved every semester, and the university accountant serves only as an advisor to the treasurer, who has the primary responsibility for keeping accurate and complete books.

- The treasurer writes a monthly report to the president and legislature of the United Students and the president of the university summarizing receipts and expenditures for the preceding month and showing funds remaining in the student government account.
- The treasurer joins with the United Students president and a committee of the legislature to decide on which student organizations get money, how much they get, and what activities are both desirable and affordable.
- The treasurer writes an annual detailed report for the president and legislature of the United Students and the president of the university accounting for the year's financial activities of student government.

The treasurer is assisted in these tasks by a full-time paid secretary, who has been serving in this capacity for the past 13 years. But in the past, several treasurers have submitted very inaccurate accounts of money taken in and spent, and one was even in danger of being charged in court with misspending funds. The treasurer, like the other student officers, also regularly comes under fire from student organizations that are furious because they don't get the funds they think they should get. It is important to have in this position someone who is hard working and conscientious and can stand up to heavy pressure.

To avoid possible bias because of sex or ethnicity, the applicants' names are not given to the hiring committee, and the treasurer has been chosen in recent years on the basis of the following documents applicants must submit: transcripts of their grades, a short autobiography, and a statement explaining what they believe to be their qualifications. Candidates are also invited to submit letters of recommendation from three persons.

You have read all this material from the three people applying for this year's job and made the following notes. Now you have to rank the three candidates in your order of preference and explain your ranking to the other members of the committee.

### Candidate X

X had a B– average in his/her first two years in college and a B+ average in the junior year. Grades in math were in the A/A– range while grades in English and speech were in the C+/B– range. All courses except required general education ones were in business.

Candidate X has not yet participated in any extracurricular activities at the university.

Candidate X has submitted two letters of recommendation. His/her accounting teacher wrote that he/she was very conscientious in doing all assigned work on time and was a straight A student. The teacher concluded the letter with this sentence: "I believe X is a capable person who will do a good job as United Students treasurer." A second letter came from X's supervisor in a job off campus. This person wrote, "X has worked for us for almost three years now, mainly filing, word processing, and taking telephone orders. X is quiet but very reliable and conscientious, has always done an excellent job, and gets along very well with supervisors and other employees. I believe X would be an excellent choice for treasurer."

Candidate X's autobiography, which is very simply, almost childishly written, indicates that the clerical job is the only one that he/she has ever had. His/her statement reads in full: "I am an excellent student in mathematics, and I plan to major in accounting. I plan to be an accountant when I leave school. I have worked in a business for three years. I have a good understanding of how businesses work. I get along very well with my coworkers in the business world. I am very reliable. I follow directions well, and I do my jobs accurately. I think that these qualities make me a good candidate for United Students treasurer."

### Candidate Y

Candidate Y has an A– average in math classes and a B+ average in speech and English classes and has done equally well in his/her other work. In six semesters, however, Y has taken five incompletes though he/she has always made up the incompletes in time. He/she has also withdrawn from three other courses, all three of them science courses. In the last semester of Y's junior year, for the first time, he/she took no incompletes and did not withdraw from a course.

During his/her freshman and sophomore years, Y was very involved in extracurricular activities, serving as a cheerleader and joining three student organizations. In his/her sophomore year, Y served as secretary of the Accounting Club and membership director of the Student Fellowship Congregation (SFC).

Letters of recommendation for Y come from two professors and the president of the SFC. A math professor Y had last semester wrote that Y was "intelligent, quick, and an active participant in class activities, one of the best students I've had in recent years." An English professor from whom Y took two classes, a freshman composition class and an introduction to the novel, wrote, "Y is very bright, a better-than-average writer, and a person with unusually good insights into literature.

Y relates extremely well with his/her classmates. In both classes, Y sometimes tried to tackle subjects in his/her papers that were a little bit too ambitious, which produced some problems, but he/she always came through in the end."

The SFC president wrote that Y "was the best membership director I've seen in my three years in the organization. Y put in longer hours and worked harder than anyone I've seen before."

Y's autobiography and statement are very well written. Y has participated in many activities both on and off campus, including a community tutoring program for middle-school children, and writes, "As my record shows, I have a strong commitment to my fellow students and to the community where I live. I am not afraid of hard work, and I believe that my commitment to people and my willingness to work hard are a strong recipe for success in the treasurer's job."

### Candidate Z

Like Candidates X and Y, Z has an almost A average in math and also has almost straight As in science courses. Z's grades in business, English, and speech courses are in the C+ to B+ range. Z has been a member of a number of student organizations but hasn't stayed long with any of them. Z was a member of the Management Club for one semester, the Accounting Club for two semesters, the Students for Participatory Democracy for one semester, the Student Fellowship Congregation for one semester, and the Cinema Guild for two semesters. Z lists a current membership in the University Mathematics Society.

Letters of recommendation from one math professor and one physics professor stress Z's extreme intelligence and meticulously careful work. His/her math professor writes, "Z never seems to make a mistake. I wish I could say the same thing about myself."

In his/her autobiography, Z writes, "My main strength is that I always do whatever I commit myself to. I never leave things unfinished. My main weakness is that I don't socialize with as many people as I think I ought to. I have three really close friends, people I've known since high school and, in one case, since grade school, and I mostly do things with them. I think I should get more involved with more people. People often think I'm kind of cold, but I'm really not."

Z thinks that his/her main qualifications for treasurer are knowing mathematics really well, getting things done, and working well with people.

**ASSIGNMENT**

Write an essay in which you examine the qualifications of all three candidates and rank them in your order of preference, considering the job requirements. You should explain why you have ranked them as you have—why, for example, you put Z before X and X before Y, or Y before X and X before Z.

## Discussion

It is clear from the history of the United Students treasurer position that this is a sensitive job and that there is a great potential for trouble if the wrong person is selected. In trying to decide which candidate will probably be the best choice, you will need to begin not with the candidates' qualifications but with the requirements of the job. These are crucial. After you have listed these requirements, you will be in a position to see which candidates match up best with which requirements.

### Step One: Make Notes and Compare Them with Others

After you have underlined or highlighted the requirements of the treasurer's job and the main strengths and weaknesses of each candidate, list each of these on a piece of paper. In one column, write down all the main job requirements. In another column write down in note form how X, Y, and Z match up with each of these requirements.

In class, work with two other students to compare your notes. If you find disagreements or omissions, try to come to a consensus on each point. If you find that you continue to disagree, that's all right. The point here is to listen to other points of view and at least consider them.

Each group should now report on the points the group has listed so that the teacher can write them on the board for class discussion. Now the class as a whole can attempt to come to a consensus on these points. Take notes on this discussion so that if you hear good ideas from other students you won't forget them. (You may think you'll remember them, but if you don't write them down, you won't.)

### Step Two: Make an Outline and Compare It with Others

Read the following guidelines for organizing "Choosing a Treasurer." At home, go over your notes and decide how you think you might organize them into an essay. Make a rough list outline just as you did for your previous assignment, and bring your outline to class for discussion of ways to organize the paper.

### Organizing "Choosing a Treasurer"

Your introduction should provide background information for your readers; briefly describe the position the three candidates are applying for and what your essay is going to do. You may state in a thesis which candidate you think is most qualified. Or you can save your recommendation for the conclusion.

Since the whole point of writing is to communicate your ideas, you need to do everything you can to help your reader follow them. If you write "sack" paragraphs, putting all of the strengths and weaknesses of Candidate X in one body paragraph or section of your essay, all of the strengths and weaknesses of Candidate Y in another, and those of Candidate Z in another, it will be impossible for your reader to compare the candidates with each other. A more effective approach is to organize point by point.

In this assignment, you essentially have two lists that can serve as the basis of a point-by-point organization plan. The first list that you can base your organization on is your list of requirements for the job of treasurer. Since each candidate has to match up with these requirements, you can devote a body paragraph to each one of the requirements and discuss all three candidates together, making your comparisons of their strengths. You will still need a conclusion following these discussions in which you make a final judgment on the total strengths and weaknesses of the candidates and rank them.

The second list that could serve as a basis for an organization is the list of qualifications of the candidates—their academic records, their work records and histories of extracurricular activities, their recommendations, and their personal statements. Again, this approach enables you to compare them as you go along, but you will still need a conclusion in which you make a final judgment on their overall strengths and weaknesses.

Whichever approach you choose, be sure to start each body paragraph with a topic sentence that states what the paragraph will cover. Topic sentences will help the reader and will help you stick to one point in the paragraph instead of wandering off into unrelated matters.

If you use the *first* organization plan, with each body paragraph focusing on a requirement for the job, you might have a body paragraph beginning with a topic sentence like this:

**One of the really important qualifications for the treasurer's job is a strong background in mathematics and accounting, and there are some differences among our candidates here.**

If you use the *second* kind of organization plan, one of your body paragraphs might begin with a topic sentence like this:

**The candidates' academic records show that . . . (whatever you think they show).**

### Step Three: Write a Rough Draft

At home, using your list outline as your basis, write a rough draft of your essay. Try to get all of your information on paper in a logical order without worrying about misspellings or other errors at this point. Use the following Checklist for Evaluating Rough Drafts to see whether you think your draft meets the requirements for the assignment, and you should also use it in class when your group members are reading their rough drafts to the group.

Make two copies of your draft so that you have three copies to bring to class.

---

**CHECKLIST FOR EVALUATING ROUGH DRAFTS**

1. Does the introduction indicate what the essay will be about and why the subject is important?
2. Is the essay divided into body paragraphs that cover single subjects?
3. Does each body paragraph have a topic sentence, a sentence telling what the paragraph will discuss?
4. Are all the sentences in each body paragraph related to the point expressed in the topic sentence? Are there any places where unrelated ideas seem to come into any paragraphs?
5. Are all of the job requirements and candidates' qualifications covered?
6. Are the body paragraphs in a logical order?
7. Is there a conclusion explaining which candidate is the most qualified and why?

*Step Four: Peer Review*

In class, in groups of three, exchange your rough drafts and take turns reading your own drafts aloud. If you spot any errors as you read, correct them. Using the Checklist for Evaluating Rough Drafts, go over each paper question by question to identify both strengths and weaknesses. It is just as important to tell when something works really well as when it doesn't. Call in your teacher if you need help or advice.

*Step Five: Write a Final Draft*

At home, write the final version of your paper, using your peers' and teacher's suggestions. Review the proofreading tips in Chapter 1 and the following Special Proofreading section, and then proofread a printed copy of your paper.

## Special Proofreading

- As you did on your last paper, proofread for subject-verb agreement.
- Now that you have completed the Getting Your Writing Right section in this chapter, you understand the function and importance of *-ed* endings on verbs. In this paper you are writing about things that happened in the past; be sure that all sentences about those past events are in the past tense. Check your verbs for past-tense *-ed* endings. Also check for *-ed* endings on verb forms following forms of *be, have, get,* and *become*.
- You have also worked on plural *-s* endings on nouns. Check your writing for these features also.

## Getting Your Writing Right

### Past-Tense Verbs

As you know, English shows the time of its sentences through their verbs. Present time or tense uses the base form of the verb (except for the verb *be*). This is the form you would look up if you were looking up the word in a dictionary:

| Verb | Base Form | Sentence (present tense) |
|------|-----------|--------------------------|
| dance | dance | They *dance* extremely well. |
| talk | talk | She *talks* very slowly. |

THE FUTURE TENSE PUTS THE WORD *WILL* IN FRONT
OF THE BASE FORM:

> They *will dance* better eventually.
> She *will talk* to her boss tomorrow.

THE PAST TENSE USUALLY ADDS *-D* OR *-ED* TO THE BASE FORM:

> They *danced* better last year.
> She *talked* until dawn.

There are two problems with this nice neat system:

1. Not all past-tense verbs add *-d* or *-ed*. Some go off in ways all their own:

   | verb/base | past |
   |-----------|---------|
   | think | thought |
   | drink | drank |
   | eat | ate |

   *irregulars*

2. The other problem applies only to the *-ed* ending verbs. The trouble is that when we speak we don't always pronounce those *-ed* endings. For example, say the following sentence aloud as you would if you were talking to a friend:

   *"silent" -ed*

   Yesterday, I walked to school.

   The chances are that you didn't pronounce the ending of the verb; the sentence probably came out sounding like this:

   Yesterday, I walk to school.

   > or maybe,

   Yesterday, I walkt to school.

There's nothing wrong with this pronunciation. The problem comes when we write. Since we don't pronounce the *-ed* ending in speech, we often don't "hear" it in our minds when we write and so we may leave it off. It's a spelling problem like any other, but it's a very basic one, one that an educated person shouldn't make.

The first step in eliminating this problem is to check all your verbs when you are writing in the past tense. It is also important to remember that two common expressions always have *-ed* endings—*used* to and *supposed* to.

*Note:* Verb forms beginning with the word *to* never have *-ed* endings.
correct:     He wanted to *walk* across the United States.

### Exercise 2A

Rewrite the following sentences, using the past-tense (*-ed*) form of the verb in parentheses. Remember that *used to* and *supposed to* <u>always</u> have *-ed* endings, and that verb forms following the word *to* <u>never</u> have *-ed* endings.

EXAMPLE:  Many people (*want*) their own car.
          Many people *wanted* their own car.

1. Tommy (*hate*) to take the bus to college.
   _____

2. In high school, he (*walk*) to school every day, and he was (*use*) to that.
   _____

3. He was not (*use*) to long, overcrowded bus trips, and he truly (*dislike*) them.
   _____

4. He (*want*) to get a car and drive to school.
   _____

5. His father (*promise*) him that if he got a B average, he could have a car.
   _____

6. He (*work*) harder than he ever had before.
   _____

7. He (*imagine*) himself driving a brand new car, but his father never (*promise*) him a new car.
   _____

8. The new car he (*suppose*) he would get (*turn*) out to be a used car.
   _____

9. The parking space he (*suppose*) he would find at school (*turn*) out not to exist.

_____

10. The first day in his new used car he (*park*) so far from school, he was (*force*) to take a shuttle bus.

_____

### Exercise 2B

The following passage is in the past tense, but many of the verbs, including *used to* and *supposed to,* are missing their *-ed* endings. On a separate sheet, rewrite the passage to correct these errors. There are 15 of these mistakes.

> EXAMPLE:  In World War II, the United States *battle* Japan.
> In World War II, the United States *battled* Japan.

> *Remember:* Verbs beginning with *to* do <u>not</u> get *-ed* endings while verbs following the word *had* <u>do</u> get them.

During World War II, the Japanese Navy start the war much stronger than the United States Navy. It own more aircraft carriers, more destroyers and cruisers, and more modern battleships. It hope to draw the American fleet into a decisive battle and to destroy it. It sail from Japan in enormous force to invade Midway Island in the Pacific. There it plan to lure the Americans into the decisive battle. The U.S. fleet was suppose to appear to defend Midway and be surprise and destroy. But the U.S. Navy had broken the Japanese naval code and was use to reading the Japanese messages. It realize what the Japanese plan. So the American fleet ambush the Japanese fleet and sank all four of the Japanese aircraft carriers. This was the decisive battle the Japanese plan for, but it turn out differently than they expect.

### Past Participles

When you look up a verb in the dictionary, if it is a *regular verb*, like "walk," you will find it listed like this:

walk, walked, walking

If it is what's called an *irregular verb*, you will find it listed like this:

take, took, taken, taking

All English verbs have four forms, but for the ones that have *-ed* endings, only three forms are listed in the dictionary because two of the forms are the same. Yet some other verbs do not have two forms the same, so all forms have to be listed. Compare the following pairs of sentences based on *walk* and *take:*

I *walk* to school.
I *take* a bus.
Yesterday, I *walked* to school.
Yesterday, I *took* a bus.
Often I *have walked* to school.
Often I *have taken* a bus.

The forms of verbs that follow *have* are called *past participles,* but we will just call them *have* forms from now on.

Actually, these *have* forms are used following four verbs: *be, become, have,* and *get.* Again, these are places where you need to be alert to use *-ed* endings, just as you do when writing in the past tense.

### Exercise 2C

In the following sentences, forms of the verbs <u>be</u>, <u>become</u>, <u>have</u>, and <u>get</u> are underlined. Rewrite the sentences, writing the correct *-ed* ending versions of verb forms following the underlined forms of <u>be</u>, <u>become</u>, <u>have</u>, and <u>get</u>.

EXAMPLE:　Juan <u>became</u> concern that he hardly <u>had</u> date.
　　　　　　Juan *became concerned* that he hardly *had dated.*

1. Juan's dating experiences <u>had</u> <u>been</u> limit when he first <u>got</u> acquaint with Alicia.

_____

2. He <u>had</u> never really ask a girl out in high school so he <u>was</u> unacquaint with these rituals when he got to college.

_____

3. He <u>was</u> use to going places with both his male and female friends, so in college he needed <u>to get</u> use to a whole new way of doing things.

4. He knew that he <u>was</u> suppose to ask the girl to a movie or a dance, but when he thought about it, he <u>became</u> fill with dread.

5. His stomach <u>became</u> unsettle, and he <u>became</u> terrify.

6. He <u>was</u> totally entrance by Alicia, but he <u>was</u> worry that she <u>wouldn't</u> <u>be</u> interest in him.

7. Finally he <u>got</u> motivate to ask her to a dance.

8. He <u>was</u> not convince she <u>was</u> interest in him, but he decided to do it anyway.

9. He <u>became</u> determine to approach her after their math class.

10. He <u>was</u> relieve when she said, "You want to see a movie tonight?"

## Exercise 2D

Rewrite the following sentences, underlining the verbs <u>be</u>, <u>become</u>, <u>have</u>, and <u>get</u> and changing the verbs following them to their *-ed* form. (Note that these four verbs aren't followed by another verb every time they appear.)

> EXAMPLE: Most people have try to get a good job.
> Most people <u>have</u> <u>tried</u> to get a good job.

1. Anyone who has work at very many jobs has experience plenty of bad ones.

2. To be sure, most people have gotten hire by nice people to do acceptable work.

3. But it is probably more common to get a job that seems good and then to become disillusion with it.

4. I have often gotten tire of jobs that were a challenge at first but then seemed routine.

   _____

5. I had work at my first job for only two or three weeks when I became tire and disgust with doing the same things over and over.

   _____

6. Of course, I was initially thrill with my impressive pay envelope, $65.34 for a week's work.

   _____

7. If you have work very much when you are young and unspoil, you will have learn that low-paying jobs for unskilled workers do not make a good career.

   _____

8. You quickly get bore at jobs like these and start to become skill at spotting them ahead of time.

   _____

9. But unfortunately you have to get train and become qualify to do anything better.

   _____

10. That's where college has play an important part in my working life.

    _____

## Exercise 2E

The following passage is written in the past tense. Proofread it for both past-tense verbs missing their -ed endings and verbs after *be, become, have,* and *get* that need -ed endings.

The Second Amendment to the U.S. Constitution says, "A well regulated militia being necessary to the security of a free state, the right of the people to keep and bear arms shall not be infringed." The men who inscribe these words believe that the United States should not have a strong army. They had experience the evils of armies, and were wary of them. They believe that citizen-soldiers—state militias—could provide defense without being a danger to the country. Washington's army in the Revolution consist mostly of state militias, bands of men the states had recruit to do the fighting. The militias had not really work very well, but the U.S. had succeed in winning that war. It was not so lucky the next time. During the second war with England, the War of 1812, the United States again depend primarily on militias to do the fighting. They consistently fail. When the British invade Maryland and march on Washington, the militia met them at a place call Bladensburg. The British attack and defeat the militia. The militia ran so fast the battle became call "The Bladensburg Races." After the militia had been defeat, the British march into Washington and burn the White House, the Capitol, the treasury, and other government buildings. The United States had learn its lesson about the value of militias, but we still have the Second Amendment.

### Plural *-s* on Nouns

Most nouns in English come in both singular and plural forms, and most of the plural nouns end in *-s*. We talk about *cats* and *books* and *vacations*. But because, as in the case with *-ed* endings, we don't always pronounce those *-s* endings, we may sometimes forget to put them on our nouns in writing. This is a very basic error that creates a bad impression on readers.

Many noun plurals are what are called redundant plurals. That is, the noun is preceded by a word that already indicates that it is plural—a number, for example, or a word like *several* or *many*. But the noun still has to have its own plural *-s* ending.

English has another odd pattern where plurals are called for. Normally, of course, the word *one* would mean a single thing, and no plural would be involved:

one movie
one book

But when we have the words *one of*, then the noun following has to be plural:

one of the movies
one of the books

These phrases mean one out of two or more movies or one out of two or more books.

### Exercise 2F

In the following exercise, find all the words that indicate plurals, words like *two, many, several, all,* and *one of*. Underline these words and then find the nouns that follow them, make them plural by adding *-s* endings, and underline them too.

Sometimes making a noun plural near the beginning of the sentence will mean that other nouns further along should also be changed to plural. Make these changes and underline them also.

EXAMPLE:  Our team lost several game, and these failure depressed them.

Our team lost several games, and these failures depressed them.

1. One of my friend got a video camera for his birthday, and he and several friend decided to become filmmaker.

   _____

2. They were only missing two thing: a script and a cast.

   _____

3. They worked on four or five script, but all their plot were stupid and trite.

   _____

4. So they decided to start with some actor and actress rather than a story.

   _____

5. They found two amateur actor who both wanted to be star.

   _____

6. They found a couple of aspiring actress who wanted to be queen or at least princess.

   _____

7. They started working on a script that would feature two male star and two female queen, but these part didn't really add up to a good story.

   _____

8. Then one of the actress revealed that her secret ambition was to play a Shakespeare heroine.

   _____

9. So they wrote a script about a woman who persuaded her husband to commit several murder, like Shakespeare's Lady MacBeth.

   _____

10. They had their hope up for an exciting experience as film director, but the actress left to play a surf lifeguard on TV.

   _____

### Exercise 2G

Do the following exercises using noun plurals:

1. Write two sentences in which you use numbers before nouns (for instance, *two dogs*).

   _____

   _____

2. Write two sentences in which you use *one of.*

   _____

   _____

3. Write two sentences in which you use either *many of* or *several of.*

   _____

   _____

4. Write a sentence in which you use *many.*

   _____

5. Write a sentence in which you use *several.*

   _____

6. Write a sentence in which you use *a family of.*

   _____

7. Write a sentence in which you use *a group of.*

   _____

## Summary and Review of Chapter 2

### Body Paragraphs

Body paragraphs contain one major point each. They start with a topic sentence, a sentence that tells the reader what the point of the paragraph will be, and then they usually examine, support, or argue that point.

### Verb Endings

Most past-tense verbs end in *-ed.* Even though we do not always pronounce this ending in speech, it must be there in writing.

Other verb forms must end in *-ed* when they follow the verbs *be, become, have,* or *get*.

## Plural Noun Endings

Most nouns have plural forms, and in most cases that means that these plurals end in *-s*. This is true even when the noun plural is redundant—that is, when the noun follows a word (like *many*) that indicates the noun will be plural.

A noun following *one of* must have a plural ending.

# THREE
# Making Comparisons

---

**CASE STUDY ONE: LUIS CARDENAS'S CAREER POSSIBILITIES**

Read the following case, which concerns a young man's career choices. It will be your job to evaluate his options and recommend the one you think is best. To do this well, you must do three things:

a. read the case,
b. read the assignment carefully to see exactly what you are being asked to do, and
c. read the discussion section on making comparisons.

When you have done these three things, go back over the case, reading it closely and underlining or highlighting the most important points, the ones you will want to consider in your essay. Don't try to find these points on your first reading.

---

### Luis Cardenas's Career Possibilities

Luis lives in the largest city in the state, where he was born and has deep family roots and many friends. He has completed his B.A. and a teaching credential. He decided to go into teaching nine years ago, between his sophomore and junior years in high school, when he worked in a summer camp teaching crafts to 10-year-old boys. He enjoyed the experience so much that he decided teaching was for him. Since then, a year and a half as a paralegal in a large law firm and another six months as a junior executive in a large corporation have only confirmed his desire to become a teacher. He hated being a slave to routine and doing work that was meaningless to him. He got into the habit of coming home and saying, "Well, there goes another eight hours of my life down the drain." Although he did not find all of his education courses particularly challenging, he felt that his student teaching, with classes of third and fourth graders, was exciting and rewarding, and he looked forward to it every day.

The student-teaching experience was an eye-opener in negative ways too. He was assigned to an elementary school in his hometown, where he worked with a master teacher named Mrs. Galbraith. He really admired Mrs. Galbraith's inventiveness and skill in working with the children, and as he came to know other teachers in the school, he was a little surprised and very pleased to discover that they were hard working and dedicated, people he liked and respected.

But Mrs. Galbraith and the other teachers were also bitter and disillusioned about their jobs, about the school, and about the whole district. They felt that they were badly underpaid, that they often didn't have the support of the school board, and that the increasingly large classes they were being forced to teach were making their jobs nearly impossible.

While Luis really enjoyed his work at the school, he could see that most of the teachers' complaints were legitimate. It was distressing to discover that the schools of his hometown had such problems, but the teachers told him that most of these problems existed everywhere else in the state as well.

Now Luis faces an unexpected choice. When he finished his degree and credential work, he did not expect to find a full-time teaching job in his hometown and had resigned himself to finding some sort of part-time job and working for several years as a substitute until something came open. He had even allowed a friend of his to talk him into interviewing for a management trainee position with a large bank, Sunset National. Now he suddenly finds that because of several faculty retirements and because he made a good impression as a student teacher, the school where he worked is offering him a permanent teaching position starting at $29,000 a year.

At the same time, Sunset National Bank has chosen him over 15 other candidates for the trainee position because of his excellent academic background, fine references from his previous jobs, and outstanding interview. Sunset National Bank would pay him $38,000 a year for the first year. He would undergo training to become a Commercial Loan Officer, taking courses in subjects he had not had in school and doing internship work in satellite banks in other parts of the state. When promoted to Loan Officer, he would receive an initial $3,000 raise and could be assigned to one of the bank's offices in any part of the state. The committee who interviewed him stressed that possibilities for eventual promotion to higher positions were very good, although it would be wise for him to consider acquiring a master's degree in business administration to improve his chances.

Salary increases in the city's school system are slow in coming, and the top salary in the system is currently $60,000. On the other hand, full-time teachers who are kept for three years receive tenure—that is, they essentially cannot be fired unless the school district goes broke—and teachers get about three months a year of vacation, while in the bank job Luis would get two weeks a year until he was promoted to Loan Officer, when this vacation time would increase to three weeks. Luis knows that it is also possible to work summers and evenings toward an administrative credential so that he might become a principal or assistant principal one day.

**ASSIGNMENT**

Discuss in detail the advantages and disadvantages to Luis Cardenas of each of his choices and make a recommendation about which job he should take. Note that you are comparing the choices, not just the jobs, although a comparison of the jobs is, of course, involved in the choice he will make.

### Discussion: Making Comparisons

In comparing two or more ideas or things or actions, the most important step is to identify all of the factors that must enter into an intelligent comparison. For instance, if you were trying to decide which of two cars to buy and you compared them only on the basis of how they looked, you would be overlooking some of the most important factors in an intelligent comparison. Once you have identified all of the significant characteristics to be compared—in the case of a car, cost, gas mileage, frequency-of-repair history of the model, special features, costs of desirable options, and so on—you would want to make a list of these characteristics so you could weigh them against each other.

The problem you are dealing with here is more complex than comparing two cars because it has more factors and because some of the factors are not as obvious as the features of cars. Try to identify the main factors involved here, the largest ones, and then see whether there are subelements within them. For instance, a main factor is income, and some subelements of income are starting income and potential income. The groupings of related characteristics will help provide you with your essay and paragraph organization when you begin writing.

### Step One: Make Notes and Compare Them with Others

Go back over the case carefully and start a list of the most important factors in making a comparison between Luis Cardenas's two career choices. You will want to include factors like his potential income and potential job satisfaction and all of the other factors you think are most important, and make notes about these factors for each career choice. Note also points that you think are important based on your own experience.

In class, work with two other students to compare your notes. Try to come to a consensus on the points involved in making a comparison between the two choices.

Each group should now report on the points the group members consider most important so that the teacher can write them on the board for class discussion.

### Step Two: Make an Outline and Compare It with Others

Read the section on organizing "Luis Cardenas's Career Possibilities." Then go over your notes and decide how you think you might organize them into an essay. Make a rough list outline as you did for your previous assignments, and bring your outline to class for discussion of ways to organize this paper.

## Organizing "Luis Cardenas's Career Possibilities"

Your introduction should briefly introduce Luis Cardenas and state the decision he has to make. You can give your recommendation in a thesis statement in your introduction, or you can save it for your conclusion.

While textbooks and teachers often suggest that one way of organizing comparisons is to list all the qualities of the two things being compared in separate paragraphs or separate sections of the paper—say everything about one job in one section and everything about the other one in another—this is not usually good advice because it leads to "sack" paragraphs, and it is very rare to find organizations like this in professional writing.

It is much more common for writers to break down the things being compared into factors, as you have done in your notes, and then compare them point by point so that readers can think about related points together. In this assignment, you could carry that too far. For instance, it would be silly to have a paragraph in which you compared only the vacations offered by the two jobs. But it might be appropriate to have one comparing what are called the "benefits" of the two jobs—that is, such things as vacation time and financial considerations other than just salaries.

You need to decide on the *main* points of comparison and plan body paragraphs for them, with the subpoints included where they logically go.

Remember: Good body paragraphs begin with topic sentences that tell what the paragraphs will cover.

In your conclusion, explain why you are recommending one career path for Luis.

### Step Three: Write a Rough Draft

At home, using your list outline as your basis, write a rough draft of your essay on Luis's decision. Do not worry about spelling and other mechanics while you are trying to get all of your information on paper in a logical order. Refer to the Checklist for Evaluating Rough Drafts to see whether your own draft meets the requirements for this assignment, and use it during peer review.

Make two copies of your draft so that you have three copies to bring to class.

---

**CHECKLIST FOR EVALUATING ROUGH DRAFTS**

1. Does the introduction indicate what the essay will be about and why the subject is important?
2. Is the essay divided into body paragraphs that cover the main points involved in comparing the two choices?
3. Does each body paragraph start with a topic sentence, a sentence that tells what the paragraph will discuss?
4. Are all the sentences in each paragraph related to the point expressed in the topic sentence? Are there any places where unrelated ideas seem to come into any body paragraphs?
5. Are all the important points involved in the comparison covered, or is anything missing?
6. Does the order of the points seem logical, or does anything seem out of place?
7. Is there a conclusion explaining what Luis should do and why?
8. Has the writer used joining words, in particular the words *and*, *but*, *or*, and *so* (or *and so*) to show the relationships between closely related points or ideas?

*Step Four: Peer Review*

In class, in groups of three, exchange your rough drafts and take turns reading your own drafts aloud. If you spot any errors as you read, correct them. Using the Checklist for Evaluating Rough Drafts, go over each paper question by question to identify both strengths and weaknesses. Call in your teacher if you need help or advice.

*Step Five: Write a Final Draft*

At home, write the final version of your paper, using your peers' and teacher's suggestions for guidance.

Check to see whether you've used the words *and, but, or, so* (or *and so*) to join logically related ideas.

Review the proofreading tips in Chapter 1 and in the following Special Proofreading section, and then proofread a printed copy of your paper.

## Special Proofreading

- As you have been doing, proofread for subject-verb agreement and for *-ed* endings on verbs and *-s* endings on nouns.
- Since you have completed the Getting Your Writing Right section in this chapter, you know how to proofread for correct pronouns:

    Are all your pronouns at the beginning of sentences subject pronouns?

    Are all your pronouns after your verbs object pronouns?

    Check to be sure that you have used the pronouns *they* or *them* when you referred to a noun that means more than one person or thing.

- *New Point:* Every time you've used Luis Cardenas's name, check to see whether it is a possessive—that is, whether you are writing about something he has (such as his name, decision, problem, career, or whatever). Look at the first sentence of this paragraph to see how the word *Cardenas* gets punctuated to show possession.

### CASE STUDY TWO: LAVONNE WILLIAMS'S WORKING FUTURE

Read the following case, which concerns a young woman's potential career choices. It will be your job to evaluate her options and recommend the one you think is best. To do this well, you must do three things:

a. read the case,

b. read the assignment carefully to see exactly what you are being asked to do, and

c. read the discussion sections.

When you have done these three things, go back over the case, underlining or highlighting the most important points, the ones you will want to consider in your essay. Don't try to find these points on your first reading.

### Lavonne Williams's Working Future

It is July, and Lavonne Williams has a decision to make. She has worked part-time (20 hours a week while in school, 40 hours a week during the summers) at the Chicken Empire outlet in her neighborhood, and she knows the operations of the place inside and out. In addition to knowing how to prepare the food and serve the public, she has worked with the manager on inventory control and ordering supplies, and she has served as acting manager three times, once when the manager was ill, and twice when he was on vacation. Now she is being offered the job of manager itself. She will receive $1,635 a month, before taxes, a huge raise over the $7.50 an hour she now makes, and, as the regional supervisor himself has told her, the job of station manager, as it is called in the chain, can be a stepping-stone to higher positions in the company. The regional supervisor also told Lavonne that if she accepts the job, she will be the youngest station manager in the company's history.

As station manager, Lavonne will have to put in between 30 and 40 hours a week at the outlet itself and, if she intends to do the job really well, another 5 to 10 hours working at home, depending on the time of year. The salary is the same regardless of the hours worked. New managers also have to attend monthly training sessions during their first year on the job, and these sessions run all day Saturday. Twice-yearly regional meetings are held on Fridays and Saturdays in February and August. The previous station manager, Lavonne's boss, held the job for almost five years before he quit to take a similar job with Burger Prince.

Lavonne will be a sophomore in the coming semester, and she intends to major in political science. She has aspirations of "going into government," but she doesn't yet know what form her career in government might take. By taking 15 units a semester, she has finished her freshman English, speech, and math requirements and taken several lower-division courses in her major. Between work and school, she has had very little time for a social life, but she has maintained a B+ average.

In one of her major courses, she met Professor Hamilton, an authority in the field of public housing. This subject is one that especially interests Lavonne, since she spent part of her childhood in public housing and has many friends who still live in housing projects. Professor Hamilton has told her that he can almost certainly get her an internship in the city's Housing Authority, and he has even introduced her to a Mr. Kellogg, the assistant director of the Housing Authority, who expressed great interest in having an intern with knowledge of the city's housing projects. The internship would probably require 15 to 20 hours of work a week and pay about $9.00 an hour. It would involve something like taking "problem inventories" of the city's housing projects—that is, visiting each project and drawing up lists of the problems at each, carefully annotated and arranged in a recommended order of priorities.

Other matters Lavonne has on her mind:

She has been trying to save to buy a car, but has only a little over $500 in the bank.

She is paying her own tuition and fees, without help from her family, who cannot afford to help pay her school costs.

She has financial aid from school, but to keep it, she has to take 12 units a semester, and it is good for only four years. On the other hand, her higher salary would mean that she could get along without this aid, though it would be tight.

Lavonne now has to decide whether she will accept the promotion in the Chicken Empire chain. Her initial impulse was to say "Yes!" at once, but her natural caution held her back. The money would be wonderful, and she likes the idea of being the youngest station manager in the company's history; she is an ambitious person, and that kind of distinction appeals to her ambition. But she is also very impressed that her professor thinks so well of her that he is recommending her to a fairly important city official for an internship. What should she do?

## ASSIGNMENT

Discuss in detail the advantages and disadvantages of the different courses of action open to Lavonne Williams and come to a conclusion as to which one you think she should take and why.

## Discussion: Questions to Consider

Here are a few of the most important questions you will have to consider as you analyze Lavonne Williams's problem and begin making your notes:

If she takes the job, what would seem to be her prospects for future promotion? What specific evidence do we have that her prospects might be good? What specific evidence do we have that they might not be good?

If she takes the job, how will her finances be affected?

If she takes the job, to what extent will her schoolwork be affected and how?

If she takes the internship, to what extent will her schoolwork be affected and how? What benefits to her would the internship have?

If she takes the internship, how will her work hours be affected?

If she takes the internship, how would her finances be affected?

## Discussion: Making Comparisons

In comparing two or more ideas or things or actions, the most important step is to identify all of the factors that must enter into an intelligent comparison. For instance, if you were trying to decide which of two cars to buy and you compared them only on the basis of how they looked, you would be overlooking some of the most important factors in an intelligent comparison. For two cars, you would want to compare such things as cost, gas mileage, frequency-of-repair history of the two models, special features, costs of desirable options, and so on. It would be a good idea to make a list of these characteristics so you could weigh them against each other.

The problem you are dealing with here is more complex than comparing two cars because it has more factors to consider and because some of the factors are not entirely clear. Try to identify the main factors involved, the largest ones, and then see whether there are subelements within them. For instance, a main factor is income, and some subelements of income are starting income and potential future income. The classifying of related characteristics will help provide you with your essay and paragraph organization when you begin writing.

### Step One: Make Notes and Compare Them with Others

After you have underlined or highlighted the most important points in this assignment, write these points down on paper. Then go back through the assignment again to find the answers to the questions to consider. You will find some of the answers in the case itself, but you'll have to figure out some other answers by thinking about the information in the case. There are *specific* answers possible for each question.

In class, work with two other students to compare your notes and the answers to the questions. If you find some disagreements, try to figure out what the best answers are. Try to come to a consensus on the important points and the best answers.

Each group should now report on the points the group members consider most important so that the teacher can write them on the board for class discussion. Now the class as a whole can come to a consensus on the most important points. Write these points down since they will form the basis for the next step in the assignment.

### Step Two: Make an Outline and Compare It with Others

Read the following section on organizing "Lavonne Williams's Working Future." At home, go over your notes and decide how you think you might organize them into an essay. Make a rough list outline and bring the list to class for a discussion of ways to organize this paper.

### Organizing "Lavonne Williams's Working Future"

In your introduction, you should briefly introduce Lavonne Williams and state the decision she has to make. You can give your recommendation in a thesis in your introduction, or you can save it for your conclusion.

While textbooks and teachers often suggest that one way of organizing comparisons is to list all the qualities of the two things being compared in separate paragraphs or separate sections of the paper—say everything about one job in one section and everything about the other one in another—this is not usually good advice because it calls for "sack" paragraphs; it is rare to find an organization plan like this in professional writing.

It is much more common for writers to break down the things being compared into their parts, or factors, as you have done in your notes, and then compare them point by point so that readers can see related factors together. In this assignment, there are many points of comparison that could serve to organize the essay, and each one of these would make a good topic for a body paragraph. Some of these points are Lavonne's financial situation, her career prospects, her education, and her job satisfaction now and in the future. When you look at your list outline, identify the main points of comparison you will be covering and decide which ones you think will be body paragraphs. When you actually start writing, you may change your mind about what points you want to make into body paragraphs, but start with an idea ahead of time.

Be sure to start each body paragraph with a topic sentence that says what the paragraph will cover. For example, you might start a body paragraph with a sentence like this: "Lavonne Williams's financial situation would improve greatly if she took the manager's job." You would then show what her financial situation would be in both jobs, and how it would improve if she took the manager's job.

In your conclusion, explain why you have recommended one of Lavonne's options.

### Step Three: Write a Rough Draft

At home, using your list outline as your basis, write a rough draft of your essay on Lavonne's case. Do not worry about spelling and other mechanics as you are trying to get all of your information on paper in a logical order.

Refer to the Checklist for Evaluating Rough Drafts to see whether your own draft meets the requirements for this assignment, and use it during peer review.

Make two copies of your draft so that you have three copies to bring to class.

### CHECKLIST FOR EVALUATING ROUGH DRAFTS

1. Does the introduction indicate what the essay will be about and why the subject is important?
2. Is the essay divided into body paragraphs that cover single subjects?
3. Does each body paragraph start with a topic sentence, a sentence that tells what the paragraph will discuss?
4. Are all the sentences in each paragraph related to the point expressed in the topic sentence? Are there any places where unrelated ideas seem to come into any paragraphs?
5. Are all of the important issues covered?
6. Does the order of the points covered seem logical, or does anything seem out of place?
7. Is there a conclusion explaining what Lavonne should do *and why*?
8. Has the writer used joining words, in particular the words *and, but, or,* and *so* (or *and so*) to show the relationships between closely related points or ideas?

*Step Four: Peer Review*

In class, in groups of three, exchange your rough drafts and take turns reading your own drafts aloud. If you spot any errors as you read, correct them. Using the Checklist for Evaluating Rough Drafts, go over each paper question by question to identify both strengths and weaknesses. It is just as important to tell when something works really well as when it doesn't work. Call in your teacher if you need help or advice.

*Step Five: Write a Final Draft*

At home, write the final version of your paper, using your peers' and teacher's responses for guidance.

Check your writing to see if you've used the words *and*, *but*, *or*, and *so* (or *and so*) to join logically related ideas.

Review the proofreading tips in Chapter 1 and the following Special Proofreading section, and then proofread a printed copy of your paper.

## Special Proofreading

- As you have been doing, proofread for subject-verb agreement and for -*ed* endings on verbs and -*s* endings on plural nouns.
- Since you have completed the Getting Your Writing Right section in this chapter, you know how to proofread for correct pronouns:

  Are all your pronouns at the beginning of sentences subject pronouns?
  Are all your pronouns after your verbs object pronouns?
  Check to be sure that you have used the pronouns *they* or *them* when you referred to a noun that means more than one person or thing.

- *New Point:* Every time you've used Lavonne Williams's name, check to see whether it is a possessive—that is, whether you are writing about something she has (such as her name, decision, problem, career, or whatever). Look at the first sentence of this paragraph to see how the word *Williams* gets punctuated in such cases.

### CASE STUDY THREE: CHOOSING AN ADMINISTRATIVE ASSISTANT

Read the following case, which involves a company's hiring decision. You will evaluate the company's two most promising applicants for the position of administrative assistant and recommend the one you think is best for the company. You must do three things:

a. read the case,

b. read the assignment carefully to see exactly what you are being asked to do, and

c. read the discussion section on making comparisons.

When you have done these three things, go back over the case and read it closely, underlining or highlighting the most important points, the ones you will want to consider in your essay. Don't try to find these points on your first reading.

## Choosing an Administrative Assistant

You are one of the partners in a new company that has quickly outgrown its part-time secretary and temporary help. You need a full-time administrative assistant to oversee other clerical employees and run your office. This person will largely be working on his or her own, and so must be independent, hard working, and reliable. Your company runs the following ad in the local newspaper:

**Administrative Assistant** New Internet start-up seeks a detail-oriented, self-motivated, dependable, well-organized person able to take direction and follow through. Must be able to work independently in a fast-paced environment and have good oral and written communication skills. Must be able to oversee others productively. Excellent knowledge in Word and Excel required.

You have received several resumes that look promising, but two stand out, and you have asked the two applicants to submit letters of recommendation from previous employers. You have also made follow-up phone calls to two of these employers. On paper, both of the candidates are equally qualified, with the technical skills you require. Following are excerpts from the letters and calls you've made.

## Candidate A: Thomas
### Letter No. 1 (from Marian McCormick: Fitch, Wilson Company)

Thomas did a very good job in the two years he was with us, and we would have been happy if he had decided to stay. Unfortunately, he wanted to take classes toward a master's degree, and we could not find a work schedule for him that would enable him to do so.

He did not have to create correspondence for us, but he did prove very useful editing the letters of the three people he worked for, and so I assume he is a good writer. He was tactful and helpful in his limited telephone contacts with clients. Above all, he was reliable, always at work on time, never missing days for suspicious reasons. You would not call Thomas a very colorful or outgoing person, but his supervisors all reported that he always carried out whatever responsibilities they gave him, and that they were happy with his work.

*dull*

### LETTER NO. 2 (FROM JONATHAN CHU: FITCH, WILSON COMPANY)

I was one of the three people to whom Thomas was assigned as a kind of combination secretary and assistant. All three of us were more than satisfied with his work. With three people giving you work and assigning you different responsibilities, you had better be well organized and able to work well under pressure, and Thomas was both. I was particularly impressed that he never complained about his workload or deadlines assigned him, and he always managed to get everything done on time. He is very reserved, not the kind of person you would particularly want to have a drink with after work, but for us he was solid and reliable. We were sorry to see him go (although his replacement has been a lot more fun to be around).

*ouch!*

### LETTER NO. 3 (FROM PROFESSOR ROOSEVELT WHITSON: FARRELL UNIVERSITY)

Thomas took two classes from me, one undergraduate and one graduate, in our International Studies program, earning an A- in one and a B+ in the other. He was a diligent and careful student. He was always prepared and participated rather modestly in class discussions; his papers were well written and carefully researched, though they somewhat lacked originality. In the graduate class, he gave an oral presentation on our problems with North Korea and did a thorough job, missing nothing important, though, typically perhaps, his recommendations were conventional. I would give him high marks for being motivated and able to work independently. If he hadn't had to leave school because of financial problems, he would have completed his M.A. on time, though probably not with distinction.

### Candidate B: Margaret
### LETTER NO. 1 (FROM SAU-LING TANG: METRO CORP.)

Margaret is an exceptionally lively person, outgoing and with a ready smile for everyone. She was extremely popular with both her supervisor and her fellow employees in the 18 months she was with us, and I *great personality* believe she made some lasting friendships while she was here.

She is intelligent and has excellent secretarial skills, and she had numerous occasions to greet and work with clients. All praised her to me as an efficient and delightful person. With our professional clientele, she upheld the image of our firm extremely well.

## LETTER NO. 2 (FROM JAMES HODGES: JOS. FARNSWORTH AND CO.)

Margaret was a very popular employee who helped create a cheerful and positive atmosphere in our little part of the company. On the occasions when she was absent for whatever reason, people clearly missed her positive presence. I was quite happy with the professional level of her work. She has excellent verbal and written skills, and, when directed, pays close attention to detail. She is a hard worker, though she does not seem to work as well as some others when under great pressure. But in the normal course of business, she did an excellent job.

*cracks under pressure*

Because it wasn't clear, in her resume or letters of recommendation, why Margaret left her two previous jobs, your company has decided to call her previous employers.

## TELEPHONE CALL TO MS. TANG

Q: Do you know why Margaret left your company?

A: She didn't leave exactly. We had to let her go. *uh-oh*

Q: Why was that, can you say?

A: Well, as you know, personnel questions are confidential. It's hard for me to go beyond what I said in the letter I wrote for her. We were in a situation where we were somewhat overstaffed, and we had to cut several people. She was one of them.

Q: I understand. We are very interested in Margaret as an employee who will have a good deal of responsibility, have to supervise a few others, and need to be able to work without much supervision. Do you think, from your experience, that she would fit our requirements?

A: Possibly. It's hard to say what kind of a supervisor anyone would be when they've never done that sort of thing before, but Margaret is certainly warm and outgoing—very thoughtful in her personal relationships. People like her.

Q: You haven't said anything about carrying out responsibilities or working independently.

A: I would have to say that Margaret works best under fairly steady supervision.

*uh-oh*

**TELEPHONE CALL TO MR. HODGES**

Q: Can you tell me how long Margaret worked for you?

A: A little over a year.

Q: And did she quit, or did you let her go?

A: We let her go.

Q: Can you tell me why?

A: Well, I wasn't directly involved in that decision. I know the company was feeling a financial pinch and had ordered all its offices to cut back on personnel, so probably Margaret was just one of the unlucky ones.

Q: In your letter, you mentioned that she doesn't work well under pressure.

A: I didn't mean to give the wrong idea. When we were busy, she worked as well as anyone else. Basically, she's a good worker. It was just that it was hard to give her an assignment outside of her normal routine work and expect it to get done very expeditiously. She would tend to put off things like that. Once, in a case like that, I was having trouble getting her to finish a project, and then after she completed it, I found out that someone else had done it for her. But she did her regular work very well.

Q: But she was popular? Other workers didn't resent that?

A: Oh, no. Everyone liked her. Nobody complained.

---

**ASSIGNMENT**

You and your colleagues have already decided to interview both of these applicants. It is your job to write a report in which you evaluate what you have learned about the two applicants, recommend which one you think is the more qualified, and explain why. You will need to consider the strengths and weaknesses of both candidates. In doing so, you must consider each of the criteria your company has established for filling this position and the ways each candidate does or does not fulfill each criterion.

---

## Discussion: Making Comparisons

When we compare two or more people, ideas, things, or actions, the most important step is to identify all of the factors that must enter into an intelligent comparison. For instance, if you were trying to decide which of two cars to buy, and you compared them only on the basis of how they looked, you would be overlooking some of the most important factors in an intelligent comparison. Once you have identified all of the significant characteristics to be compared—in the case of two cars, cost, gas mileage, frequency-of-repair history of the two cars, special features, costs of desirable options, and so on—you would want to make a list of these characteristics so that you could compare the two cars in each category.

The hiring decision you are dealing with in this assignment is more complex than comparing two cars because it has more factors to compare, and because some of the factors are not as clear. A good starting point is the criteria the company has established for the position. Try to identify the main categories, or criteria, to compare, and then see whether there are subcategories within them. The groupings of related characteristics will help provide you with your essay and paragraph organization when you begin writing.

### Step One: Make Notes and Compare Them with Others

Go back over the case carefully and start a list of the most important factors in making a comparison between the two applicants, using the job requirements as a starting point. You can make a list of job requirements in one column; next to this column you can make two more—one for Thomas, and one for Margaret, in which you write whatever you know about their ability or inability to meet each job requirement. Note also any points that you think are important based on your own experience.

In class, work with two other students to compare your notes. Try to come to a consensus on the points involved in making a comparison between the two applicants.

Each group should now report to the teacher on the points the group members consider most important so that the teacher can write them on the board for class discussion.

### Step Two: Make an Outline and Compare It with Others

Read the following section on organizing "Choosing an Administrative Assistant." Then go over your notes and decide how you think you might organize them into an essay. Make a rough list outline as you did for your previous assignments, and bring the outline to class for discussion of ways to organize this paper.

## Organizing "Choosing an Administrative Assistant"

In your introduction, you will want to briefly introduce the applicants and the job they are applying for, and let your reader know what your essay will do. You can state your recommendation in a thesis in your introduction, or you can save it for your conclusion.

Although textbooks and teachers often suggest that one way of organizing comparisons is to list all the qualities of the two things being compared in separate paragraphs or separate sections of the paper—for instance, everything about Thomas in one section and then everything about Margaret in another—this is not usually good advice because it leads to "sack" paragraphs, which do not line up related points of comparison about the two applicants.

*"Sack" para.*

It is much more common for writers to compare two things point by point, that is, to write about both applicants together, comparing them characteristic by characteristic. In this assignment, it makes sense to evaluate the applicants according to the requirements for the job, writing one body paragraph about each requirement and how each applicant meets or does not meet it.

Remember that good body paragraphs begin with topic sentences that tell what the body paragraphs will cover.

Your conclusion should make clear why you have chosen one applicant over the other.

### Step Three: Write a Rough Draft

At home, using your list outline as your basis, write a rough draft of your essay, without worrying about spelling and other mechanics as you just get all of your information on paper in a logical order. Use the following Checklist for Evaluating Rough Drafts to see whether your essay meets the assignment requirements, and use it for peer review.

Make two copies of your draft so that you have three copies to bring to class.

### CHECKLIST FOR EVALUATING ROUGH DRAFTS

1. Does the introduction indicate what the essay will be about and why the subject is important?
2. Is the essay divided into body paragraphs that cover the main points involved in comparing the two candidates for the job?
3. Does each body paragraph start with a topic sentence, a sentence that tells what the paragraph will discuss?
4. Are all of the sentences in each body paragraph related to the point expressed in the topic sentence? Are there any places where unrelated ideas seem to come into any body paragraphs?
5. Are all the points of comparison covered, or is anything missing?
6. Does the order of the points seem logical, or does anything seem out of place?

> 7. Is there a conclusion explaining what the company should do, and why?
>
> 8. Has the writer used joining words, in particular the words *and, but, or,* and *so* (or *and so*) to show the relationships between closely related points or ideas?

### Step Four: Peer Review

In class, in groups of three, exchange your rough drafts and take turns reading your own drafts aloud. If you spot any errors as you read, correct them. Using the Checklist for Evaluating Rough Drafts, go over each paper question by question to identify both strengths and weaknesses. Call in your teacher if you need help or advice.

### Step Five: Write a Final Draft

At home, write the final version of your paper, using your peers' and teacher's advice for guidance.

Check to see that you've used the words *and, but, or,* and *so* (or *and so*) to join logically related ideas.

Then proofread a printed copy of your paper, after reviewing the proofreading tips in Chapter 1 and the following Special Proofreading section.

### Special Proofreading

- As you have been doing, proofread for subject-verb agreement and for *-ed* endings on verbs and *-s* endings on nouns.
- Check your pronouns:

   Are all your pronouns at the beginning of sentences subject pronouns?
   Are all your pronouns after your verbs object pronouns?
   Check to be sure that you have used the pronouns *they* or *them* when you want to refer to a noun that means more than one person or thing.

- *New Point:* Every time you've used Margaret's or Thomas's name, check to see whether it is a possessive—that is, whether you are writing about something he or she has (such as his or her name, decision, problem, career or whatever). Look at the first sentence of this paragraph to see how the words *Margaret* and *Thomas* get punctuated in such cases.

Proofread your paper for possessive apostrophes on Margaret's and Thomas's names throughout your paper.

## Getting Your Writing Right

### Using Coordinators

As you know, everyone, whether students or professionals, has to write rough drafts. Even very experienced writers are not able to produce a polished, finished text the first time. The following paragraph is from the very first draft of this book, and it's about using words called coordinators.

> Coordinators are words that show logical relationships between complete sentences. English has seven coordinators. We use four of them more often than the others. We'll focus on those four: *and, but, or,* and *so* (or *and so*). You use these words all the time when you're talking. Many people who haven't written much get so focused on getting individual sentences on paper that they forget to join them when they should. Sometimes they are afraid to join them. They fear that the sentences will get too long. The result is that readers spend their time trying to make the connections. The readers can't concentrate on the ideas.

I suppose the information in that paragraph is clear, but I wasn't happy with it, so I rewrote it as follows. See if you can find the changes I made.

> Coordinators are words that show logical relationships between complete sentences. English has seven coordinators, but we use four of them more often than the others, and so we'll focus on those four: *and, but, or,* and *so* (or *and so*). Many people who haven't written much get so focused on getting individual sentences on paper that they forget to join them when they should, or sometimes they are afraid to join them, fearing that the sentences will get too long. The result is that the readers spend their time trying to make the connections, and they can't concentrate on the ideas.

You probably noticed that in the second version the sentences are a lot longer, primarily because some of them have been joined with the four coordinators—*and, but, or,* and *so* (or *and so*). As you can see, longer sentences actually read better than a lot of very short ones, and they aren't hard to write.

In addition to joining sentences, the four main coordinators can also be used to introduce sentences. This is very common in good published writing. For now, however, you should work on using these words to join sentences.

While you know what these four coordinators mean, it's a good idea to know it consciously as well, so here is a quick review:

**and**     indicates addition of something similar to what one just wrote:

She made a living working as a waitress, *and* her parents gave her a little extra money.

**but**     indicates contrast or opposition between two things:

She made a living working as a waitress, *but* it wasn't a very good one.

**or**     indicates that two things are alternatives:

They said the medicine would work, *or* they'd give us our money back.

**so/and so**     mean the same thing, and you can use either one you like; they indicate cause-result relationships, that something has caused something else.

He insisted on driving far too fast, *and so* he eventually had an accident.

## Exercise 3A

Combine the following pairs of sentences using one of the four coordinators. The relationship between the sentences is indicated after each pair. Use a comma in front of the coordinator when it joins two complete sentences.

EXAMPLE:  They had to stop fighting.
They would get in trouble. (alternatives)
They had to stop fighting, *or* they would get in trouble.

1. John was a big sports fan.
He watched as many games on television as possible. (cause-result)

_____

2. Mary hated sports.
   She loved cooking shows. (contrast)

   _____

3. On Saturday mornings John could watch sports.
   Mary could watch Julia Child and the Frugal Gourmet. (alternatives)

   _____

4. John wanted to get to the television first.
   He tried to get up earlier than Mary. (cause-result)

   _____

5. Mary pointed out that she would watch her cooking shows.
   John would eat hot dogs. (alternatives)

   _____

6. John didn't mind hot dogs.
   He didn't want to eat them all the time. (contrast)

   _____

7. The ideal solution would be that he could watch sports.
   At the same time, Mary could watch cooking shows. (addition)

   _____

8. There had to be a solution to the problem.
   John couldn't think of one. (contrast)

   _____

9. Finally, he bought a huge screen television.
   He could watch sports as though he were at the games. (cause-result)

   _____

10. The next Saturday he got up at his usual time.
    There was Mary watching Julia Child in full size. (addition)

    _____

## Exercise 3B

Combine the following pairs of sentences as you did in exercise 3A. In this exercise, you will have to figure out the relationship between the sentences and decide which coordinator to use. After each sentence is a question to help you figure out the right one. _Don't guess._ If you think a particular coordinator is the right one, try it out; see whether the sentence sounds right, _whether it makes sense._ If it doesn't really, try another word.

Example: Most people like to give presents.
They forget how hard it is to choose a gift.
(Is this alternatives or contrast?)
Most people like to give presents, *but* (or *yet*) they forget
how hard it is to choose a gift. (contrast)

1.  Both men and women love to receive presents.
    They do not necessarily like to receive the same kinds of presents.
    (Is this alternatives or <u>contrast?</u>)
    _____ but _____

    _____

2.  Of course, some men like to receive the same kinds of presents most
    women like.
    Some women like to receive the same kinds of presents that most men
    like.
    (Is this contrast or <u>addition?</u>)     and
    _____

    _____

3.  But most men would rather get new tools than clothes.
    It is generally not a good idea to buy them a new pair of silk boxers for
    a special occasion.
    (Is this addition or <u>cause-result?</u>)        so
    _____ (either one seems ok?)

    _____

4.  Most women would usually rather get clothes or jewelry for their
    birthday.
    It would be a mistake to bring them a nice chainsaw.
    (Is this <u>cause-result</u> or alternatives?)
    _____ so _____

    _____

5.  All of this seems rather obvious.
    Some people do not understand these basic rules.
    (Is this <u>contrast</u> or addition?)
    _____ but _____

    _____

6. They must not have been paying attention when they were growing up.
   They spent their childhoods living in a cave.
   (Is this cause-result or alternatives?)

   _____

   _____

7. Children, of course, don't usually understand these things.
   They have to learn them from their parents.
   (Is this alternatives or cause-result?)

   _____

   _____

8. Little boys want to give little girls toy trucks for their birthdays.
   Little girls think little boys would really like new clothes.
   (Is this contrast or addition?)

   _____

   _____

9. Of course, some little girls really would like to get a toy truck.
   Their relatives usually make sure they get a doll instead.
   (Is this contrast or alternatives?)

   _____

   _____

10. The safest gift is a gift certificate.
    Then you have to choose the right store.
    (Is this contrast or addition?)

    _____

    _____

## Exercise 3C

Combine the following pairs of sentences as you did in exercises 3A and 3B. In this exercise, you will have to figure out the relationship between the sentences and decide which of the coordinators to use. *Don't guess.* If you think a particular coordinator is the right one, try it out; see whether the sentence sounds right, *whether it makes sense.* If it doesn't really, try another word.

EXAMPLE:  New teachers are usually full of enthusiasm.
          They want their students to be appreciative.
          New teachers are usually full of enthusiasm, so they want
          their students to be appreciative. (cause-effect)

1. New teachers usually start out their careers full of wonderful ideas about how great they will be and how much their students will like them. *but* They quickly discover a few basic facts of life.

   _____

   _____

2. They adapt to these facts quickly. *or*
   They don't continue long as teachers.

   _____

   _____

3. They usually want their students to like them. *and*
   They forget that liking the teacher is not what the students are there for.

   _____

   _____

4. They sometimes forget that the students are there to learn. *and*
   The teacher is there to teach.

   _____

   _____

5. If the teacher and students like each other, that's good. *but*
   It isn't the point of education.

   _____

   _____

6. New teachers sometimes think that since all students want to learn, their job is just to tell the students what they need to know. *so*
   They design lessons that are informative but boring.

   _____

   _____

7. Boring teachers quickly become unpopular and ineffective. *or, and, so*
   They quit teaching early.

   _____

   _____

8. Sometimes disappointed teachers blame the students for their problems. *and , w*
   Then they become unpleasant.

   _____

   _____

9. Of course, sometimes lazy students blame their teacher for their problems. *so*
   Then they fail the course.

   _____

   _____

10. School is not supposed to be entertaining.

    It should not be tedious.

    It is up to the teacher to try to make things as interesting as possible.

_____

_____

## Using Pronouns

**Subject Pronouns and Object Pronouns** Pronouns are words that (usually) substitute for nouns, and it's a good idea to use them frequently in your writing so that it isn't repetitious. You already know that. The challenge, however, is to use them correctly, which isn't hard to do if you pay attention. Let's quickly review the way pronouns work.

Some pronouns are *subjects* of verbs, and just like noun subjects, they precede the verb:

George ate the cake.
*He* ate the cake.

Some pronouns are *objects* of verbs, and just like noun objects, they follow the verb:

Maria bought a car.
Maria bought *it*.

Here is a list of subject and object pronouns:

| Subject | Object |
|---------|--------|
| I       | me     |
| you     | you    |
| he      | him    |
| she     | her    |
| we      | us     |
| they    | them   |
| it      | it     |

Subject and object pronouns get misused in two ways:

(1) In some cases, people put object pronouns in the position of subject pronouns—that is, in front of the verb:

Me and her went to a club last night.

Would you say "Me went to a club last night"?

Would you say "Her went to a club last night"?

If those two sentences are incorrect, then the sentence "Me and her went to a club last night" is also incorrect. You can test whether two pronouns joined with *and* are right or not by trying out each pronoun alone.

Although many people say a sentence like "Me and her went to a club last night," to educated people—like those who do the hiring and promoting for companies—it sounds childish because it is mainly children and high school students who do it.

(2) In other cases, people put subject pronouns in the position of object pronouns—that is, after the verb:

Juan gave the money to she and I.

Would you say "Juan gave the money to she"?

Would you say "Juan gave the money to I"?

Again, you can test whether two pronouns joined with *and* are right or not by trying out each pronoun alone.

## Exercise 3D

Check the pronouns in the sentences below. Rewrite the sentences, correcting the pronouns that are incorrectly used. Not every pronoun is wrong.

EXAMPLE: My best friend and me go dancing a lot.
My best friend and *I* go dancing a lot.

1. Me and Juan and Sandy went to a club last night.

_____

2. The club let Sandy in because she looked 21, but the doorman gave Juan and I a lot of trouble.

_____

3. He wanted to know if he and I were old enough.

_____

4. Me and Juan showed him our IDs, but he wasn't convinced.

_____

5. When we finally got in, Juan and I finally spotted Sandy dancing with a guy.

   _____

6. She and him were great dancers.

   _____

7. When she spotted Juan and me, she waved.

   _____

8. He and I started looking for someone to dance with.

   _____

9. Juan asked a girl to dance, and she and him just forgot about the rest of the world.

   _____

10. Finally, I found someone to dance with, and her and me danced all night.

   _____

## Pronoun Agreement

Pronouns come in two other varieties besides subject pronouns and object pronouns. There are also singular pronouns and plural pronouns, like this:

| Singular | Plural |
|----------|--------|
| I | we |
| he | they |
| she | they |
| it | they |
| you | you |

Nobody ever has problems with _I_, or _we_, or _you_, but the others can get mixed up. For one thing, it is important to remember that the pronoun _they_ can refer to more than one thing as well as more than one person. Both of the following sentences are correct:

Sylvia and Jamaal liked to work together on their math, but sometimes _they_ got distracted by each other. (_They_ refers to _Sylvia_ and _Jamaal_.)

The teacher assigned three math problems for homework, and _they_ were difficult. (_They_ refers to _problems_.)

The only difficulty with the other pronouns is to remember to use the right ones. Usually, pronoun errors arise when writers use a singular noun to refer to a lot of people, like this:

The housewife in Puritan New England had none of today's modern conveniences.

or a plural noun to refer to some group of people in general, like this:

Housewives in Puritan New England had none of today's modern conveniences.

In the first case, it is easy to forget that one has used a singular noun, and in the second case, it is equally easy to forget that one has used a plural noun, and so in either case errors like the following are easy to make:

The housewife in Puritan New England usually managed the family finances and was responsible for all housework, including making the family's clothes. *They* were not allowed to take jobs outside of the home.
[The second sentence should read, *She was* not allowed to take *a job* outside of the home.]

Housewives in Puritan New England had to give up all their property to their husbands after marriage, and *she* became completely dependent on *him* for her financial well-being.
[The second part of the sentence should read, and *they* became completely dependent on *them* for *their* financial well-being.]

## Exercise 3E

In the following passage, fill in the correct singular or plural pronouns and underline the noun each pronoun refers to.

Childcare is one of the major problems that keep poor people from achieving greater prosperity. Their financial situation puts (____) at a great disadvantage. A woman's best years for childbearing are also the time when (____) needs to get an education, get a good job, and get promotions. In years past, when only the husband worked, (____) could concentrate on his education and training when (____) was in his teens and twenties while his wife had the babies. Wives got high school or college educations, but basically (____) stayed home and raised the children. Now, when both partners work, wives must either postpone having children, or (____) can have (____) and get someone else to take care of (____). But if the woman has a child early or if (____) can't afford childcare, (____) has to work harder for an education and a career. Women from families with money do not have this problem. (____) can afford childcare. The woman from a poor background has a big problem. (____) cannot afford it.

## Summary and Review of Chapter 3

### Making Comparisons

In comparing two or more ideas or things or actions, the most important step is to identify all of the factors that must enter into an intelligent comparison. Once you have identified these factors, you can make your comparison point by point in the body of your essay.

Avoid "sack" paragraphs in which you write everything you know about one thing in one body paragraph or section of your essay, and everything you know about the other thing in another section.

### Coordinators

Four coordinators are particularly important for joining ideas in your writing: *and, but, or,* and, *so* (or *and so*).

Coordinators can also introduce sentences; when you put a coordinator on the front of a sentence, you still have a complete sentence.

### Pronouns

*Subject pronouns* precede their verbs. The subject pronouns are *I, you, he, she, we, they, it.*

*Object pronouns* follow their verbs. The object pronouns are *me, you, him, her, us, them, it.*

Pronouns can be singular or plural.

Remember that the pronouns *they* and *them* can refer to things as well as people.

**FOUR**

# Arguing
# a Position

**CASE STUDY ONE: JONETTA GRISSOM'S FUTURE**

Read the following case, which involves a personnel decision in a restaurant business. You will examine the arguments in this case and come to a conclusion about what you think should be done. To begin well, you must do three things:

    a. read the case,
    b. read the assignment, and
    c. read the discussion.

When you have done these three things, go back over the case, reading closely and underlining or highlighting the most important points, the ones you will want to consider in your essay. Don't try to identify these points on your first reading.

## Jonetta Grissom's Future

The manager of the local branch of a chain of national restaurants is facing a personnel problem. The restaurant chain is extremely well known and popular, serving everything from a cup of coffee at the counter to full dinners with wine. It is open 24 hours a day. Restaurants like this one do everything they can to keep their prices low, one of the reasons they are popular. But the single best way of keeping down expenses is to keep down employee costs, which are usually the single highest budget item for most businesses. As a result, pay at this place is not very good. The cooks are mostly immigrants who work for little more than minimum wage, and the waitresses are only slightly better paid, though they are eligible for small annual raises if they stay long enough. Turnover among the wait staff, is, however, quite high. The manager and assistant manager were both hired by the owner of the local franchise, as is customary in this chain. Both are quite young; the manager is in his early thirties, and the assistant manager is in his late twenties. Three of the waitresses—one black and two white—have been with this restaurant longer than any of the others, four years in one case and a little over three in the other two. Now one of these women, Jonetta Grissom—the African-American one—has asked the manager for a big favor.

She has discovered that she is eligible for a fully paid computer training class sponsored by the state government. The program was designed primarily to help women on welfare acquire job skills, but it is also open to working women under a certain annual income, and Jonetta qualifies. The problem is that the course begins at 7:00 P.M. on Tuesday and Thursday evenings, while her shift runs from 11:00 A.M. to 7:00 P.M. every day, with Wednesdays and Sundays off. She figures that she will need to leave work at 5:00 P.M. on the class days in order to get home, change, grab a quick bite to eat, and take the bus to the course. She is not asking to be paid for the four hours of lost work each week, just the time off. She hopes that with computer training, she will be able to get out of the dead-end, low-paying waitress job and get work that will enable her to lead a better life. She is 26 years old. The manager has asked the woman who works the 7:00 P.M. to 3:00 A.M. shift if she would be willing to come in two hours early on Tuesdays and Thursdays for overtime pay, but she says that childcare problems make that impossible.

The manager likes Jonetta and sympathizes with her desire to better herself. He knows how poor a life his single waitresses live on their incomes. And there is another reason to try to help Jonetta. Because of past discrimination against African-American employees by restaurants in this chain in other parts of the country, the entire chain is under court order to maintain nondiscriminatory practices in all aspects of its personnel policies. The manager has checked with the home office of the chain and been told that this situation does not fall under the court order, but at the same time he has been urged to try to find a helpful solution to the problem.

There is a simple solution, of course, but like most simple solutions, it creates its own set of problems. The solution is to hire someone part-time to fill in for Jonetta during the four hours she needs to be away. But this solution creates two big problems and possibly a third. One of the two big problems is that it's virtually impossible to hire someone to work four hours a week, and not even four hours on the same day. The pay is simply too little to make it worth anyone's while. So the manager would have to hire someone to work longer, including hours when he doesn't need an extra person, and, of course, he would have to pay these wages out of his already tight budget. The point of the restaurant, after all, is to make as much money as possible, not to waste it on unneeded help. The second big problem is that the hours when Jonetta needs to be away are among the restaurant's busiest during the day, the very time when good quick efficient service is most essential, and the manager would have to hire and train an inexperienced person to work these hours, not something that can be done overnight, or even in a month. Losing customers because of poor service during the dinner hour is, again, not a recipe for running a profitable business. The third possible problem is that giving one waitress time off during the restaurant's busiest hours might create morale problems among the other waitresses, who would likely think that the management is playing favorites. Morale is always a problem anyway at a place like this, and it could be disastrous to make it worse.

Following are opinions and information the manager has gotten on this issue.

### The Manager's Discussion with the Assistant Manager

AM: How long is this course supposed to last?

M: Eight weeks.

AM: That's a long time to be trying to fill in.

M: Tell me about it.

AM: Well, I'm against it. It just creates too many problems. I mean we're not running a welfare program here. If Jonetta needs to work a different shift, she can work a different shift.

M: Sure, John, but we don't have any openings in the 3:00 to 11:00 A.M. shift.

AM: We will. We always do eventually.

M: Yeah, but her class doesn't start eventually. It starts in two weeks. Anybody given us notice they're quitting in two weeks?

AM: No. But how can we hire someone totally new? We'd have to give her at least 20 hours a week, which we can't afford, and we'd have a screwed-up mess at dinnertime for at least three weeks, maybe longer, if the person even stayed that long.

M: I know, I know. Of course, we might luck out and get a vacancy on the morning shift. I've asked Jonetta if she could work that one, and she said she could. But in the meantime, the home office and the owner would have to cut us some slack on our profit margin.

AM: What if we don't lose anybody off the morning shift for the whole eight weeks? It could easily happen.

M: We have to assume that's what will happen. Worst-case scenario.

AM: Not good. Not at all good. Besides, I don't think this class will do her any good anyway. These waitresses don't know what studying is like. They never did it in school, which is why they're in these lousy jobs, and even when they get the chance, they don't do it later. She'll sign up for this class and be all gung-ho for about a month, and then she'll start falling behind and missing classes, and the whole thing will turn out to have been a huge waste of time.

M: Maybe. But she's been a really good worker for us, and she seems motivated. I'd like to help her if I can.

**The Last Paragraph of a Letter from the Home Office on This Issue.**
Although, as you know, we consider personnel decisions to be entirely up to our individual outlets, we would urge you, in this case, to consider Ms. Grissom's request carefully. As I said, this is clearly not a case that falls under the current court order, but at the same time, the company is particularly sensitive just now to its image as an equal opportunity employer, and we hope you will consider that as you make your decision.

**News Item from a National News Service Reprinted in the Local Newspaper.**
A recent study of federal and state programs designed to train welfare recipients in job skills has shown a disturbing trend. According to the National Survey Research Foundation, the training provided by these programs has often proven remarkably ineffective. Dawn Adams, spokesperson for NSRF, says, "The programs tend to have two chief flaws that prevent them from accomplishing their aims. First and probably most important is that those enrolling in the programs aren't paid to do it. They must take the courses, often at inconvenient times, while still managing to keep sufficient income and take care of children. Often, these two problems overwhelm them." Adams notes that it's hard to succeed, particularly at a brand-new task, "when you've never succeeded before." She adds, "Without adequate support, they are practically guaranteed to fail."

The second problem, according to Adams, is that "many of the programs are so badly designed that they do not actually teach marketable skills." The NSRF study notes, in particular, that many courses purporting to teach computer skills really teach only the most basic kinds of word processing, a skill with very little market value.

As Adams says, "Courses like these are a cruel hoax. They raise the hopes of poor people, women especially, who invest time and energy in them only to find that they have learned nothing of value."

At the same time, Adams warns that not all programs and courses are badly designed. "While we would strongly suggest that most of them be reviewed and, if necessary, changed," she says, "some are very good and should provide genuinely helpful training to people with few if any marketable skills."

**ASSIGNMENT**

Write an essay in which you evaluate the arguments for and against granting Jonetta the time off she has requested and explain what decision you think the manager should make and why.

### Discussion

As you make your decision about what the manager should do, you will want to consider the arguments for and the arguments against allowing Jonetta to take the time off for a computer course. You may find that you think it's a good idea to grant Jonetta the time off, but also feel that it would be difficult to find a solution to the staffing problem. If so, can you think of a way that the manager can deal with the staffing problem that her absence could create? You will want to show how the arguments in favor of allowing her the time off are stronger than the opposing arguments. Or you may think that Jonetta should not be granted the time off. In this case, you will want to show how the arguments against allowing her the time off are stronger than the opposing arguments.

Whichever position you take, you will need to consider both sides of the issue. If you present only your side, your reader will think of arguments opposing your position, and you won't have a chance to respond to them. By presenting both sides of the issue, you show your reader that you have carefully considered all of the arguments and have come to a reasonable conclusion.

*Step One: Make Notes and Compare Them with Others*

Go back over the case and write down the most important points. You will need to write down the basic problem and list the arguments for and against allowing Jonetta to take time off of work to attend a course.

In class, work with two other students to compare your notes. Exchange views on the points you and they think are important, and make any additions or subtractions from your list if you change your mind about anything.

Each group should now report to the teacher on the points the group members consider most important.

*Step Two: Make an Outline and Compare It with Others*

Read the following section on organizing "Jonetta Grissom's Future." At home, go over your notes and decide how you think you might organize them into an essay. Make a rough outline as you did for your previous assignments, and bring the outline to class for discussion of ways to organize this paper.

## Organizing "Jonetta Grissom's Future"

In your introduction, you will need to briefly state the problem the manager is facing so that your readers understand the basic situation. You can state your opinion about what the manager should do in a thesis statement in your introduction, or you can state it in your conclusion.

In the body of your essay, you will want to discuss why the manager should or should not grant Jonetta the time off. When you plan the organization of a position paper, you follow essentially the same process you follow with a comparison paper. You will want to match related arguments, in this case the matching arguments for and against allowing Jonetta to take time off work to attend a computer course. For instance, one argument in favor of giving Jonetta the time off is that the national restaurant chain is trying to be supportive of minorities because of its past history of discrimination against African-American employees. However, the home office has decided that Ms. Grissom's situation is not covered by the court order requiring the restaurant chain to maintain nondiscriminatory practices in its personnel policies. These two opposing points both address the issue of discrimination, and so you can discuss them together, in the same body paragraph. What other factors must the manager consider as he makes his decision? As you look over your notes, decide which opposing arguments match up, and plan the body of your essay so that each body paragraph focuses on a matching set of opposing arguments. Make sure that each body paragraph has a topic sentence.

Be sure to avoid "shopping bag" or "sack" paragraphs in which you consider all of the arguments in favor of allowing Jonetta the time off in one paragraph or section of your essay, and all of the arguments against allowing her the time off in another. "Sack" paragraphs do not give your readers the opportunity to see how you've compared related arguments and reached your decision about what the manager should do.

Since you will be taking a stand in this essay, you will want to emphasize your own points of view while, at the same time, acknowledging the opposing arguments. The concessive subordinators will help you concede points you oppose while downplaying them and stressing your own position.

In your conclusion, explain why you have recommended the action you think the manager should take.

### Step Three: Write a Rough Draft

At home, using your outline as a basis, write a rough draft of your essay. Do not worry about spelling and other mechanics while you are trying to get your ideas down on paper in logical order. Use the following Checklist for Evaluating Rough Drafts to see whether your draft meets the assignment's requirements, and use it in peer review.

Make two copies of your draft so that you have three copies to bring to class.

### CHECKLIST FOR EVALUATING ROUGH DRAFTS

1. Does the introduction indicate what the essay will be about and why the subject is important?
2. Is the essay divided into body paragraphs that cover the main points?
3. Does each body paragraph start with a topic sentence, a sentence that tells what the paragraph will discuss?
4. Are all of the sentences in each body paragraph related to the point expressed in the topic sentence? Are there any places where unrelated ideas come into any paragraphs?
5. Are all the most important points involved covered, or is anything missing?
6. Does the order of points seem logical, or does anything seem out of place?
7. Is there a conclusion explaining what the manager should do and why?
8. Has the writer used the joining words *and*, *or*, and *so* (or *and so*) to join logically related ideas?
9. Has the writer used the words *but*, *while*, *whereas*, *although*, *even though*, and *though* to show contrast and concession?

*Step Four: Peer Review*

In class, in groups of three, exchange your rough drafts and take turns reading your own drafts aloud. If you spot any errors as you read, correct them. Using the Checklist for Evaluating Rough Drafts, go over each paper to identify both strengths and weaknesses. Call in your teacher if you need help or advice.

*Step Five: Write a Final Draft*

At home, write the final version of your paper, relying on your peers' and teacher's suggestions for guidance.

Check each paragraph to see if you've used the coordinators *and, or,* and *so* (or *and so*) to join logically related ideas.

Check to make sure you've used *but, while, whereas, although, even though,* and *though* to show contrast and concession.

Finally, review the proofreading guidelines in Chapter 1 and the following Special Proofreading section, and proofread a printed copy of your paper.

## Special Proofreading

- As you did in your previous papers, proofread for subject-verb agreement, *-ed* endings on verbs, and *-s* endings on plural nouns.
- Check to see that you've used subject pronouns in front of your verbs and object pronouns after verbs.
- Check to see that you've used the pronoun *they* or *them* to refer to plural nouns.
- Check to see whether any of your nouns are possessives and whether you've used apostrophes in those cases.
- When you've started sentences with *while, whereas, although, even though,* or *though,* make sure that these words join two logically related ideas into one sentence.
- Check your spellings of *whereas.* It is one word, not two. Check your spellings of *even though.* They are two words, not one.

### CASE STUDY TWO: THE ATHLETES CLUB

Read the following case, which concerns the issue of sexual harassment at a high school. It will be your job to evaluate the case and recommend the solution you think is best. To do this well, you must do three things:

a. read the case,

b. read the assignment, and

c. read the discussion.

When you have done these three things, go back over the case, reading closely and underlining or highlighting the most important points, the ones you will want to consider in your essay. Don't try to find these points on your first reading.

### The Athletes Club

For many years, your high school has had, in addition to the usual student government, what it calls a Student Judicial Court. The court is an elected body of six seniors who help the school administration decide whether or not students who have violated rules will be punished. The judicial court also recommends the kind of punishments it thinks should be administered. The court doesn't have any real power, of course. Only the principal or district superintendent can actually punish students, but tradition has established that except in rare instances, the principal and superintendent will normally follow the court's recommendations.

The Student Judicial Court has had a long history of making essentially Mickey Mouse decisions—recommendations to the principal on matters such as too many absences, fighting on campus, disobeying teachers, and so on. The court made headlines in the local newspapers seven years ago when some students used the journalism facilities after hours to put out a parody edition of the school newspaper announcing that the principal and superintendent had been caught in a love triangle with the algebra teacher, a woman in her late sixties. The principal and superintendent had urged the court to recommend expulsion of the students, but after the algebra teacher testified that she thought the parody issue was funny and had sent copies to her son and daughter, the court recommended that the students perform 15 hours of after-school services to the school doing such chores as cleaning up the gym after basketball games and the lunchroom after lunch. The local newspapers both wrote editorials praising the student court for being wiser than the principal and the superintendent.

Now a more serious matter has come up, and the Student Judicial Court is on a real hot seat for the first time in its existence. In fact, the principal and superintendent jointly announced that, for the first time in its existence, the court would not be allowed to make a recommendation on this matter, but protests among the students, a petition signed by many of the teachers, and editorials in the local newspapers caused this decision to be reversed. The court will make a recommendation.

Here is the case.

A number of years ago, no one is sure quite when, a small in-group of athletes formed an informal club or fraternity, getting together once in a while to celebrate a win or discuss what to do about a losing team or just drink some beer and hang out. The group never gave itself a name and was never acknowledged by the school, but everyone knew it existed and who was in it at any given time. At worst the group was fairly harmless, despite the beer drinking, and at best it sometimes had a positive effect on the play of the school's teams. Beginning a few years ago, however, some members of the group began acting in ways that were unpleasant to some students, mainly females.

Everyone understands that adolescents engage in a certain amount of more or less serious sexual teasing, and as long as it doesn't get out of hand in one way or another, most adults look the other way. Most students are having enough problems with their own lives to worry about anyone else's.

So at first no one thought anything about how some of the club members were beginning to behave. They tended to tease a small number of girls, always freshmen, always ones who dressed in a feminine way and seemed shy and vulnerable. At first, they made obscene proposals under their breaths in the hallways, and then they began to graduate to sly touching in crowded places. Usually, they would leave their victims alone after a couple of weeks of this behavior, and the girls were too insecure and frightened to say anything. Most of the other students either thought it was funny or none of their business when the girls suddenly reddened or made shrieks of surprise.

As time went on, however, the group began to get bolder. The whispered propositions began to get longer and more detailed, the touching more intimate. The group members began to give their victims obscene nicknames that they used aloud in the hallways or classrooms to make them blush and make the other students laugh.

Finally, last year, one of the girls told her parents what had been happening, and the parents went to the principal. He promised that the behavior would stop and called into his office the group members the girl had identified. He explained to them why this behavior was unacceptable and warned them that they could be expelled if they continued. At that point, the boys stopped the worst of their behavior, but they continued more subtle forms of harassing the girl who had complained, and at the end of the school year, she transferred to another school.

Now, during the fall semester, the behavior has resumed. When one girl threatened to tell the principal, three of the boys pushed her into one of the boys' lavatories, threatening that it would be worse if she talked. But she did talk, and when she did, other girls who had been harassed also came forward along with their parents. Again, the principal called in the offenders, and again the boys discontinued their physical attacks, but they continued their verbal teasing, making the girls objects of laughter in their classes. Now the girls' parents have hired a lawyer, and the lawyer has written the principal and superintendent that unless this behavior ceases entirely and in all of its manifestations, the families will sue the principal and superintendent personally and the school district for damages caused by emotional stress. The boys named in the lawyer's letter are two juniors and three seniors, all of whom are average to good students who plan to attend college. One of the seniors is being recruited as a football player by several major colleges.

Although the principal and superintendent have informed the Student Judicial Court that they will not feel themselves bound by any decision it makes, they have reminded the court that whatever it decides will reflect on the school and on the students attending it. Students talking to court members have generally fallen into two camps on this issue. The minority group, mostly girls but with a few boys, feel that the behavior of the athletes has been totally out of bounds and that they should be expelled. Most of the students, however, the majority of them boys but with a fairly large number of girls too, think that this whole thing has been overblown and that the victim girls are overreacting to normal teasing. Most students don't think that girls should be grabbed or touched against their will, but they don't see anything particularly wrong with verbal teasing or using mildly obscene nicknames.

At its first meeting, the members of the court got into a heated discussion that led nowhere, and so the president of the court asked each of the members to write a paper stating their opinions in this case, to back up the opinions with specifics as they know them, and to make a tentative recommendation as to what, if any, penalties they think the athletes should be given. The court may decide that the behavior of the boys is acceptable or unacceptable, or they may decide that some of it is acceptable and some of it isn't. They may recommend that no action be taken against the boys or that actions be taken. In the latter case, they may decide that the boys be warned only. They may decide that they be warned and threatened with probation or expulsion. They may decide that they be put on probation, in which case they must decide what the terms of the probation are and how long it should last. Finally, they may decide that some or all of the boys should be expelled from the school.

You are a member of the Student Judicial Court, and you are now to write your paper.

---

**ASSIGNMENT**

Write an essay in which you discuss how serious you believe the offenses of the members of the Athletes Club are, and following that, what punishment, if any, you think should be given them and why you think that punishment (or lack of it) would be appropriate.

---

### Discussion

The issue here, "sexual harassment," is one that is being taken seriously by schools and the larger society. Sexual harassment is both socially undesirable and illegal. At question is whether members of the Athletes Club caused mental or physical suffering to others, and whether their actions prevented other students from fulfilling their purpose in attending school.

The most important aspects of this essay will be your evaluation of the seriousness of the behavior and the reasoning behind your recommended punishment or your recommendation that no punishment be handed out. Judgments of this kind must very carefully supported.

Whichever position you take, you must consider both sides of the issue. If you present only your side—that is, only your arguments in favor of punishing the students, or only your arguments against punishing them—your readers will think of arguments opposing your position, and you won't have a chance to respond to them. By presenting both sides of the issue, you show your readers that you have carefully considered all of the arguments and have come to a reasonable conclusion.

*importance of recognizing opposition*

### Step One: Make Notes and Compare Them with Others

On paper, write down the facts that led to the lawyer's letter to the principal. Then make two lists: One list will cover the points that show whether or not the students' behavior was serious enough to deserve punishment, and the second list will show all of the possible punishments you can think of that might be applied. Make notes about the appropriateness or inappropriateness of these punishments.

In class, work with two other students to compare your notes, checking to make sure none of you has left out any important points. Try to come to a consensus on what these points are. Discuss the seriousness of the offenses, and discuss the question of punishment. It is not important to agree on these points, but it is important for each of you to hear what the others have to say.

Each group should now report to the teacher on the points the group members consider most important, and the class should discuss these points.

### Step Two: Make an Outline and Compare It with Others

Read the following section on organizing "The Athletes Club." At home, go over your notes and decide how you think you might organize them into an essay. Make a rough list outline as you did for previous assignments, and bring the outline to class for discussion of ways to organize this paper.

## Organizing "The Athletes Club"

In your introduction, you should briefly summarize the background of this case. You may state your recommendation in a thesis, or you can save your recommendation for your conclusion.

In the body of your essay, you need to first explain the degree to which you think the problem is serious or not, and the reasons you think it is serious or not. Following will be the section in which you discuss the different options for either punishing or not punishing the boys involved. Here you need to decide why each possible punishment is either appropriate or inappropriate and explain why.

The body of your essay will probably be fairly easy to organize. You will take essentially the same approach that you would take with a comparison/contrast paper; that is, you will compare matching sets of opposing arguments and discuss each set, point by point, in the body paragraphs. Remember that your body paragraphs will need topic sentences so that their points are clear.

Be careful to not write "shopping bag" paragraphs. In other words, do not discuss all of the reasons in favor of punishment in one body paragraph or section of your essay and all of the reasons against punishment in another.

Since you are taking a position, you will want to acknowledge arguments that you do not agree with and emphasize your own point of view. You can use the concessive subordinators to acknowledge the opposition and, at the same time, emphasize your own position.

In your conclusion, explain your recommendation and the reasons for it.

### Step Three: Write a Rough Draft

At home, using your list outline as your basis, write a rough draft of your essay. As usual, do not worry about spelling and other mechanics while you are getting your ideas down on paper in a logical order. Refer to the following Checklist for Evaluating Rough Drafts to see whether your own draft meets the requirements for this assignment, and use it during peer review.

Make two copies of your draft so that you have three copies to bring to class.

---

### CHECKLIST FOR EVALUATING ROUGH DRAFTS

1. Does the introduction indicate what the essay will be about and why the subject is important?
2. Is the essay divided into body paragraphs that cover the main points involved in this issue?
3. Does each body paragraph start with a topic sentence, a sentence that tells what the paragraph will discuss?
4. Are all the sentences in each body paragraph related to the point expressed in the topic sentence? Do any sentences seem out of place?
5. Are all the most important points involved in the issue covered, or is anything missing?
6. Does the order of the points seem logical, or does anything seem out of place?
7. Is there a conclusion explaining what the school should do and why?
8. Has the writer used the joining words *and, or, but,* and *so* (or *and so*) to show the relationships between closely related points or ideas?
9. Has the writer used *but, while, whereas, although, even though,* and *though* to show contrast and concession?

---

### Step Four: Peer Review

In class, in groups of three, exchange your rough drafts and take turns reading your own papers aloud. If you spot any errors as you read, correct them. Using the Checklist for Evaluating Rough Drafts, go over each paper question by question to identify both strengths and weaknesses. Call in your teacher if you need help or advice.

### Step Five: Write a Final Draft

At home, write the final version of your paper, relying on your peers' and teacher's advice for guidance.

Check each paragraph to see whether you've used the coordinators *and, or,* and *so* (or *and so*) to join logically related ideas.

Check to make sure that you have used *but, while, whereas, although, even though,* and *though* to show contrast and/or concession.

Print a copy of your paper and proofread it. Review the proofreading tips in Chapter 1 and the following Special Proofreading section.

## Special Proofreading

- As you did in your previous papers, proofread for subject-verb agreement, *-ed* endings on verbs, and *-s* endings on nouns.
- Check to see that you've used subject pronouns in front of your verbs and object pronouns after verbs.
- Check to make sure that you have used *they* or *them* to refer to plural nouns.
- Check to see whether any of your nouns are possessives and whether you've used apostrophes in those cases.
- When you've started sentences with *while, whereas, although, even though,* or *though,* make sure that these words join two contrasting ideas.
- Check your spellings of *whereas.* It is one word, not two. Check your spellings of *even though.* They are two words, not one.

---

**CASE STUDY THREE: GENERAL EDUCATION AT ADDAMS STATE**

Read the following case, which concerns the general education requirements at a four-year college. You will evaluate two proposed general education plans and recommend what you think is the best program for the college to adopt. To do this well, you must do three things:

    a. read the case,
    b. read the assignment, and
    c. read the discussion section.

When you have done these three things, go back over the case, reading closely and underlining or highlighting the most important points, the ones you will want to consider in your essay. Don't try to find these points on your first reading.

### General Education at Addams State

In many colleges, particularly four-year schools, general education programs are an ongoing source of conflict. Historically, the purpose of general education courses was to give freshmen and sophomores a broadly based education before they began majoring in a specific subject. The heart of general education was usually subjects such as English, history, one of the "hard" sciences (physics, chemistry, botany, biology, and so on), a foreign language, and perhaps a social science (sociology, psychology) or an arts course.

Recently these programs have been under attack and have undergone changes. Few colleges require a foreign language now, and new courses such as ethnic studies have sometimes been added.

Not surprisingly, academic departments that have traditionally offered general education courses have wanted to keep them, but some departments would like to see general education reduced so that their majors can be expanded. There is a conflict here between the educational "breadth" supposedly provided by large general education programs and an increased opportunity for students to receive technical training in specialized fields, which would mean reducing general education.

Students, too, have tended to have mixed feelings about general education. Many students have enjoyed such courses, but many others see such requirements as an intrusion on their right to take what they want. They often see general education as something to get out of the way so they can take what they are really interested in.

For almost three years, the faculty members at Addams State University have been debating a new general education program, and they are divided between two plans. One of the plans, the Williams Plan, was developed by Dr. Randolph Williams, professor of African-American studies, and modified by colleagues in the Creative Arts, History, and English Departments. The other plan, the Ozawa Plan, was developed by a committee of business and engineering faculty headed by Dr. Mason Ozawa, professor of electrical engineering. Here are the two plans:

### The Williams Plan

| | |
|---|---|
| English composition | 6 units |
| English/American literature (including one course in ethnic American literature) | 9 units |
| American history | 6 units |
| European history | 3 units |
| African or Asian history | 3 units |
| Creative arts | 6 units |
| Science | 6 units |
| Social science | 6 units |
| Senior seminar | 3 units |
| Total | 48 units |

### The Ozawa Plan

| | |
|---|---|
| English composition | 6 units |
| Speech | 3 units |
| Critical thinking | 3 units |
| History | 3 units |
| Literature and the arts | 3 units |
| Science | 3 units |
| Total | 21 units |

Currently, most majors at Addams State run between 39 and 60 units. Engineering majors are 99 units and business majors are 70 units, although the School of Business wishes to increase its required units to 76 with two more courses. Addams State requires 120 units for graduation as do all the universities in the state university system. The 48 units of the Williams Plan are the traditional number of G.E. units required at Addams.

A number of articles about this issue have appeared in the school newspaper, the *Campus Outlook*, and in the nearby *Capital City Post*. Following are excerpts from some of those articles.

### From the *Campus Outlook*

As the fight over a new General Education program continues unabated in the Academic Senate, a new voice has suddenly been heard—that of the students. The students of Sociology 220, guided by Professor Mary MacArthur, have taken a poll of 100 students chosen at random in the main cafeteria of the Student Union to see which of the contending plans they prefer.

Not surprisingly, perhaps, 68 percent of the students favored the Ozawa Plan, which calls for a minimal G.E. program of only 21 units. Twenty percent favored the Williams Plan, which would require 48 units of General Education courses, as is required under the existing plan. The rest said they didn't care.

But the students taking the poll are not sure that this landslide for the Ozawa Plan necessarily means what it seems to mean.

Joanne Silva, representing the students of Sociology 220, said, "There are two problems here. First, everyone hates the current program, and when they see that the Williams Plan calls for the same number of units, they tend to just reject it automatically."

The other problem, according to Silva, is that almost none of the students knew any of the details of the two plans before encountering the pollsters, who had to outline the plans for them. "How informed do you think those preferences can be, under these circumstances?" Silva asked. "Nobody has given the issue any thought."

A sampling of student opinions by the *Outlook* got pretty much the same response. As Marcus Smith, a Business Administration major, put it, "I just want to get on with my career. I don't need all this history and English, and I don't want to take it. The G.E. classes I've had to take have been lousy. Half the teachers don't even care whether you learn the stuff. It's been a waste of time."

## From the *Campus Outlook*

When it comes to General Education, the faculty divides into two camps along departmental lines. The humanities and fine arts departments—like the English, History, Art, Music, Philosophy, and Ethnic Studies Departments—favor the Williams Plan, while the Schools of Business and Engineering favor the Ozawa Plan.

The sciences and social sciences seem split. Most of the Economics and Physics Departments, for example, favor the Williams Plan, but most of the Psychology and Chemistry Departments favor Ozawa.

Professor Donald Chan in the English Department expressed the sentiment of most of the Williams advocates: "We think that students should get an education here, not just get trained in a technical subject. We want students to graduate with an awareness of how rich this world is and how they can be a part of that richness."

On the other hand, Professor Lillian Frost of the Business Computing Department argues, "Students can't spend their lives here. They can't take everything. And if they're going to be competitive on the job market, they have to take the courses that will make them competitive. Low-unit majors just don't cut it anymore."

The one thing everyone agrees on is that the current system is so complicated and unpopular that it has to go.

### From the *Campus Outlook,* Letters to the Editor Section

My colleague, Professor Chan, was quoted in your last issue on the merits of what has traditionally been called a "liberal education," that is, a broad schooling in a diverse number of traditional subjects.

There are two problems with his argument. First, we have something like that now, and the students hate it. Second, the faculty hates it too. Why else do the English and History and Ethnic Studies faculties give most of their G.E. courses to brand-new teachers and part-timers?

If they think General Education is so great, how come the senior professors aren't lining up to teach these classes instead of relegating them to the powerless and the underpaid? If they believed what they are saying, they would surely be teaching these great courses themselves, wouldn't they? A survey of this semester's offerings by our department shows that only 14 percent of our G.E. courses are being taught by senior faculty.

Could this be one of the reasons students seem to hate these classes?

—Mariette E. Johnson
Professor of Marketing

### From the *Campus Outlook*

At yesterday's convocation of business leaders from Capital City, as well as nearby Tampa and Seattle, the students and faculty at Addams State got an earful on what is wanted in our graduates.

In the words of Sherman Grant of the Monolith Corporation, "What we're getting from the schools is a bunch of trained seals who can't read and write and think for themselves. They don't know anything except accounting, or whatever they've majored in."

Other speakers weren't quite so negative as Mr. Grant, but they tended to say the same sort of thing. Again and again, they said they wanted applicants who could read, write, and think well more than they wanted people with narrow expertise in particular fields.

"Of course," said Marjorie Paderewski, director of recruitment for State Utilities, "we'd really like to have it all—people both well trained and well educated. The people with the training do get most of the entry-level jobs. But the people with the education too get most of the promotions."

**From the *Capital City Post***

A poll of University of Virginia alumni released today indicated that 91 percent believe a liberal arts education is good preparation for fulfilling careers.

The alumni recommended liberal arts majors to students planning to enter their own fields. About 20 percent were in law, nearly 10 percent each were in medicine and finance, and more than 5 percent were in electronics and government.

Many of the alumni, who have been out of college between 5 and 15 years, are working in fields with no apparent connection to their undergraduate majors.

**From the *Capital City Post***

Washington—The Carnegie Foundation for the Advancement of Teaching issued a report today that was highly critical of the nation's colleges, claiming that instead of educating students they are simply handing out degrees.

The 242-page report, titled "College: The Undergraduate Experience in America," concluded: "Driven by careerism and overshadowed by graduate and professional education, many of the nation's colleges and universities are more successful in credentialing than in providing a quality education for their students."

The report recommends the following changes:

- Make all college seniors write a senior thesis and defend it orally in a seminar with classmates.
- Restrict the growing use of part-time faculty members. It said part-timers are "often insecure and unconnected to the college" and are not given adequate time and office space to help their students.
- Bolster general education requirements and require students to study an integrated core of seven broad areas: language, art, cultural heritage, the social web of institutions, nature, work, and self-identity.

**ASSIGNMENT**

Examine carefully the issue facing the Addams State faculty and write an essay in which you recommend a course of action for the school—whether to adopt the Williams Plan, the Ozawa Plan, or some other solution to the problem.

## Discussion

The Addams State problem represents a classic one in American education. Most American colleges originally stressed a general education in languages, history, the arts, and science as the key to success not only in a profession but in one's personal life. As knowledge in all fields grew and the fields became more specialized, and as the world of work became more technically oriented, college curriculums changed to adapt to the new realities. Now many schools—and many employers—debate whether a broad education or a highly specialized one is better. Of course, one place where specialized training is assumed to be appropriate is graduate programs, and some argue that it is better to get a broad education as an undergraduate and a more specialized one as a graduate student. Others feel, however, that since not everyone can go to graduate school, schools should offer the best possible technical programs to their undergraduates.

As you study this issue, consider not only your own needs as a student but also the needs of an entire student body. In other words, you will be making a recommendation for a general education program, not a specific course of study designed to meet just one student's needs.

Remember to consider arguments opposing your position. If you present only your side, your readers will think of arguments opposing your position, and you won't have a chance to respond to them. By presenting both sides of the issue, you show your readers that you have carefully considered all of the arguments and have come to a reasonable conclusion.

### *Step One: Make Notes and Compare Them with Others*

Go back over the case and write down what you consider to be the most important points. Be sure to take into consideration the number of units involved in relation to the overall number of units students are expected to take in order to graduate, and be sure also to consider the issues raised in the newspaper articles. You should also think about your own education and make any notes you wish about your own views on the issue.

In class, work with two other students to compare your notes. Exchange views on the points you and they think are important and make any additions or subtractions from your list if you change your mind about anything.

Each group should now report on the points the group considers most important so that the teacher can write them on the board for class discussion.

*Step Two: Make an Outline and Compare It with Others*
Read the following section on organizing "General Education at Addams State." At home, go over your notes and decide how you think you might organize them into an essay. Make a rough outline as you did for your previous assignments, and bring the outline to class for discussion of ways to organize this paper.

## Organizing "General Education at Addams State"

In your introduction, you should briefly state the decision Addams State has to make. You can state your opinion in a thesis in your introduction, or you can state it in your conclusion.

As you plan the organization of your essay, remember that you are essentially planning a comparison paper; that is, you are comparing related opposing arguments. Use your notes on the number of units each plan would require and your notes on the important issues raised in the newspaper articles as your starting point. You can compare the units required by each plan and discuss the related arguments on unit load. Then, point by point, in the body paragraphs, consider the issues raised in the newspaper articles, matching related arguments. Each body paragraph should have a topic sentence that makes the point of the paragraph clear.

Be sure to avoid "sack" paragraphs, in which you write all of the arguments in favor of one plan in one body paragraph or section of the essay, and all of the arguments in favor of the other plan in another. "Sack" paragraphs do not give you or your readers the opportunity to compare related points together.

Since you are arguing a position, you will want to emphasize your point of view as you acknowledge arguments you do not agree with. You can use the concessive subordinators to acknowledge an argument you are opposed to, and at the same time, give it less emphasis than your own position.

In your conclusion, explain your recommendation and the reasons for it.

*Step Three: Write a Rough Draft*
At home, using your list outline as your basis, write a rough draft of your essay. As usual, do not worry about spelling and other mechanics while you are just getting your ideas down on paper. Use the following Checklist for Evaluating Rough Drafts to see whether your own draft meets the requirements for this assignment, and use it also in class during peer review.

Make two copies of your draft so that you have three copies to bring to class.

**CHECKLIST FOR EVALUATING ROUGH DRAFTS**

1. Does the introduction indicate what the essay will be about and why the subject is important?
2. Is the essay divided into body paragraphs that cover the main points?
3. Does each body paragraph start with a topic sentence, a sentence that tells what the paragraph will discuss?
4. Are all the sentences in each body paragraph related to the point expressed in the topic sentence? Are there any places where unrelated ideas seem to come into any paragraphs?
5. Are all the most important points involved covered, or is anything missing?
6. Does the order of the points seem logical, or does anything seem out of place?
7. Is there a conclusion explaining what the school should do and why?
8. Has the writer used the words *and, or,* and *so* (or *and so*) to join logically related ideas?
9. Has the writer used the words *but* or *while* or *whereas* or *although* to show contrast or concession?

### Step Four: Peer Review

In class, in groups of three, exchange your rough drafts and take turns reading your own drafts aloud. If you spot any errors as you read, correct them. Using the Checklist for Evaluating Rough Drafts, go over each paper question by question to identify both strengths and weaknesses. Call in your teacher if you need help or advice.

### Step Five: Write a Final Draft

At home, using your peers' and teacher's suggestions, write the final version of your paper.

Check each paragraph to see whether you've used the coordinators *and, or,* and *so* (or *and so*) to join logically related ideas.

Check to make sure you have used *but, while, whereas, although, even though,* and *though* to show contrast and/or concession.

Print a copy of your paper and proofread it. Review the proofreading tips in Chapter 1 and the following Special Proofreading section.

### Special Proofreading

- As you did in your previous papers, proofread for subject-verb agreement, *-ed* endings on verbs, and *-s* endings on nouns.
- Check to see that you've used subject pronouns in front of your verbs and object pronouns after them.
- Check to make sure that you have used *they* or *them* to refer to plural nouns.
- Check to see whether any of your nouns are possessives and whether you've used apostrophes in those cases.
- When you've started sentences with *while, whereas, although, even though,* or *though,* make sure that those words join two contrasting ideas.
- Check your spellings of *whereas.* It is one word, not two. Check your spellings of *even though.* They are two words, not one.

## Getting Your Writing Right

### Using Subordinators

Subordinators are just like coordinators in most respects. Mainly, they join sentences to show the logical relationships between them. There are a lot more subordinators than coordinators, but we will focus on just five of them:

> *while    whereas    although    though    even though*

These are the ones you will find most useful in writing essays in which you examine complex issues or argue one point over another one.

A very important point to remember is that while coordinators can be used to start sentences, subordinators can only be used to *join* sentences. In other words,

> *But Carlos decided to go anyway* <u>is a sentence</u>, while
> *Although Carlos decided to go anyway* <u>is not a sentence</u>.

All the subordinators we are looking at here function like the word *but;* that is, they tell us that the two sentences they join are opposites or in contrast with one another. The two subordinators that are closest to *but* in meaning are *while* and *whereas*:

Alicia decided to major in math, *but* Jorge wants to study Greek.
Alicia decided to major in math *while* Jorge wants to study Greek.
Alicia decided to major in math *whereas* Jorge wants to study Greek.

## Exercise 4A

Join the following pairs of sentences, first with *but* and then again with *while* or *whereas*. When you do the *while/whereas* version, decide whether you think the subordinator should come at the beginning of your sentence or in the middle.

EXAMPLE:  The Super Bowl is the biggest sports event of the year.
The World Series is usually more exciting.

a. The Super Bowl is the biggest sports event of the year, *but* the World Series is usually more exciting.

b. Which sounds better to you?

The Super Bowl is the biggest sports event of the year, *while* the World Series is usually more exciting.

*or*        *While* the Super Bowl is the biggest sports event of the year, the World Series is usually more exciting.

1. Doreen and Cosmo loved each other.
   They disagreed about almost everything.

   _____

   _____

2. Doreen was a vegetarian.
   Cosmo loved meat, especially beef.

   _____

   _____

3. Cosmo loved watching sports on TV.
   Doreen liked romantic movies.

   _____

   _____

4. Doreen enjoyed hiking and swimming.
   Reading and watching TV were Cosmo's greatest pleasures.

   _____

   _____

5. For vacation, Cosmo wanted to go to the beach and lie in the sun.
   Doreen preferred to go to the mountains to hike and rock climb.

   _____

   _____

6. On one vacation at the seaside, Doreen spent all her time sailing.
   Cosmo lay on the beach reading.

   _____

   _____

7. On another one in the mountains, Cosmo sat in the sun on the deck of
   their cabin.
   Doreen climbed two 14,000-foot mountains.

   _____

   _____

8. Cosmo's favorite reading was books about the Civil War.
   Doreen liked to read novels.

   _____

   _____

9. Cosmo enjoyed cooking.
   He preferred to make meat dishes rather than vegetarian meals.

   _____

   _____

10. Doreen and Cosmo seemed totally mismatched as a couple.
    They had a completely happy marriage.

    _____

    _____

The three *although* words could be used in the sentences above too, but they really have a different function. Rather than just expressing contrast/opposition, the *although* words express what is called *concession*.

To concede something is to admit that it's true. Suppose you are arguing the merits of a new movie. It's an action thriller that keeps you on the edge of your seat, but you don't really like it because it is extremely violent. You might say to someone who likes it, "*Although* it is really exciting, I didn't like it because of the extreme violence." Concessive subordinators can put two ideas into new perspectives with one another. Look at these two sentences; suppose your teacher wrote them in a note at the end of your essay:

I really like your ideas. Your writing is full of errors.

It would be hard, just from reading these two sentences, to know whether you were going to get a good grade or not. Suppose your teacher wrote the sentences this way:

> I really like your ideas, and your writing is full of errors.

Do you have a better idea? Probably not. So suppose your teacher wrote the sentences this way:

> I really like your ideas, but your writing is full of errors.

Not so good. Looks like bad news. But suppose your teacher wrote the sentences this way:

> Although your writing is full of errors, I really like your ideas.

How do you feel about it now? How would you feel if your teacher wrote it this way:

> Although I really like your ideas, your writing is full of errors.

As you can see, when you begin a part of a sentence with *although* (or *though* or *even though*) you play down that part of the sentence and give emphasis to the other part. The part you *concede* gets less importance, and you actually give the other part more importance.

Concessive subordinators are extremely important in arguing a position. When you write in college and the professional world, you cannot simply ignore what you don't like or what you disagree with. Using concessives like *although* enables you to give both sides of a position while still stressing your own.

## Exercise 4B

Join the following sentences with *although, even though,* or *though.* These words mean exactly the same thing. *Although* is the one most frequently used; *even though* gives a little more emphasis, and *though* is a little more informal. In each pair of sentences, you are asked to emphasize one sentence. To do that, you put the subordinator in front of the *other* sentence. Remember that *even though* is two words.

EXAMPLE:  The Super Bowl is the biggest sports event of the year.
The World Series is usually more exciting.

Emphasize the first sentence:

> The Super Bowl is the biggest sports event of the year,
> *although* the World Series is usually more exciting.

*or*       *Although* the World Series is usually more exciting, the Super
Bowl is the biggest sports event of the year.

1. Doreen's hobby was gardening.
   She was a good sport about going along with Cosmo's hobbies.
   Emphasize the second sentence.

   _____

2. Cosmo was fascinated by the American Civil War and by railroads.
   Doreen was interested in neither.
   Emphasize the second sentence.

   _____

3. Cosmo liked to go on tours of famous Civil War battlefields.
   He understood that they rather bored Doreen.
   Emphasize the first sentence.

   _____

4. One time Doreen went with Cosmo on a two-day walking tour of the
   battlefield at Gettysburg, Pennsylvania.
   She was pretty bored by the whole thing.
   Emphasize the first sentence.

   _____

5. Cosmo didn't insist that Doreen accompany him on these trips.
   He liked to have her company.
   Emphasize the second sentence.

   _____

6. Doreen wasn't interested in old battlefields.
   She understood and appreciated the importance of what had taken
   place there.
   Emphasize the second sentence.

   _____

7. She was willing to go along on visits to major battlefields like Gettys-burg.
   She usually stayed home when Cosmo wanted to visit some place of no real importance.
      Emphasize the second sentence.

   _____

8. She found Cosmo's interest in railroads a lot harder to share.
   She still tried to go along with it.
      Emphasize the first sentence.

   _____

9. Cosmo, on the other hand, hated gardening.
   He joined Doreen in working on her garden.
      Emphasize the second sentence.

   _____

10. He did his best to be helpful without doing too much damage.
    He had a hard time remembering the difference between a dandelion and a petunia.
       Emphasize the first sentence.

   _____

## Exercise 4C

In the following exercises, use the subordinators *while, whereas,* and the three *although* words to join the sentence pairs. Use this chart as your guide:

| | | |
|---|---|---|
| *whereas* | = | contrast/opposition |
| *while* | = | contrast/opposition |
| *although* | = | concession |
| *though* | = | concession |
| *even though* | = | concession |

When expressing contrast or concession, remember that you emphasize one sentence and play down the other. Attach the subordinator—*whereas, while,* or *although* (or *though* or *even though*)—to the sentence that you want to play down, *not* to the one you want to emphasize.

EXAMPLE:  Felicia enjoyed her job.
          She really preferred not to work at all.

a.　concession: emphasize the second sentence

> *Although* Felicia enjoyed her job, she really preferred not to work at all.

b.　contrast: emphasize the first sentence

> *While* [or *whereas*] Felicia really preferred not to work at all, she enjoyed her job.

[Notice that the sentence to be played down has been moved to the front of the new sentence.]

1. Some logging practices are very harmful for the environment.
   A few communities depend on logging for their survival.

   a.　concession:　　　emphasize the second sentence
   b.　contrast:　　　　emphasize the first sentence

   _____

   _____

2. The right to own guns of almost any kind is an American tradition dating from the sixteenth century.
   We have by far the highest rate of gun deaths of any country in the world.

   a.　contrast:　　　　emphasize the second sentence
   b.　concession:　　　emphasize the first sentence

   _____

   _____

3. We say our political leaders should have high principles.
   We want them to do what we tell them to do.

   a.　concession:　　　emphasize the first sentence
   b.　contrast:　　　　emphasize the second sentence

   _____

   _____

4. Most Americans believe in freedom of speech.
   Many of the same people would actually censor speech and books they disagree with.

   a.　concession:　　　emphasize the second sentence
   b.　contrast:　　　　emphasize the first sentence

   _____

   _____

5. Laboratory testing of animals is often cruel and inhumane.
   Animal testing has resulted in numerous health benefits for human beings.

   a.  contrast:        emphasize second sentence
   b.  concession:      emphasize first sentence

   _____

   _____

6. We know that we should eat a healthy diet and stay away from fats and sugars.
   Most of us still prefer fats and sugars.

   a.  concession:      emphasize second sentence
   b.  contrast:        emphasize first sentence

   _____

   _____

7. Many Americans are highly critical of the honesty of politicians.
   Many Americans do not vote in most elections.

   a.  contrast:        emphasize first sentence
   b.  concession:      emphasize second sentence

   _____

   _____

8. Most Americans think that people should be informed on the issues of the day.
   Most Americans do not read newspapers or newsmagazines.

   a.  contrast:        emphasize second sentence
   b.  concession:      emphasize first sentence

   _____

   _____

9. Many Americans think that there is too much violence in the media.
   In many cases, the most violent shows receive the biggest audiences.

   a.  concession:      emphasize the first sentence
   b.  contrast:        emphasize the second sentence

   _____

   _____

10. Exercise is said to prolong life.
    The amount of extra life one gets is about the same as the amount of time one has spent exercising.

    a.  concession:     emphasize the second sentence
    b.  contrast:       emphasize the first sentence

    _____

    _____

## Exercise 4D

The following exercise works in the same way as the one you have just done, with one slight difference. The point in learning to use subordinators of contrast and concession is not just to throw them into your papers here and there. The point is to use them to stress the points you want to stress and play down the points you want to play down. Look at the following sentences:

War is always an evil.
War is sometimes necessary.

You would join these sentences differently depending on the paper you were writing. Suppose you were writing a paper in which you basically argued against wars. In this case, you would want to stress the first sentence and play down the second:

*Although* war is sometimes necessary, it is always an evil.

But if you were writing a paper about the need to fight wars, you would do it differently:

*Although* war is always an evil, it is sometimes necessary.

You need to shape your sentences according to the larger purpose of your paragraph or essay. The following exercises ask you to shape the sentences according to some purpose, as in the examples above.

In these sentences, give emphasis to what Carmen thinks or wants and play down what Ernesto thinks or wants:

1.  Ernesto hopes to go to a ballgame next Saturday.
    Carmen has her heart set on a picnic.

    _____

2. Ernesto has oiled his favorite glove and saved up for parking and hot dogs.
   Carmen has planned a menu of delicious food that can be eaten cold.

3. Ernesto has visions of a great afternoon at the ballpark.
   He is going to be disappointed when he calls Carmen.

4. Write a sentence of your own using *although* in which you tell the conclusion of this sad story.

In these sentences, give emphasis to what Henry thinks or wants and play down what My Lien thinks or wants:

1. My Lien is planning to take Henry, her boyfriend, to visit her sisters.
   Henry promised to go see My Lien's sisters but he really plans to see the latest Hong Kong kung fu movie.

2. My Lien loves her sisters.
   Henry thinks they are boring.

3. My Lien envisions a lovely afternoon with Henry and her sisters when she calls Henry.
   She is astonished to hear that he's gone to the movies.

4. Write a sentence of your own using *while* in which you tell what happens when My Lien finds out Henry is at the movies.

In these sentences, give emphasis to what Wendy thinks or wants and play down what Josmar thinks or wants:

1. Josmar needs to write a paper for his sociology class.
   Wendy considers papers a waste of time.

2. Josmar has set aside all day Saturday to work on his paper and Saturday evening to party with Wendy.
   Wendy has set aside all day Saturday for Josmar to take her shopping and Saturday evening for partying with Josmar.

3. Josmar has gotten out his books and notes and started to work.
   Wendy makes it clear that unless they go shopping, there will be no partying later on.

   _____

4. Write a sentence using *although* or *while* in which you describe the conclusion to this tragic situation.

   _____

In these sentences, give emphasis to what Alan thinks or wants and play down what Melissa thinks or wants:

1. Melissa has her heart set on a concert by the Savage Rabbits, the leading rock group in the Western world.
   Alan is planning to visit the Marine Mammal Center to see how wounded seals and sea lions are treated.

   _____

2. Melissa loves exciting music.
   Alan is fascinated by seals and sea lions.

   _____

3. Melissa expects to spend a great afternoon with Alan at the stadium moving to the rhythms of the Savage Rabbits.
   Alan has contacted the Marine Mammal Center and gotten permission to visit it.

   _____

4. Write a sentence of your own using *even though* in which you tell what happens when Melissa and Alan reveal to each other their plans.

   _____

## Exercise 4E

The following exercise asks you to shape the sentences according to some purpose, just as in Exercise 4D. But in these cases, you may have to think a little bit about the point of view of each sentence before you start working on it. You can use pronouns (*he, she, it, they*) to avoid repeating words in your new sentences.

1. Big-time, scholarship athletics have nothing ~~whatever~~ to do with the aims and purposes of universities.
   They are incredibly popular with alumni and the public at large.

a.  Join these sentences with *although* or *while* as you would if you were writing a paper in favor of big-time college sports.

b.  Join these sentences with *even though* or *while* as you would if you were writing a paper opposed to big-time college sports.

_____

_____

2.  Higher academic standards would result in more college athletes who could graduate.

   Higher academic standards may shut many athletes out from college.

a.  Join these sentences with *whereas* or *although* as you would if you were writing a paper opposing higher academic standards for athletes.

b.  Join these sentences with *whereas* or *although* as you would if you were writing a paper in favor of higher academic standards for athletes.

_____

_____

3.  Some see college athletics as a possible stepping-stone to professional careers.

   Others argue that college athletics simply exploit the athletes for entertainment purposes.

a.  Join these sentences with *whereas* or *although* as you would if you were writing a paper opposing college athletics.

b.  Join these sentences with *whereas* or *although* as you would if you were writing a paper in favor of college athletics.

_____

_____

4.  States use lotteries to get the poor to pay a higher share of government expenses than the rich.

   Lotteries are much more popular with the average person than taxes.

a.  Join these sentences with *while* or *even though* as you would if you were writing in favor of lotteries.

b.  Join these sentences with *while* or *even though* as you would if you were writing in opposition to lotteries.

_____

_____

5. The odds against winning a lottery are about the same as the odds on getting hit by an asteroid.
   Many people see lotteries as their only hope of ever achieving financial security.

   a.   Join these sentences with *whereas* or *although* as you would if you were writing an essay attacking lotteries.
   b.   Join these sentences with *while* or *even though* as you would if you were writing an essay in favor of lotteries.

   _____

   _____

6. Every student knows that attending class and doing homework are essential for success in school.
   Some students would rather hang out in the student union or party in the evenings.

   a.   Join these sentences with *even though* or *while* as you would if you were writing an essay of advice for entering freshmen.
   b.   Join these sentences with *even though* or *while* as you would if you were writing an essay critical of students.

   _____

   _____

7. The function of high school and college classes is to inform or train.
   Many students act as though they thought the function of classes was to amuse and entertain.

   a.   Join these sentences with *although* or *whereas* as you would if you were writing an essay critical of students.
   b.   Join these sentences with *although* or *whereas* as you would if you were writing an essay of advice for students.

   _____

   _____

8. We all realize that bookstores and libraries are full of books that can both entertain and instruct us.
   Many of us prefer to watch brainless television shows.

   a.   Join these sentences with *although* or *while* as you would if you were writing an essay stressing the importance of reading.

      b.   Join these sentences with *even though* or *whereas* as you would if you were writing an essay about the foolishness of human behavior.

          _____

          _____

9.  The freedom to say or print whatever we want is one of the foundations of American society.
The use of free speech to insult or demean people because of their race or their sexual orientation is deplorable.

      a.   Join these sentences with *although* or *while* as you would if you were writing an essay stressing the importance of the First Amendment to the Constitution.

      b.   Join these sentences with *even though* or *while* as you would if you were writing an essay advocating some limits on the freedom of speech.

          _____

          _____

10.  Everyone wants the right to say or print whatever he or she believes.
Many people want the right to censor those who hold unpopular beliefs.

      a.   Join these sentences with *although* or *while* as you would if you were writing a paper in favor of free speech.

      b.   Join these sentences with *even though* or *whereas* as you would if you were writing a paper on the subject of censorship.

          _____

          _____

## Summary and Review of Chapter 4

### Arguing a Position

When you argue a position in an essay, it is important that you consider both sides of the issue. You can plan the organization of the body of your essay in much the same way you plan the organization of a comparison essay—by matching related opposing points and discussing each matching set in a body paragraph. A point-by-point plan enables your reader to see how you have compared related arguments.

Using concessive subordinators is an effective way for you to acknowl-edge, and play down, points of view you are opposed to while emphasizing your own points of view.

## Subordinators

Five subordinators are particularly important for showing contrast or conces-sion between points:

| | |
|---|---|
| while | (contrast) |
| whereas | (contrast) |
| although | (concession) |
| even though | (concession) |
| though | (concession) |

*Contrast* means that two ideas are in opposition to each other (the coordinator *but* also shows contrast/opposition):

The grasshopper spent all his money as soon as he got it, *but/while/whereas* the ant saved hers.

*Concession* means that you are admitting that something is true but you are opposed to it:

Although *Birth of a Nation* is a historically important movie, it is still a racist film.

The subordinators that show contrast and concession play down the part of the sentence they are attached to so that the other part gets emphasized.

Subordinators can introduce sentences, but the part of the sentence they are attached to is not, all by itself, a complete sentence. Subordinators have to join two related ideas.

Although skateboarding is thrilling. (not a sentence)
Although skateboarding is thrilling, it is risky. (sentence)

# CHAPTER FIVE

# Responding to Arguments

## Censorship of a High School Newspaper

The student newspaper at Central High School, *The Tiger's Eye*, has published an article that the principal and superintendent consider inappropriate, and they have prevented the paper from being distributed. It is your task, as a member of the court, to read the article, read the reasons given by the principal and superintendent, read a statement made by the editor of the paper, and write a recommendation to the court on what you think should be done—

whether the paper should be distributed to the students in the school or be destroyed.

In addition to the documents just mentioned, the president of the court has written a short summary of the most important points made by the U.S. Supreme Court on exactly this issue, whether a high school administration has the right to censor its student newspaper.

Here is the article that the school does not want to see published:

### UNDERAGE DRINKING RAMPANT AT CENTRAL HIGH
#### by Shareen Donnell and John Hernandez

A pickup truck accident last week in which five students at Capital City High School were killed points to a problem that students at Central High also share.

The five had been drinking, and the driver of the truck, who was 17, had twice the legal limit of alcohol in his blood.

A quick survey of students here indicates that a lot of underage drinking also goes on and so does a lot of drinking and driving. Maybe the most typical answers in our survey were the following two:

*George M:* "Everybody drinks. Well, practically everybody. Mostly we just drink beer. I know a guy who'll get it for us, or one of my friends has a fake i.d. We just drive out in the country on Friday night or Saturday and drink a couple of six-packs. I don't see any real harm in it. Nobody gets totally wasted or anything. You have maybe three or four beers, sit around and talk and sing a few songs. It's a great way to loosen up at the end of the week."

*Juanita C:* "Sure I drink. Not a lot. Everyone I know does. I think most of us started when we were freshmen. You know, there were always some guys who could get beer or wine or whatever, and you'd just get together and party. I started when I was 14, and all my friends started then too. We have a lot of fun. Do we drink in cars? Sure. Where else you going to do it? Sometimes somebody's parents are out of town and then you can use their house if you're a little careful not to mess it up. But most of the time we just park and have a little party. I don't see a problem."

According to everyone we talked to, even those who don't drink, getting beer or wine isn't a problem. Nobody admits to buying it themselves, but everybody always knows somebody who can get it for them.

Almost no one thought it was very bad. A few kids had heard about the fatal accident at Capital City, but nobody worried about something like that happening to them.

*Alice L:* "They must have been driving like a bunch of crazies. We don't do that. Sometimes we get a little silly, but we're basically careful."

What would their parents think if they knew what was going on?

*James W:* "They'd flip out. You have to use a little discretion with the older generation, you know? You don't want to tell them everything you do."

*Roberto F:* "My mom doesn't drink at all, but my father and his brothers do. Sometimes they can get a little blasted even. Not often. But they sit around and watch football, and they aren't drinking orange juice. So what's the difference?"

When we asked about the connection between drinking and sex, we didn't get a lot of straight answers, but we got a lot of laughing. One student who wanted to stay anonymous said, "A party's a party. First you drink a little. Then you dance a little. Then you find a quiet bedroom somewhere or go out and get into your car. Everybody knows this."

One other student just said, "Get down to Planned Parenthood and get on the pill."

We don't claim that everyone here drinks or even that the majority do. We got a lot of answers like *Trisha M's:* "I'm not ready to drink yet. Maybe when I get a lot older."

But it looks to us like another Capital City could happen here any time.

### Statement by the Principal and Superintendent

A high school is a community, and it is a special kind of community.

It is a community whose members have a special obligation to take care of each other. Teachers work hard to help their students learn the information and the skills they will need to have later in life, and both teachers and administrators try to help parents at home by providing moral guidance and the standards the community would like its citizens to live by.

In the community at large, most people obey the law and live honest lives. A few do not, and that's why we must have laws and police. But we do not approve of these few; we disapprove of them.

In the community of our school, we also realize that a few will not obey the law and will not necessarily live honest lives. We know that they will do things that they would never want their parents to find out about. We understand that they are not necessarily criminals and that many of the things they do are simply honest expressions of youthful experimentation and youthful energy. But as adults charged with providing guidance as well as education, we cannot be expected to approve of these activities.

When an official publication of our school community publishes material that is likely to increase rather than decrease illegal activities by the students, it is our responsibility as educators to step in and stop it. We have no choice. This is what we are hired to do, and this is what the parents of our students expect from us.

We have decided that the article in question cannot be published for three main reasons:

First, although we understand that the authors of the article on drinking had the best possible motives for writing what they did, we feel that the article contributes to a climate in which drinking, drinking and driving, and even drinking and sexual activities are seen as acceptable. And this is unacceptable.

Second, while the authors of the article have not given the full names of the students they quoted, they have given enough that anyone attending our school will easily be able to recognize them.

Third, in writing about drinking and sexual activities in such explicit language, we feel that the authors have forgotten that many of their readers are very young indeed, only 14 and 15, and we feel that material of this sort is inappropriate for such youngsters.

We would like to stress that we have always admired the work of Penelope Elwin, our journalism teacher, and have read the wonderful work of her students with great pleasure over the years. We sincerely regret that we feel this issue of *The Tiger's Eye* cannot be distributed.

### Statement by the Editor of *The Tiger's Eye*

"Congress shall make no law . . . abridging the freedom of speech, or of the press . . . "

That's what the First Amendment to the U.S. Constitution says. Congress may not. The state legislature may not. The city council may not. But the principal and the superintendent may?

They argue that they want a community in which everyone obeys the law. Everybody but them. Do they really want to set an example to students that says you only have to obey the law if no one can stop you from disobeying it?

Are we students of Central High School citizens of the United States or not?

But wait. They say they are not suppressing our newspaper because they are petty dictators. They are suppressing it because it's good for us. When we write about what everybody knows is going on, they say we are creating a climate in which it is acceptable.

We do not create climates. We report on climates. The climate is there already. We are bringing it out into the open. If we wrote an article about AIDS, would we be creating the AIDS virus? If we wrote an article about high school pregnancies, would we be getting girls pregnant?

We must have more power than we thought.

Finally, the principal and superintendent say that we are in danger of ruining the morals of the freshmen at this school. I think that what we are doing is telling them what they could be lured into if they don't watch themselves. According to what we have been studying in my world literature class, it is a long-standing principle that we are better off knowing about the evils around us than not knowing about them.

Unfortunately, that does not seem to be one of the educational principles at work in this school.

### Excerpts from the Supreme Court decision of January 13, 1988, in *Hazelwood School District, et al., v. Cathy Kuhlmeier, et al.*

In this decision, the Court ruled five to three that high school administrations have the right to censor or forbid publication of articles in school newspapers in certain circumstances. The general principles the Court applied seem to have been these: "A school must be able to take into account the emotional maturity of the intended audience in determining whether to disseminate student speech on potentially sensitive topics, which might range from the existence of Santa Claus in an elementary school to the particulars of teenage sexual activity in a high school setting. A school must also retain the authority to refuse to sponsor student speech that might reasonably be perceived to advocate drug or alcohol abuse, irresponsible sex or conduct otherwise inconsistent with the shared values of a civilized social order."

Further, "a school need not tolerate student speech that is inconsistent with its 'basic educational mission,' even though the government could not censor similar speech outside the school." And a school need not tolerate speech that is "ungrammatical, poorly written, inadequately researched, biased or prejudiced, vulgar or profane or unsuitable for immature audiences." In short, the court majority ruled that schools must set "standards that may be higher than those demanded by some newspaper publishers or theatrical producers in the 'real' world."

---

**ASSIGNMENT**

Evaluate the arguments for and against censorship of high school newspapers, and come to your own conclusion about what the school should do—distribute the newspaper with the controversial article in place or not distribute the paper. The newspaper containing the controversial article has already been printed; the question is whether or not it should be distributed and why or why not.

---

## Discussion

If this were an easy or an obvious issue, the judges of the U.S. Supreme Court, appointed because of their intelligence, knowledge of the law, and distinguished careers as jurists, would have voted unanimously one way or another, and the lower courts would all have ruled the same way. But the lower courts disagreed with each other, and so did the judges of the Supreme Court.

The newspaper article you have to evaluate is almost identical to the ones at issue in the Hazelwood High School case that went through the court system. The arguments presented by the editor, the principal, and the superintendent are essentially the ones presented to the Supreme Court. You have the most significant excerpts from the ruling by the court's majority. The minority argued from First Amendment principles—that as citizens of the United States, high school students have the same right to a free press as adults.

### *Step One: Make Notes and Compare Them with Others*
On paper, write down the main points at issue, the arguments for and against censorship. Make notes about your views of the strengths or weaknesses of these arguments.

In class, work with two other students to compare your notes, checking to make sure none of you has left out any important points. Try to come to a consensus on what these points are. Discuss your views of the various arguments. It is not important to agree on these, but it is important for each of you to hear what the others have to say.

Each group should now report on the points the group members consider most important so that the teacher can put them on the board for class discussion. Now the class as a whole can come to a consensus on the most important points. Take notes during this discussion since your notes will be the basis for the next step in the assignment.

### Step Two: *Make an Outline and Compare It with Others*
Read the following guidelines for organizing "Censorship of a High School Newspaper." Then go over your notes and decide how you think you might organize them into an essay. Make a rough list outline as you did for previous assignments, and bring your outline to class for discussion of ways to organize this paper.

## Organizing "Censorship of a High School Newspaper"

In your introduction, you should briefly state what the controversy is at Central High School. You can give your opinion in a thesis in the introduction, or you can save it for your conclusion.

As in other assignments you have done so far, you have gone through the material you have here and written down the principal arguments for and against the censorship of high school newspapers. Now you must try to see how these opposing arguments match up with each other, and you must also note how strong or how valid you think the various arguments are. For instance, one argument in favor of censoring the newspaper is that the principal and superintendent believe that it promotes illegal activities, specifically drinking and drinking while driving. But the newspaper editor points out that the article just reports the behavior. It would make sense to consider these opposing points of view together in one body paragraph and to discuss any information related to these arguments in the same paragraph. You can plan your essay point by point, writing a body paragraph about each set of opposing arguments and their strengths and weaknesses. Be sure to rely on topic sentences to make the point of the body paragraphs clear.

Remember that when you start organizing your paper, you will *not* want to put all the pro arguments in one paragraph and all the con arguments in another, thus creating "shopping bag" paragraphs. It is essential to treat each set of opposing arguments separately.

Since you will be taking a position, you will want to both acknowledge arguments you do not agree with and de-emphasize them while stressing your own position. Use the concessive subordinators to play down viewpoints you do not agree with.

The conclusion to your essay will probably be your own summing up of what you think are the better arguments and your decision about what you believe the school should do and why.

### Step Three: Write a Rough Draft

At home, using your list outline as your basis, write a rough draft of your essay, without worrying about spelling and other mechanics at this point.

Use the following checklist to see whether your own draft meets the requirements for this assignment, and use it also in class during peer review.

Make two copies of your draft so that you have three copies to bring to class.

---

### CHECKLIST FOR EVALUATING ROUGH DRAFTS

1. Does the introduction indicate what the essay will be about and why the subject is important?
2. Is the essay divided into body paragraphs that cover single subjects?
3. Does each body paragraph start with a topic sentence, a sentence that tells what the paragraph will discuss?
4. Are all the sentences in each body paragraph related to the point expressed in the topic sentence? Are there any places where unrelated ideas come into paragraphs?
5. Are all of the arguments for and against censoring the paper covered?
6. Does the order of the points covered seem logical, or does anything seem out of place?
7. Has the writer used the words *and, or,* and *so* (or *and so*) to join logically related ideas?
8. Has the writer joined sentences with *but, while, whereas, although, even though,* and *though* to show contrast and concession?
9. Is there a conclusion that tells what the school should do, and why?

---

### Step Four: Peer Review

In class, in groups of three, exchange your rough drafts and take turns reading your own drafts aloud. If you spot any errors as you read, correct them. Using the Checklist for Evaluating Rough Drafts, go over each paper question by question to identify both strengths and weaknesses. Call in your teacher if you need help or advice.

*Step Five: Write a Final Draft*

At home, using your peers' and teacher's suggestions for guidance, write the final version of your paper.

Check to see that you've used the words *and*, *or*, and *so* (or *and so*) to join logically related ideas.

Check to see that you've joined sentences with the words *but*, *while*, *whereas*, *although*, *even though*, and *though* to show contrast and concession. Look particularly for places that you can use the *although* words to concede, and at the same time, play down, points you are opposed to.

Finally, review the proofreading tips in Chapter 1 and in the following Special Proofreading section, and proofread a printed copy of your paper.

## Special Proofreading

- As you did in your previous papers, proofread for subject-verb agreement and plural -*s* endings on nouns.
- Since your essay discusses actions that took place in the past, it is especially important to check that you've used the past tense to describe them, and that your past-tense verbs have -*ed* endings.
- Check for possessive apostrophes in phrases like "the editor's opinion" and "the students' parents."
- If pronouns have been a problem for you, check to make sure that you have used subject pronouns and object pronouns correctly, and that your pronouns agree with the nouns they refer to.
- Check your spellings of *whereas*. It is one word, not two. Check your spellings of *even though*. They are two words, not one.

---

### CASE STUDY TWO: CURFEWS FOR TEENS

Read the following case and the two articles and assignment and discussion sections following it. Then go back over the readings carefully, underlining or highlighting the most important information. Don't try to identify this information on your first reading.

---

## Curfews for Teens

Because of escalating crime among younger and younger teens, including aggravated assaults and murder, a great many American cities have instituted curfews. In most cases, the curfews require teens under 17 or 18 to be off the streets by 10:00 or 10:30 on weekdays and 12:00 or 12:30 on Friday and Saturday evenings. All such laws provide at least some exceptions. The most liberal laws allow teens to be out after curfew if:

they are accompanied by a parent or guardian,
they are running an errand,
they are working or traveling from work,
they are involved in an emergency,
they are attending a religious or recreational event,
they are exercising their First Amendment rights.

Several of these curfew laws have been taken to court on the grounds that they are unconstitutional, but so far the courts have found that they are legal.

In some cities, exemptions such as "running an errand" or "working or traveling from work" are not allowed, and parents or employers who cause underage teens to be out after curfew can be fined as much as $500.

Many people, adults as well as teens, have argued against such curfews. The principal arguments are the following. Enforcement of curfew laws will be selective and will chiefly target minority kids. The police, according to this argument, will not be found in the wealthier sections of big cities looking for teens on the streets. Rather, they will concentrate their efforts in the poorer parts of town. As a result, the children of well-to-do parents will be able to stay out as long as they wish, while those of poorer parents will be subject to arrest or detention.

A second argument is that relations between minority kids and the police are already bad enough, and a curfew will only make them worse. Police will have an additional reason to harass teens, and teens will have an additional reason to fear and hate the police. In addition, no one expects that the real criminals and troublemakers will be affected by a curfew. It's hard to imagine some tough kid with a record of muggings looking at his watch and saying, "Oops. It's 10 o'clock. I'd better get home now."

Finally, some people, including some police, argue that enforcing curfews is a misuse of police resources. In most cities, according to this argument, the police already have more to do than they can handle, and if they have to spend time detaining teenagers out after curfew, they won't be able to attend to more serious problems. The result will be that after an initial flurry of detentions, the law will largely go unenforced.

Some of the best data on the effects of a curfew law come from the city of San Jose, the second largest city in California, where, unlike most places, careful records have been kept. In San Jose, when a teenager is picked up by police, he or she is taken to a detention center and questioned, and then the teen's parents are called and the teen is released to their custody. This process does not produce a criminal record for the teen. In the first year of San Jose's curfew, 3,358 juveniles were picked up, but this number represents only 21 percent of those stopped by police. Of those detained, 40 percent had previous arrest records and 95 percent were returned to their parents. The rest were sent to shelters, hospitals, or juvenile hall. The juveniles picked up ranged in age from 7 to 17, with slightly more males than females taken in.

*[margin note: SJ stats]*

San Jose has a large Hispanic population, and the argument that enforcement of curfew laws would tend to be selective seems to have been born out there, since 60 percent of those picked up were Hispanic. However, Police Chief Louis Cobarruviaz cites a 96 percent support ratio for the law among Latino parents in San Jose, and he argues that the figures don't represent discrimination against Latino youths. The police, he says, pick up whoever is out there, and they obviously have to patrol more heavily in the areas where the crime rate is highest.

*[margin note: 60% Hispanic, but 96% Hispanic parents support it]*

During the first year of San Jose's law, the number of juvenile crime victims dropped 12 percent, and the San Jose Medical Center Trauma Service reported a 42 percent drop in admissions of juvenile victims of assault or penetrating injuries during curfew hours.

*[margin note: apparent success]*

Some of the best evidence on this issue may not be here in this writing case. This evidence may be the experiences of you and the other members of your class as grade and high school students. If your city has a curfew law, how well, in your experience, do you think it has worked? If your city does not have such a law, what has been the effect? Are the streets dangerous late at night? Could the streets be safer at night if your city enacted a curfew law?

The following two articles provide more information about curfew laws in U.S. cities and about the First Amendment issues raised by opponents of curfews.

## CURFEWS CURTAIL CRIME IN BIG CITIES, KEEP CHILDREN OFF STREETS OF TROUBLE
### by Beth Frerking

It's nearly midnight when officer Tom Pomoroski pulls the police Care-O-Van to a lurching stop alongside two teenage boys who might, or might not, be 17, old enough to ignore the city's 10:30 P.M. curfew. Pomoroski thinks not. He doubts one young man's assertion that he is 17, doesn't buy his [1]indignant excuses. ("See all this hair on my face? Do I look like a baby?") Sure enough, when Pomoroski and his partner, Debbie Egan, take the young man home, an older brother [2]inadvertently blows the gig. "How old's your brother?" Egan asks, neutrally. "Fifteen," he says, too sleepy to notice his brother's glare.

Some lie, some run, some get away. The more practiced youths spot the van at a distance and step silently into the shadows. Still, Pomoroski and the officers who staff a special curfew enforcement program in Chicago believe they net more violators than they miss, and deter even more. And they [3]contend that the neighborhood and the children who live there are safer for it.

In the past, cities passed curfews almost exclusively to keep young criminals off the streets. But around the country, a [4]spate of new curfews also is aimed at righting two wrongs of modern urban life: Innocent children, from toddlers to teens, are being injured and killed by people not old enough to legally buy a drink. And many parents seem unable to control their children without the stern backing of a city law. "When we target an area, the kids think twice about being out on the street after curfew," said Sgt. Carol McLaurin, bumping along behind the Care-O-Van one hot August night in an unmarked burgundy Chevy Caprice. "It lessens the chances of them being a young victim."

It is a [5]conviction shared nationwide, even though there [are] scant national data to support it. Of the country's 200 largest cities (with at least 100,000 residents), three-quarters have youth curfews, said William Ruefle, a criminology professor at the University of South Alabama and co-author of the most extensive study on American curfews to date. Since 1990, 53 cities have adopted curfews. Nearly 40 cities strengthened existing laws during the same period. Detroit has a year-round curfew, enacted in 1987. Frustrated citizens in San Antonio, Cincinnati, New Orleans, and, most recently, in Washington, D.C., have demanded strict curfews after watching, horrified, as children and teenagers have been cut down by street violence, guilty of no more than being in the wrong place at the wrong time.

Chicagoans joined and ended the debate long ago. The Second City has one of the nation's oldest curfew laws, passed in 1955. All patrol officers have to enforce the law, which requires youths 16 and younger to be at home by 10:30 P.M. on weekdays and 11:30 P.M. Fridays and Saturdays. For many adults, the curfew was just part of growing up in

Chicago. Natives who were teens in the 1960s and '70s still remember the televised public service spots that ominously asked parents: "It's 10:30. Do you know where your children are?" Most parents didn't have to look far. Even today, adults here express surprise that some other large cities, New York, Boston, and Los Angeles, for example, don't have curfews. As street crime increased in Chicago over the decades, curfew enforcement often got bumped down an officer's priority list. These days, Chicago police say they regularly enforce the curfew and the 100,000 curfew citations each prove it. Yet in most of those cases, neither the youthful offender nor the parents paid a penalty for the transgression. The kids simply went home.

*each year?*

*Chicago Program: Operation Timeout*

Last summer, in response to rising levels of gang- and drug-related violence, the police launched a pilot program, Operation Timeout, to turn up the heat on parents. On a first curfew offense, a child is taken home, and parents receive a written warning. The second time around, police cite parents and require them to appear in court to answer the complaint. Fines can run as high as $100 per offense. This is the second summer of Operation Timeout, and police officers who roam the streets say it's working. In two nights of riding behind the Care-O-Van, it was evident that most parents are grateful for the curfew. Some didn't understand they were required to be outside supervising. Others didn't know the children were gone. The mother of the young man who claimed to be 17 thanked Egan for bringing her son home, despite her exasperation with him. "They know the rules here," she said wearily. "I try to teach him. I'm glad somebody's doing something."

*puts the heat on parents*

*most parents are grateful*

It is precisely the public fear of crime that often makes civil rights challenges against curfews seem like so much shouting in the wind. "You get some middle-class ACLU type who is against it, who makes [6]high-minded philosophical arguments against curfews; well, they don't see their children and their children's friends dying in their neighborhood," Ruefle said. Before he proposed and implemented the nation's toughest youth curfew—8 P.M. on school nights, 9 P.M. on summer weeknights, and 11 P.M. on weekend nights—New Orleans Mayor Marc Morial commissioned a poll that found nearly 9 of 10 adults supported the idea.

*refutes civil rights argument on economic grounds*

*super strict curfew in New Orleans*

But for civil rights proponents, public opinion isn't the issue. Constitutionality is. The American Civil Liberties Union [ACLU] has been successful in striking down several city curfews because they violated constitutional rights of free speech and association. They also argue that

*ACLU position*

*age classification*

*Dallas → exceptions compromise to allow 1st amendment rights*

*ACLU Rebuttal*

*apparent success...*

*or just a shift in crime hours?*

curfews violate the equal protection clause of the Constitution by classifying suspects merely by age. Dallas found a way around that. The U.S. Supreme Court let stand a Dallas statute, upon which many cities now model their laws, that allows several exceptions for an underage person to break curfew: coming home from work, carrying a note from his or her parents, or exercising First Amendment rights. "Those [laws] are a little harder to challenge, because they've built in those exceptions," said Chris Hansen, senior staff counsel at the ACLU national office in New York. However, he added, "When you leave that much discretion to a beat cop to decide, for example, whether or not a parent's note is genuine, you are inviting discriminatory enforcement."

Meanwhile, no one has answered the question, in any broad sense, as to whether curfews reduce juvenile crime and victimization. Local statistics suggest they do. During the first year of Cincinnati's curfew, juvenile arrests dropped 18 percent, and crimes involving a juvenile victim decreased 15 percent. And in San Antonio, while juvenile arrests rose by 41 percent last year, the third year after the curfew was enacted in 1991, the victimization of youths aged 10 to 16 [7]plummeted 84 percent. Nonetheless, Ruefle says no one has done the kind of [8]empirical study that would pass the peer review required by academic journals. And the only recent study of that kind, a 1977 examination of a Detroit curfew law, showed that juvenile crime merely shifted from after curfew hours to the period between 2 and 5 P.M. Even Chicago police acknowledge that the precise reasons behind crime rate decreases are difficult to tease apart. They would like to credit the curfew for a 42 percent decrease in juvenile murder offenders from January through July 1995, compared with the same period in 1994. But they admit there are many factors—weather, for example.

Still, they know what they feel in their gut, when the streets near Marquette Park seem calmer, safer. "Is curfew enforcement the reason for this? We really don't know," Chicago patrolman Patrick Camden said. "But it doesn't take a rocket scientist to figure that if kids aren't on the streets, they're not committing crimes or becoming victims."

## COURT BLOCKS ENFORCEMENT OF WEST NEW YORK CURFEW
### by the American Civil Liberties Union

Ruling in a lawsuit brought by the American Civil Liberties Union of New Jersey, a Superior Court judge today blocked West New York from enforcing its juvenile curfew until a final determination is made about the law's constitutionality. Chancery Division Judge Martin L. Green-berg, in Hudson County, issued the preliminary [9]injunction in a suit brought by the ACLU of New Jersey on behalf of two families whose children had been arrested under the curfew. Finding that the families were likely to prevail on their claim that the curfew was unconstitu-tional, the court told West New York that it must immediately stop enforcing the ordinance and prosecuting curfew violators. The judge said that it was unlikely that West New York would be able to show that "house confinement of all minors under age 18" was a permissible restriction on minors' constitutional rights. The township's curfew, enacted in 1993, prohibits anyone under age 18 from being in a public place between 10:00 P.M. and 6:00 A.M. unless accompanied by a parent or guardian.

*judge concluded the court probably couldn't show the curfew to be constitutional*

According to the township's attorney, the ordinance provides exceptions for juveniles traveling to or from work, engaged in a medical emergency, or traveling to or from events sponsored by community or religious organizations. Curfew violators and their parents are subject to fines of up to $1,000, and up to 90 days community service.

*details of west NY law*

But the teenagers involved in the ACLU lawsuit have been arrested for curfew violations while returning home from such activities as deliv-ering cake to a grandparent, eating in a restaurant with an adult friend, walking home from work at McDonald's, and walking home with friends from a movie.          *rhetoric*

*teens arrested in apparently permissable duties*

"Placing everyone in West New York under house arrest from 10:00 P.M. to 6:00 A.M. would certainly reduce crime, but how many people would be willing to pay that price?" said David M. Kohane, an attorney in the Hackensack law firm of Cole, Schotz, Meisel, Forman & Leonard, who is handling the case for the ACLU. "It makes no sense to punish these teenagers, and thousands of other good kids like them, for prob-lems they haven't caused," he added.

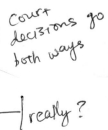

Courts around the country have reached differing conclusions regarding the constitutionality of juvenile curfews, and the U.S. Supreme Court has never ruled on their legality. Juvenile curfews have been found to be unconstitutional by the Supreme Courts of Washing-ton, Iowa, and Hawaii, and have recently been struck down by federal courts in Washington, D.C., and San Diego, California. However, courts have upheld curfews in Dallas, Texas, and Charlottesville, Virginia.

*Court decisions go both ways*

Studies have repeatedly shown that curfews are an ineffective crime-fighting tool, and many large cities have either scrapped or refused to

*really?*

*CA study*

*doesn't impact peak youth crime hours*

*— punishes the innocent?*

adopt curfew laws. A recent comprehensive study of curfew enforcement in California by the Justice Policy Institute found that curfew enforcement had no [10]discernible effect on juvenile crime, and in many jurisdictions, juvenile crime actually increased. In addition, federal crime statistics show that the majority of juvenile crimes occur during noncurfew hours, peaking between 2:00 and 6:00 P.M. "The police already have the ability to arrest juvenile criminals; the curfew adds nothing more than the obligation to arrest the innocent as well," said David Rocah, staff attorney with the ACLU of New Jersey. "The proper response to juvenile crime is to arrest the criminals, not to place thousands of law-abiding young people under house arrest."

Some of the best evidence on this issue may not be here in the readings. This evidence may be your and your classmates' experiences as elementary and high school students. If your city has a curfew law, how well, in your experience, do you think it has worked? If your city does not have such a law, are the streets dangerous late at night? Could the streets be safer at night if your city enacted a curfew law?

You and your classmates might wish to research this issue in your town. If there is a curfew law, you can contact the police department, the health department, and other branches of city government that should have statistics on the results of the curfew. If there is no such law, you might want to contact the police and members of the city council or mayor's staff to see whether anyone thinks there should be one, and why they think so (or don't). Be sure to write down the opinions of the people you speak to so that you will know the sources of the opinions when you discuss your findings in class and when you write your paper.

### ASSIGNMENT

Evaluate the arguments for and against a curfew and come to your own conclusion about whether or not a curfew is a good policy.

### Discussion

This issue can be seen as one in which teens (and younger children) are not allowed all of the constitutional rights enjoyed by adults. However, the courts have not agreed with this point of view, and anyone who wishes to argue it will have to come to terms with the courts' reasons. We do not, for example, grant the right to vote to 17-year-olds, and no one thinks that their constitutional rights are being violated in this area.

The question of constitutional rights is just one question to consider in your essay. Look closely at the opposing arguments regarding the effectiveness of curfew laws, that is, whether or not they produce positive results or create more problems than they solve.

### Step One: Make Notes and Compare Them with Others

On paper, write down the main points at issue, the arguments for and against a curfew. You will find these arguments in the readings and in any responses you get from government agencies in your own research. Make notes about your views of the strengths or weaknesses of these arguments.

In class, work with two other students to compare your notes, checking to make sure none of you has left out any important points. Try to come to a consensus on what these points are, and discuss your views of strengths and weaknesses of the various arguments. It is not important to agree on these, but it is important for each of you to hear what the others have to say.

Each group should now report on the points the group members consider most important, so that the teacher can write them on the board for class discussion. Now the class as a whole can come to a consensus on the most important points. Write these down since your notes will form the basis for the next step in the assignment.

### Step Two: Make an Outline and Compare It with Others

Read the following section on organizing "Curfews for Teens." Then go over your notes and decide how you think you might organize them into an essay. Make a rough list outline as you did for previous assignments, and bring the outline to class for discussion of ways to organize this paper.

## Organizing "Curfews for Teens"

Your introduction should briefly state the issue you are writing about. You can state your opinion about curfews in a thesis in your introduction, or you can save it for your conclusion.

As in other assignments you have done so far, you have gone through the material you have here (and that you found in your research) and written down the principal arguments for and against a curfew. You must try to see how these arguments match up with each other, and you must also note how strong or how valid you think the various arguments are. For instance, one argument against a curfew is that it would worsen relations between minority teens and the police. But in the case of San Jose's curfew, most Latino parents in the city support the curfew law, and San Jose Police Chief Cobarruviaz claims that the police just "pick up whoever is out there" and do not target minority youths. It would make sense to consider these opposing points of view together in one body paragraph, and to discuss any information related to these arguments in the same paragraph. You can organize the body of your essay point by point by presenting matching opposing arguments on the same point together. You will want to write topic sentences expressing the main points of the body paragraphs.

*example: opposing view on targeting of Latinos*

Since you are arguing a position, you will want to use the concessive subordinators both to acknowledge arguments you do not agree with and to deemphasize them while emphasizing your own position.

*PRACTICE*

Remember that when you start organizing your paper, you will *not* want to put all the pro arguments in one paragraph and all the con arguments in another, thus creating "shopping bag" paragraphs. It will be essential to treat these arguments separately.

The conclusion to your essay will probably be your own summing up of what you think are the better arguments and your conclusion as to what you think about curfews.

### Step Three: Write a Rough Draft

At home, using your list outline as your basis, write a rough draft of your essay. As usual, do not worry about spelling and other mechanics while you are getting your ideas down on paper. Refer to the following checklist to see whether your rough draft meets the requirements for this assignment, and use it also in class in peer review.

Make two copies of your draft so that you have three copies to bring to class.

---

#### CHECKLIST FOR EVALUATING ROUGH DRAFTS

1. Does the introduction indicate what the essay will be about and why the subject is important?
2. Is the essay divided into body paragraphs that cover the main points involved in comparing the two opposing sides?
3. Does each body paragraph start with a topic sentence, a sentence that tells what the paragraph will discuss?

4. Are all the sentences in each body paragraph related to the point expressed in the topic sentence? Are there any places where unrelated ideas seem to come into any body paragraphs?
5. Are all of the important arguments in the issue covered, or is anything missing?
6. Does the order of the points seem logical, or does anything seem out of place?
7. Does the writer use the words *and, or,* and *so* (or *and so*) to join ideas and show logical relationships?
8. Does the writer use the words *but, while, whereas, although, even though,* and *though* to show contrast and concession?
9. Is there a conclusion explaining whether a teen curfew is or is not a good policy, and why?

### Step Four: Peer Review

In class, in groups of three, exchange your rough drafts and take turns reading your own drafts aloud. If you spot any errors as you read, correct them. Using the checklist, go over each paper question by question to identify both strengths and weaknesses. Call in your teacher if you need help or advice.

### Step Five: Write a Final Draft

At home, write the final version of your paper, using your peers' and teacher's advice for guidance.

Check to make sure that you have used the words *and, or,* and *so* (or *and so*) to join logically related ideas.

Check to see that you have joined sentences with *but, while, whereas, although, even though,* and *though* to show contrast and concession. Look particularly for places to use the *although* words to concede, and at the same time, play down points you are opposed to.

Finally, review the proofreading tips in Chapter 1 and the following Special Proofreading section and proofread a printed copy of your paper.

### Special Proofreading

- As you did in your previous papers, proofread for subject-verb agreement and plural -*s* endings on nouns.
- This assignment asks you to discuss a number of actions that took place in the past, so it will be especially important to check that you've used

the past tense in describing them and that you have -*ed* endings on your past-tense verbs.

- Check also for possessive apostrophes in phrases like "a teenager's rights" or "many teenagers' parents."
- If pronouns have been a problem for you, check to make sure you've used subject pronouns in front of your verbs and object pronouns after them, and check to make sure that you have used *they* or *them* to refer to plural nouns.
- Check your spellings of *whereas*. It is one word, not two. Check your spellings of *even though*. It is two words, not one.

---

**CASE STUDY THREE:**
*SANTA FE INDEPENDENT SCHOOL DISTRICT V. DOE*

Read the following case and the assignment and discussion sections following it. Then go back over the case, reading closely and underlining or highlighting the most important information. Don't try to identify this information on your first reading.

---

### Santa Fe Independent School District v. Doe

The First Amendment to the U.S. Constitution reads as follows:

> Congress shall make no law respecting an establishment of religion, or prohibiting the free exercise thereof; or abridging the freedom of speech, or of the press, or the right of the people peaceably to assemble, and to petition the Government for a redress of grievances.

High school football in Texas is a community institution second to few others in importance, and in some communities, a prayer preceding the games was customary. In 1998, however, in the Santa Fe Independent School District in southern Texas, a Mormon family and a Catholic family brought suit against the district objecting to the Christian prayers being offered. The prayer was declared unconstitutional by the U.S. Court of Appeals for the Fifth Circuit in New Orleans. At the same time, however, Sim Lake, a federal district court judge in Galveston, Texas, ordered the Santa Fe Independent School District to permit the prayer, saying the prohibition amounted to "state-sponsored atheism." And in the same year, the U.S. Court of Appeals for the Eleventh Circuit in Atlanta, Georgia, ruled that school districts must permit prayers of a religious nature at graduations and football games because to forbid them would be a "form of content-based censorship" and thus would violate the First Amendment guarantee of freedom of speech. Understandably confused, the Santa Fe Independent School District appealed its case to the U.S. Supreme Court.

Meanwhile, the district decided to change its prayer policy. The district knew that it was up against the first clause of the First Amendment, the so-called "establishment clause." The establishment clause is the part that says "Congress shall make no law respecting an establishment of religion, or prohibiting the free exercise thereof. . . ." A series of Supreme Court decisions had ruled that this clause prohibited government—whether federal, state, or local—from supporting any aspect of any religion. A public, taxpayer-supported school or school district is considered to be a part of the government. The problem, from the school district's point of view, was how to continue the popular pregame prayer without violating the establishment clause. As Attorney General John Cornyn of Texas said, "They were trying to work their way out of a very practical problem: how do we avoid being sued."

The school district came up with a compromise that it hoped would satisfy the Supreme Court. According to the new policy, the student body would elect a student to serve during the football season as a speaker prior to each game. The student could say whatever he or she wanted, with no attempt by the school to dictate the nature or content of his or her speech. The lawyer for the school district argued that because the speaker would be elected by the students and not told what to say by the school, he or she would be acting as an "independent speaker" when leading a prayer, and so the district would not be in violation of the establishment clause. In fact, the lawyer continued, if the district tried to prevent the student from offering a prayer, it would be acting as a censor, and, he continued, "All speech is protected by the First Amendment."

But the new school policy was not quite as this lawyer represented it. In fact, there were two policies, an August policy and an October policy. The August policy required two student body votes. The first vote was to decide whether "a student would deliver prayers at varsity football games," and the second vote was to select the person to deliver them. The [11]explicit mention of prayers in the August policy worried the district, so it tried again. The October policy was the same, but it omitted the word "prayer" and referred instead to "messages," "statements," and [12]"invocations" and stated that the purpose of the policy was to [13]"solemnize the event." It was the October policy that the U.S. Supreme Court considered.

The U.S. Supreme Court was not persuaded by the arguments of the school district and, in June 2000, voted six to three against the October policy. Prayers, even if disguised as "messages," "statements," or "invocations," cannot be offered before football games in public schools.

Before getting further into the particulars of the Santa Fe case, it may be helpful for you to know something of the background of the establishment clause of the First Amendment.

It is sometimes argued that keeping government strictly out of religious affairs and institutions is antireligion and atheistic. If we look back at the writing of the Constitution and the Bill of Rights and the men who wrote them, we find that nothing could be less true. These men were religious, though not all of the same religion, and they believed in God. As Professor William Lee Miller has noted, "When the Americans provided . . . for a presidential veto [of a bill from Congress], they simply put in parentheses an absent-minded but significant phrase: 'If any bill shall not be returned by the President within ten days (Sunday excepted).'" They took for granted that Sunday, the traditional Christian day of worship, would not be a work day. When they came to the end of the new Constitution, they began the date with the phrase "In the year of our Lord . . . " (*The Business of May Next*, Charlottesville: University Press of Virginia, 1992, 112–13). And when they completed work on the Bill of Rights, they declared a day of "public thanksgiving and prayer."

But, as Miller also notes, "In the body of the Federal Constitution . . . we discover that the topic of religion is treated primarily, although not quite entirely, by negation, silence, exclusion, and inference. There is in this Constitution . . . no formal commitment to Christianity, or to belief in God, or to any religious belief whatsoever" (106). "Usually now," Miller continues, "our American disengaging of church from state is found to rest in the First Amendment, but one may find it already in a negative way in the silence of the rest of the Constitution. These Americans . . . said nothing whatsoever about the church or the churches that had figured large for fourteen hundred years in the formal makeup of the states of Christendom from which they had come" (108–9). The single exception occurs at the end of Article VI, where the Constitution says, "No religious test shall ever be required as a Qualification to any Office or public Trust under the United States." That's it for religion in the Constitution.

In his review of the writing of the First Amendment and of the laws governing the relationship between government and religion in the various states, Professor Leonard W. Levy has noted that "an [14]uncontested and

[15]incontestable fact that stands out from the establishment clause is that the United States cannot constitutionally enact any law preferring one church over others in any manner whatsoever" (*Origins of the Bill of Rights*, New Haven: Yale University Press, 1999, 79). He also notes that James Madison, often called the Father of the Constitution and of the Bill of Rights, "did not believe that religion needed government support any more than government needed religious support. . . . His antagonism to government-assisted religion was extreme, even as to trifling matters" (85–86).

Professor Jack N. Rakove has pointed out an important difference between the establishment clause of the First Amendment and everything else in the Bill of Rights. Rakove argues that the establishment clause, unlike the other protections in the Bill of Rights, attempts to protect the people not from government tyranny but instead from the tyranny of other more numerous citizens. In other words, the establishment clause says that if the majority where you live [16]subscribe to religion A, they cannot make you subscribe to it too. Madison worried that legislators might act "in response to the passions and interests of the constituents. And this meant that the problem of rights was no longer to protect the people as a collective whole *from* government, but to defend minorities and individuals against popular majorities acting *through* government." In the area of religious freedom, Madison "now concluded that the people themselves, acting through their representatives, were the chief danger" (*Original Meanings*, New York: Alfred A. Knopf, 1996, 313).

As we mentioned earlier, the U.S. Supreme Court voted that the Santa Fe, Texas, school district could not allow prayers before high school football games. Writing for the majority, Justice John Paul Stevens concluded that the school's policy permitting prayer at football games violates the establishment clause of the First Amendment.

The entire majority and minority decisions in this case are too long to reprint here, but the main arguments made on both sides are particularly interesting.

### JUSTICE JOHN PAUL STEVENS WRITING FOR THE MAJORITY

The first clause in the First Amendment to the federal Constitution provides that "Congress shall make no law respecting an establishment of religion, or prohibiting the free exercise thereof . . . "

The principle that government may accommodate the free exercise of religion does not [17]supersede the fundamental limitations imposed by the establishment clause. It is beyond dispute that, at a minimum, the Constitution guarantees that government may not coerce anyone to support or participate in religion or its exercise, or otherwise act in a way which establishes a religion or religious faith, or tends to do so.

[In the Santa Fe Independent School District], once the student speaker is selected and the message composed, the invocation is then delivered to a large audience assembled as part of a regularly scheduled, school-sponsored function conducted on school property. In this context, the members of the listening audience must perceive the pregame message as a public expression of the views of the majority of the student body delivered with the approval of the school administration.

While Santa Fe's [18]majoritarian election might ensure that most of the students are represented, it does nothing to protect the minority; indeed, it likely serves to intensify their offense. . . . The controversy in this case clearly demonstrates that the views of the students are not unanimous on [the pregame prayer] issue.

In addition to involving the school in the selection of the speaker, the [school's] policy . . . invites and encourages religious messages. The policy itself states that the purpose of the message is "to solemnize the event." A religious message is the most obvious method of solemnizing an event. . . . Indeed, the only type of message that is expressly endorsed in the text is an "invocation," a term that primarily describes an appeal for divine assistance. . . .

Regardless of whether one considers a sporting event an appropriate occasion for solemnity, the use of an invocation to foster such solemnity is [19]impermissible when, in actuality, it constitutes prayer sponsored by the school. And it is unclear what type of message would be both appropriately "solemnizing" under the district's policy and yet nonreligious.

We explained [in a previous case] that the "preservation and transmission of religious beliefs and worship is a responsibility and a choice committed to the private sphere." The two student elections authorized by the policy, coupled with the debates that presumably must precede each, impermissibly invade that private sphere. . . . The election, when considered in light of the history in which the policy in question evolved, reflects a device the district put in place that determines whether religious messages will be delivered at home football games. The mechanism encourages [20]divisiveness along religious lines in a public school setting, a result at odds with the establishment clause.

The district argues that the football games "are 'decidedly extracurricular,' thus [21]dissipating any coercion." . . . There are some students, however, such as cheerleaders, members of the band, and of course, the team members themselves, for whom season commitments mandate their attendance, sometimes for class credit. . . . Undoubtedly, the games are not important to some students, and they voluntarily choose not to attend. For many others, however, the choice between whether to attend these [football] games or to risk facing a personally offensive religious ritual is in no practical sense an easy one. The Constitution, moreover, demands that the school may not force this difficult choice upon these students.

### CHIEF JUSTICE WILLIAM REHNQUIST WRITING FOR THE MINORITY

(Note: When Justice Rehnquist refers to "the court," he means the majority opinion.)

The court holds that the school district's student-message program is invalid on its face under the establishment clause. But even more disturbing than its holding is the tone of the court's opinion; it bristles with hostility to all things religious in public life. Neither the holding nor the tone of the [majority] opinion is faithful to the meaning of the establishment clause, when it is recalled that George Washington himself, at the request of the very Congress which passed the Bill of Rights, proclaimed a day of "public thanksgiving and prayer, to be observed by acknowledging with grateful hearts the many and signal favors of Almighty God. . . . "

We did not learn until late in the court's opinion that [22]respondents in this case challenged the district's student-message program at football games before it had been put into practice. . . . Therefore, the question is not whether the district's policy may be applied in violation of the establishment clause, but whether it inevitably will be . . . . The court, venturing into the realm of prophesy, decides that it "need not wait for the inevitable" and invalidates the district's policy on its face.

First, the court [23]misconstrues the nature of the "majoritarian election" permitted by the policy as being an election on "prayer" and "religion." . . . The election permitted by the policy is a twofold process whereby students vote first on whether to have a student speaker before football games at all, and second, if the students vote to have such a speaker, on who that speaker will be. . . . It is conceivable that the election could become one in which student candidates campaign on platforms that focus on whether or not they will pray if elected. . . . It is also conceivable that the election could lead to a Christian prayer before 90 percent of the football games. If, upon implementation, the policy operated in this fashion, we would have a record before us to review whether the policy as applied violated the establishment clause or [24]unduly suppressed minority viewpoints. But it is possible that the students might vote not to have a pregame speaker, in which case there would be no threat of a constitutional violation. It is also possible that the election would not focus on prayer, but on public-speaking ability or social popularity. And if student campaigning did begin to focus on prayer, the school might decide to implement reasonable campaign restrictions.

But the court ignores these possibilities by holding that merely granting the student body the power to elect a speaker that may choose to pray, "regardless of the students' ultimate use of it, is not acceptable." The court so holds despite that any speech that may occur as a result of the election process here would be private, not government, speech. The elected student, not the government, would choose what to say. [The court's decision] essentially invalidates all student elections. A newly elected student body president, or even a newly elected prom king or queen, could use opportunities for public speaking to say prayers. Under the court's view, the mere grant of power to the students to vote for such offices, in light of the fear that those elected might publicly pray, violates the establishment clause.

Second, with respect to the policy's purpose, the court holds that "the simple enactment of this policy, with the purpose and perception of school endorsement of student prayer, was a constitutional violation." But the policy itself has [25]plausible [26]secular purposes: "To solemnize the event, to promote good sportsmanship and student safety, and to establish the appropriate environment for the competition."

The policy at issue here may be applied in an unconstitutional manner, but it will be time enough to invalidate it if that is found to be the case. I would reverse the judgment of the Court of Appeals.

**ASSIGNMENT**

While the U.S. Supreme Court ruled that the October policy of the Santa Fe, Texas, school district on student speakers before football games was unconstitutional, not all nine justices agreed. Three disagreed. There have been many times in the past when a majority ruling in the Supreme Court has been overturned by later courts. What is your view on this issue? After evaluating all of the evidence, write a paper in which you either support or disagree with the U.S. Supreme Court's ruling in the Santa Fe case.

In writing your paper, whichever side you take, you must consider the history behind the establishment clause, and you must refute the arguments of the other side. Most of these are probably included in the opinions written by Justice Stevens and Chief Justice Rehnquist, but others may come up in your class discussions.

## Discussion

There have been arguments over the years about what the phrase "an establishment of religion" was intended to mean. Some have insisted that the establishment clause was meant to prevent the federal government from making one religion a state religion. In Europe in the past, there have been state religions, religions to which one had to belong in order to hold office or even, in some cases, to do business. For several centuries, the Anglican Church was the state church of Great Britain, the Catholic Church the state church of Spain, Italy, and France, The Russian Orthodox Church the state church of Russia, and so on. And when the Constitution was written, a few of the American states had state churches—for example, the Episcopal Church in South Carolina and the Congregational in Massachusetts. But Article VI of the Constitution already in effect prohibits the federal government from favoring one church as a national church. Too many different religions were thriving in the United States for there to be any sentiment anywhere for a national church.

In fact, because of all the differences in religious belief, the consensus was that the government should stay out of religion altogether. New Hampshire wanted an amendment to the Constitution saying "Congress shall make no laws touching Religion, or to infringe the rights of Conscience." Virginia, North Carolina, and Rhode Island urged wording that said "no particular religious sect or society ought to be favored or established, by law, in preference to others." New York urged similar wording.

You must be careful not to read too much into the Supreme Court's decision. The establishment clause as interpreted by the Court does not prohibit private acts of religious observance in public schools. Students can wear t-shirts with religious (or antireligious) messages; they can pray silently any time they want; they can form religious clubs and meet on campus. What is forbidden is school-sponsored religious activities.

## Discussion: Questions to Consider

1.  Consider the intent of the establishment clause, after reading and taking notes on the three historians' viewpoints and on the information in the preceding discussion. In this assignment, it can be easy to start saying silly things, such as Judge Lake's assertion that opposing school prayer amounts to "state-sponsored atheism." The citizens of New Hampshire, Virginia, North Carolina, Rhode Island, New York, and the other states were not atheists, and as far as we know, the judges of the Court of Appeals in New Orleans and the Supreme Court aren't either, although the First Amendment protects the rights of atheists just as much as it does those of believers. If the school allowed the student body to elect a pregame speaker who said a prayer, would the school then be respecting an establishment of religion?

2.  If the student body can't pray before a football game, is the students' right of freedom of speech being violated? The Court of Appeals in Atlanta thought so when it ruled that forbidding prayer at football games would be a "form of content-based censorship." It is possible to see that a situation like the one in the Santa Fe School District might pit two parts of the First Amendment against each other—the establishment clause against freedom of speech. In your essay, you will need to decide what you think about the conflict between the establishment clause and freedom of speech. Is there a real conflict between the establishment clause and freedom of speech, or does there just seem to be one?

### *Step One: Make Notes and Compare Them with Others*

You will need to take notes on the events that led to the U.S. Supreme Court's hearing of the case. Then take notes on the background of the establishment clause of the First Amendment. What do the three historians—Professor Miller, Professor Levy, and Professor Rakove—say about the establishment clause? Make notes on their opinions.

Next you should consider the main arguments of the U.S. Supreme Court majority and minority opinions. List the arguments for the majority presented by Justice John Paul Stevens, and list the arguments for the minority presented by Chief Justice William Rehnquist. Make notes about how strong or weak you think these arguments are.

Review your notes and answer the questions to consider.

In class, working with two other students, compare your notes. If you find disagreements or omissions, try to come to a consensus on the important points.

Each group should report on the points the group members consider most important so that the teacher can write them on the board for class discussion. Now the class as a whole can come to a consensus on the most important points and answer the questions to consider. Take notes during this class discussion since these notes will form the basis for the next step in the assignment.

### Step Two: Make an Outline and Compare It with Others

Read the following section on Organizing *"Santa Fe Independent School District v. Doe."* Then go over your notes and decide how you think you might organize them into an essay. Make a rough list outline as you did for your first assignment, and bring your outline to class for discussion of ways to organize this paper.

## Organizing *"Santa Fe Independent School District v. Doe"*

In your introduction, you should briefly state the highlights of the case so that your reader understands why the U.S. Supreme Court considered it. You can state your opinion in a thesis statement in your introduction, or you can save it for your conclusion.

You can begin the body of your essay by explaining the three historians' interpretations of the establishment clause in the First Amendment, since the meaning of this clause is central to the case.

As in other assignments you have done so far, you have gone through the material and written down the opposing majority and minority arguments. Now, working with your lists of these arguments, try to see how the opposing arguments match up with each other, and note how strong or how valid you think the arguments are. For instance, the court majority argued that the Santa Fe Independent School District, representing government, may not force students to participate in religion by sponsoring a pregame prayer, but the minority argued that, in the student election, the students might vote to *not* have a speaker give a pregame prayer. You should organize the body of your essay point by point, writing a paragraph about each set of opposing arguments and their strengths and weaknesses. Remember that each body paragraph should have a topic sentence, so that its main point is clear.

You can use the concessive subordinators to acknowledge arguments you do not agree with, and at the same time, de-emphasize them and emphasize your own point of view.

Be sure to not present all of the majority arguments in one body paragraph and all of the minority arguments in another; this plan will create "sack" paragraphs, which do not give your readers the opportunity to see how you've evaluated opposing arguments together.

Your conclusion will contain your own summing up of what you think are the better arguments and your position on the Supreme Court decision.

### Step Three: Write a Rough Draft

At home, using your list outline as your basis, write a rough draft of your essay. As usual, do not worry about spelling and other mechanics at this point. Refer to the following checklist to see if your own rough draft meets the requirements for this assignment, and use it also in class in peer review.

---

### CHECKLIST FOR EVALUATING ROUGH DRAFTS

1. Does the introduction indicate what the essay will be about and why the subject is important?
2. Is the essay divided into body paragraphs that cover the meaning of the establishment clause and the majority and minority opinions?
3. Does each body paragraph start with a topic sentence, a sentence that tells what the paragraph will discuss?
4. Are all the sentences in each body paragraph related to the point expressed in the topic sentence? Are there any places where unrelated ideas seem to come into any paragraphs?
5. Are the most important majority and minority opinions covered, or is anything missing?
6. Does the order of the points seem logical, or does anything seem out of place?
7. Is there a conclusion explaining the writer's position on the issue?

8. Does the writer use the words *and, or,* and *so* (or *and so*) to join logically related ideas?
9. Does the writer use the words *but, while, whereas, although, even though,* and *though* to show contrast and concession?

### *Step Four: Peer Review*

In class, in groups of three, exchange your rough drafts and take turns reading your own drafts aloud. If you spot any errors as you read, correct them. Using the checklist, go over each paper to identify both strengths and weaknesses. Ask your teacher if you need help or advice.

### *Step Five: Write a Final Draft*

At home, write the final version of your paper, using your peers' and teacher's advice for guidance.

Check to make sure you have used the words *and, or,* and *so* (or *and so*) to join logically related ideas.

Check to see that you have joined sentences with *but, while, whereas, although, even though,* and *though* to show contrast and concession. Look particularly for places to use the *although* words to concede, and at the same time, play down points you are opposed to.

Review the proofreading tips in Chapter 1 and the following Special Proofreading section, then proofread a printed copy of your paper.

### Special Proofreading

- As you did in previous papers, proofread for subject-verb agreement and plural -*s* endings on nouns.
- This assignment asks you to discuss actions that took place in the past, so be sure to check that you've used past-tense verbs in describing them, and that your past-tense verbs have -*ed* endings.
- Check for possessive apostrophes in phrases like "Justice Rehnquist's opinion," and "the students' rights."
- If pronouns have been a problem for you, make sure you've used subject pronouns in front of verbs and object pronouns after them, and make sure that you have used the pronouns *they* and *them* to refer to plural nouns.
- Check your spelling of *whereas;* it is one word, not two. Check your spelling of *even though;* they are two words, not one.

## Getting Your Writing Right

### Using Quotations

Often when we are writing essays based on sources, we use quotations to report someone's ideas, or to back up our own points. For example, in Case Study One, the controversial article in the student newspaper contains many comments from students, and you may want to quote a couple of them.

There are two common patterns for introducing quotations.

> 1. *According to* author's name, + quotation

> According to George M., "We just drive out in the country on Friday night or Saturday and drink a couple of sixpacks."

*or*    2. Author's name *says*, + quotation

> George M. says, "We just drive out in the country on Friday night or Saturday and drink a couple of sixpacks."

In pattern 2, we can also use the expression *says that* and there are several alternatives to the verb *says* in this pattern:

> states that        points out that
> claims that        believes that
> thinks that        argues that

Be sure that the expression you choose makes sense with the quotation. For instance, you wouldn't write a sentence like the following one, because George M. is not stating an argument:

> George M. argues that "we just drive out in the country on Friday night or Saturday and drink a couple of sixpacks."

In the following sentence, an alternative to *says* works well because the editor is arguing a point:

> The editor of the student newspaper *argues that,* "we do not create climates. We report on climates. The climate is there already. We are bringing it out into the open."

*Note:* When we use the word *that* before a quotation, we don't capitalize the first word in the quotation unless it's a proper noun.

## Exercise 5A

*Note:* When you write sentences using pattern 2, you can use alternatives to *says that* that are listed above.

### For Case Study One

1. Choose a statement by a student in the newspaper article that supports the principal and superintendent's belief that the article promotes drinking.

   Write one sentence quoting this statement using pattern 1:

   > *According to* author's name, + quotation.

   _____

   Write another sentence quoting this statement using pattern 2:

   > Author's name *says* (or *says that*), + quotation.

   _____

2. Choose a statement by the principal and superintendent that represents their opinion about censoring the article.

   Write one sentence quoting this statement using pattern 1:

   > *According to* authors' names, + quotation.

   _____

   Write another sentence quoting this statement using pattern 2:

   > Authors' names *say* (or *say that*), + quotation.

   _____

### For Case Study Two

1. Choose a statement from the readings that expresses support for a
   curfew law.

   Write one sentence quoting this statement using pattern 1:

> *According to* author's name, + quotation.

_____

Write another sentence quoting this statement using pattern 2:

> Author's name *says* (or *says that*), + quotation.

_____

2. Choose a statement from the readings that does *not* support a curfew law.

   Write one sentence quoting this statement using pattern 1:

   > *According to* author's name, + quotation.

   _____

   Write another sentence quoting this statement using pattern 2:

   > Author's name *says* (or *says that*), + quotation.

   _____

### For Case Study Three

1. Choose a statement from the majority opinion.

   Write one sentence quoting this statement using pattern 1:

   > *According to* author's name, + quotation.

   _____

   Write another sentence quoting this statement using pattern 2:

   > Author's name *says* (or *says that*), + quotation.

   _____

2. Choose a statement from the minority opinion.

   Write one sentence quoting this statement using pattern 1:

   > *According to* author's name, + quotation.

   _____

   Write another sentence quoting this statement using pattern 2:

   > Author's name *says* (or *says that*), + quotation.

   _____

### Book and Article Titles

In typewritten papers for any of your courses, there are two conventions you, like all writers, will be expected to follow:

1.  When you refer to a short work, like one of the articles in this book, a short story, a poem, or a television show, you put quotation marks around the title and capitalize the main words:

    "Underage Drinking Rampant at Central High"
    "Court Blocks Enforcement of West New York Curfew"

2.  When you refer to the title of a long work—a book, magazine, newspaper, or movie, you underline or italicize the title, and capitalize all the main words:

    <u>The Tiger's Eye</u>        or        *The Tiger's Eye*
    <u>Great Expectations</u>     or        *Great Expectations*

### Possessive Apostrophes

Through an unfortunate historical accident, English has come to use the apostrophe to show when a noun is possessive as opposed to when it is plural. There is no need for the possessive apostrophe, and none of the brother or sister languages of English use it, but there it is, and we seem to be stuck with it.

All languages indicate the concept of possession in some way or other, even though the concept itself may vary from language to language. One of the ways English does it is through possessive pronouns in front of nouns:

*my* father
*her* shoes
*our* money

So our pronouns take on a different shape when they are possessives. So do our nouns. The idea is simple enough. If the noun is a possessive, we add *'s* on the end of its regular form:

*John's* father
*mother's* shoes
*the club's* money

Of course, if a noun is plural, we also add an *s* but no apostrophe:

the movie stars
the lions
the teams

So what do we do if we want to make a plural noun ending in -*s* into a posses-sive? We can just add the apostrophe after the -*s* (or, if we want to, we can add '*s*, but this form isn't as common).

| | |
|---|---|
| the movie stars' salaries | (or the movie stars's salaries) |
| the lions' cubs | (or the lions's cubs) |
| the teams' losses | (or the teams's losses) |

If the word is singular but still ends in *s*, as some names do, add '*s*:

Charles's problem

## Exercise 5B

Rewrite each underlined group of words using apostrophes to show posses-sion.

EXAMPLES: I envied the <u>income of the baseball player.</u>
the baseball player's income

I envied the <u>income of the baseball players.</u>
the baseball players' income

1. Henry admired <u>the car of Gloria.</u>

   _____

2. Gloria admired <u>the motorcycle of Henry.</u>

   _____

3. Henry liked <u>the company of his friends.</u>

   _____

4. Gloria liked <u>the company of her sister.</u>

   _____

5. Henry was worried about <u>the math test of the professor</u>.

_____

6. Gloria was worried about <u>the nosiness of her neighbors</u>.

_____

7. The new champion was <u>the choice of the people</u>.

_____

8. The dethroned champion earned <u>the scorn of the spectators</u>.

_____

9. We were concerned about <u>the plans of their coaches</u>.

_____

10. We were not concerned about <u>the attitudes of their fans</u>.

_____

To add a little confusion to the mix, some nouns change their spelling when they are plural, and sometimes people get confused about whether the nouns are plural or possessive. A good example is the word _baby_. The plural, as you know, is _babies_.

When using the possessive of the singular form _baby_, add the _'s:_

the baby's blanket    (one baby, one blanket)

When using the possessive of the plural form _babies_, you can add just an apostrophe (or _'s_):

the babies' health    (the health of two or more babies)
_or_ the babies's health

## Exercise 5C

Following are five singular words that change their plural spelling to _-ies_. Write two sentences for each word, one using the singular possessive and one using the plural possessive.

industry, baby, lady, canary, library

_____
_____
_____
_____

_____

_____

_____

_____

_____

_____

## Summary and Review of Chapter 5

### Evaluating Arguments

When we write position papers, essays in which we take a stand, we have to consider opposing points of view. It is important not only to identify the principal arguments on both sides of an issue but also to evaluate these arguments—to judge how strong or how weak they are.

### Using Quotations

Two common patterns are useful for introducing quotations:

1. *According to* author's name, + quotation

2. Author's name *says (that)*, + quotation

### Possessive Apostrophes

When a noun is a possessive, we normally add *'s* to the end of it. When a plural noun, one that already ends in *s*, is a possessive, we have a choice. We can just add an apostrophe to it, or we add *'s*.

### Chapter 5: Glossary

| | | |
|---|---|---|
| 1. | **indignant** | angry |
| 2. | **inadvertently** | unintentionally; carelessly |
| 3. | **contend** | claim |
| 4. | **spate** | sudden rush |
| 5. | **conviction** | belief |
| 6. | **high-minded** | morally righteous |

7. **plummeted** decreased or fell suddenly
8. **empirical** based on facts
9. **injunction** legal order
10. **discernible** noticeable
11. **explicit** definite, clear
12. **invocations** appeals to a spiritual power
13. **solemnize** dignify
14. **uncontested** not challenged or disputed
15. **incontestable** not to be challenged, indisputable
16. **subscribe to** (a religion) belong to
17. **supersede** replace
18. **majoritarian election** election determined by the votes of more than one-half of the voters
19. **impermissible** not allowed
20. **divisiveness** disharmony, conflict
21. **dissipating** removing, scattering
22. **respondents** (in a court case) defendants
23. **misconstrues** misunderstands
24. **unduly** excessively
25. **plausible** possible, believable
26. **secular** nonreligious

# CHAPTER SIX
# Analyzing Primary Sources

**CASE STUDY ONE: THE ABRAHAM LINCOLN CONTROVERSY**

Read the following case and the assignment and discussion sections following it. Then go back over the case, reading carefully and underlining or highlighting the most important information. Don't try to identify this information on your first reading.

## The Abraham Lincoln Controversy

African-American students at Abraham Lincoln High School are arguing that the annual Lincoln's Birthday celebrations be canceled on the grounds that Lincoln was a racist who was not, in fact, interested in the fate of Black people. To prove their point, they cite a letter Lincoln wrote to Horace Greeley, editor of the *New York Tribune*, in 1862, during the Civil War, the year that Lincoln issued his famous Emancipation Proclamation supposedly freeing the slaves. Here is the part of the letter the students find offensive:

> My paramount object in this struggle *is* to save the Union, and is *not* either to save or destroy slavery. If I could save the Union without freeing

*any* slave I would do it, and if I could save it by freeing *all* the slaves I would do it; and if I could save it by freeing some and leaving others alone I would also do that. What I do about slavery, and the colored race, I do because I believe it helps to save the Union; and what I forbear, I forbear because I do *not* believe it would help to save the Union.

You are part of the History Team, a team of students studying American history who have volunteered to learn about Lincoln's feelings about African-Americans and discover what his role really was in abolishing slavery. Your team has come up with the following document. It consists of a brief summary of the situation with regard to slavery just prior to the Civil War, followed by a list of Lincoln's statements or positions on African-Americans and on slavery. The team has arranged this list chronologically, year by year.

## Slavery in the United States Before the Civil War

Not counting California, which was too far away to matter, before the Civil War there were 16 free states in the north and 15 slave states in the South. Slavery also existed in the District of Columbia. When the U.S. Constitution was adopted in 1789, one of the compromises that made it possible was an understanding that Congress would not even discuss the issue of slavery in the states where it existed. Slavery was such a touchy issue in both the north, which was against it, and the South, which was for it, that the southern states would not agree to the Constitution unless the northern states would agree that slavery could not even be discussed in Congress. It was not until 1844 that this "gag rule" was overturned, and Northerners could begin to attack slavery in the Congress.

Numerous loud and even violent disputes followed over whether slavery could be extended into the territories to the west, which would one day become states. The country was divided into three basic parties. One, the Abolitionists, mostly from New England, wanted slavery abolished entirely. Most, but not all, Southerners wanted it protected and extended into the west. A third group opposed slavery but did not mind it being extended to the west if settlers there should vote for it.

In 1857, a slave named Dred Scott sued for his freedom after his master died, on the grounds that he had previously lived in two free states. In its decision, the U.S. Supreme Court held that slaves were property, not citizens with the right to sue, and that their owners had the right to take their property with them to free states. The Chief Justice of the Supreme Court, Roger B. Taney, wrote that when the Constitution was written, Blacks "had for more than a century been regarded as beings of an inferior order . . . so far inferior that they had no rights which the white man was bound to respect" and that there was nothing in the Constitution to forbid slavery anywhere. This decision caused a furor among the Abolitionists and even some others, but many American citizens saw nothing wrong with it.

Many citizens of the northern states were opposed to slavery, but they had little idea of what it really involved. The average farmer in the north had never even seen a Black person and had no idea of what kind of treatment African-Americans were receiving on the plantations in the South. The whole idea of there even being Black people was, to most Northerners, like the idea of there being Martians.

In 1861, the first year of the Civil War and of Lincoln's presidency, the country divided into two warring factions, the Union and the Confederacy, but there were also four border states that each side tried to get for its cause: Delaware, Maryland, Kentucky, and Missouri. Although these border states were slave states, there were many Union supporters in them, and they had governments that were generally pro-Union. Part of Lincoln's problem in the early years of the war was to keep these states as much on his side as he could, which meant that he had to leave their slave institutions alone. By 1863, when the Union armies were defeating the Confederates, Lincoln was freer to act on the slavery issue.

### Lincoln's Views

1857    In a speech, Lincoln responded to Chief Justice Taney's decision in the Dred Scott case with these words: "All the powers of earth seem rapidly combining against [the Negro]. They have him in his prison house; they have searched his person, and left no prying instrument with him. One after another they have closed the heavy iron doors upon him, and now they have him, as it were, bolted in with a lock of a hundred keys, which can never be unlocked without the concurrence of every key; the keys in the hands of a hundred different men, and they scattered to a hundred different and distant places; they stand musing as to what invention, in all the dominions of mind and matter, can be produced to make the impossibility of his escape more complete than it is." Lincoln felt that Taney's views were completely wrong and that African-Americans were being unjustly imprisoned in slavery.

1858    In a speech, Lincoln outlined his position on many of the key slavery issues of the time:

He supported the Fugitive Slave Act, which required that slaves who escaped to free states had to be returned to their owners.

He was not opposed to adding more slave states to the Union, though he wished it would not happen.

He did not pledge himself to abolish slavery in the District of Columbia, though he would be happy to see it done.

He was opposed to permitting slavery in territories not yet admitted to statehood.

In another speech he said, "I am not, nor ever have been, in favor of bringing about in any way the social and political equality of the white and Black races. I am not, nor ever have been, in favor of making voters or jurors of negroes, nor of qualifying them to hold office, nor to intermarry with white people." Still, he argued that there was a fundamental difference "between the men who think slavery a wrong and those who do not think it wrong." He considered slavery "a moral, a social, and a political wrong."

*Seems totally at odds!*

**1861** In 1860, Lincoln was elected president of the United States. But, in February 1861, before Lincoln could take office, the secessionist states set up a southern nation, wrote a new constitution declaring the secessionist states independent, and elected Jefferson Davis as their president. As president of the Confederacy, Davis claimed that the Confederacy just wanted to be left alone, but if attacked, it would defend itself against the Union "aggressors." Two weeks later, Lincoln took the oath of office and expressed his intention to avoid war and at the same time to keep and defend the Union.

During the first year of his presidency, Lincoln signed a law prohibiting slavery in the territories and signed a treaty with Britain to eliminate the slave trade. This meant that British and American ships could not transport slaves from Africa to the United States. But during this year, which was also the first year of the Civil War, he refused to make slavery a war issue. He would fight to restore the Union but not to get rid of slavery.

**1862** Shortly after writing the letter to Horace Greeley, in which he wrote that his main objective in the Civil War was to save the Union, Lincoln told his closest advisors that he had changed his mind. He now thought that slavery should be an issue in the war. He was, however, opposed to enrolling Black soldiers in the Union Army. He issued the Emancipation Proclamation, which freed the slaves in areas controlled by the Confederacy. It did not free slaves in the slave states that were part of the Union. *!!!*

He did this in order to keep Britain and France from joining the war on the southern side. These two countries were suffering because their factories that made cloth could not get cotton from the American South, and Lincoln was afraid that they would help the South in order to get the cotton. But *tactical move*

both Britain and France had outlawed slavery, so if he "freed" the slaves in the southern states, he knew that they could not help the South to win the war because then they would be supporting slavery.

1863  Lincoln continued to change his mind about slavery and about African-Americans. For the first time, he now recognized that African-Americans would become full citizens of the United States after the war, and he author-ized the army to enlist Black soldiers.

In response to those who said that they would not fight to free the Negro, Lincoln said, "Fight you, then, exclusively to save the Union. But when peace comes, there will be some Black men who can remember that, with silent tongue, and clenched teeth, and steady eye, and well-poised bayonet, they have helped mankind on to this great consummation; while, I fear, there will be some white ones, unable to forget that, with malignant heart, and deceitful speech, they have strove to hinder it."

In the Gettysburg Address he reaffirmed the words of the Declaration of Independence, that "all men are created equal." This was understood everywhere to include African-Americans.

1864  Under pressure from many of his political supporters in Congress to end the war without abolishing slavery, Lincoln said, "I should be damned in time and in eternity" for betraying the Black soldiers fighting for the Union. He wrote a letter to these supporters in which he tried (1)to be conciliatory, but he showed it to Frederick Douglass, the great Black leader, and on Dou-glass's advice tore it up. No president in American history had ever admitted an African-American into the White House as anything but a servant. Lin-coln was the first to bring Blacks into the White House to discuss important issues and the first to take the advice of a Black leader.

In his annual message to Congress, he strongly urged passage of the Thir-teenth Amendment, to abolish slavery in the United States, and worked hard to persuade those who were opposed or unsure to vote for it. It passed, and slavery was forever ended as a legal institution in the United States.

## ASSIGNMENT

Write an essay in which you examine Lincoln's different opinions on the issues of slavery and African Americans and come to a conclusion as to whether you think Abraham Lincoln High School should, or should not, cel-ebrate Lincoln's Birthday.

## Discussion

As you read the background paragraphs, notice the climate in the country regarding slavery and African-Americans. This climate is especially important since most of us—and Lincoln was no different than anyone else—think pretty much like those around us. For example, you probably find it hard to imagine thinking human sacrifice is a good idea, but if you were a member of the ancient Inca civilization in South America, you probably would have been like everyone else and thought that it was fine. If you were born a Roman in the fourth century A.D., you probably would have been in favor of persecuting Christians. It's very difficult to hold completely different values from those around us.

### Step One: Make Notes and Compare Them with Others

After you have underlined or highlighted the most important points in the reading, make two pairs of lists: The first pair will contain a list of the points indicating that Lincoln can be seen as pro-African-Americans, and a list indicating that he can seen as against them; the second pair of lists will contain opposing points showing Lincoln's attitudes toward the institution of slavery. Be sure to write down the dates of each different position, since it is clear that he changed his mind over the years.

In class, work with two other students to compare your notes. If you find disagreements or omissions, try to come to a consensus on the important points.

Each group should now report to the teacher on the points the group members consider most important so that the teacher can write them on the board for class discussion. Now the class as a whole can come to a consensus on the most important points. Take notes during class discussion since these notes and your original ones will form the basis for the next step in the assignment.

### Step Two: Make an Outline and Compare It with Others

Read the following guidelines on organizing "The Abraham Lincoln Controversy." At home, go over your notes and decide how you think you might organize them into an essay. Make a rough list outline, and bring the list to class for discussion of ways to organize this paper.

## Organizing "The Abraham Lincoln Controversy"

In your introduction, you will want to briefly state the controversy at Abraham Lincoln High School so that your readers will understand why you have researched the subject of Lincoln's opinions on slavery and on African

Americans. You can state your opinion about whether the school should celebrate Lincoln's Birthday in a thesis statement in your introduction, or you can save your opinion for your conclusion.

This assignment can be organized in several different ways. The most obvious is to put all the arguments for celebrating Lincoln's Birthday into one paragraph and all the arguments against in another. But this is also the poorest way of organizing. As you know, a body paragraph usually contains one major point in an essay, and the topic sentence tells what the point is. A paragraph that begins "There are many reasons why we should not celebrate Lincoln's Birthday" obviously will not make one main point; it will make a lot of them. It will be a "shopping bag" paragraph.

In this assignment, there are many points that could serve to organize the essay, and each one of these would make a good body paragraph. There probably should be a body paragraph telling how Americans in general felt about slavery before the Civil War. There might be one on Lincoln's early attitudes toward slavery and another one on his later attitudes. And so on. Remember that you are looking at Lincoln's attitudes not toward one thing, but toward two—his attitude (or attitudes) toward slavery as an institution, and his attitude (or attitudes) toward African-Americans as people, as human beings. When you are listing his different feelings in these two respects, be sure to note the different years he felt the way he did.

Since you will be taking a position in this essay, you will want to concede points that you do not agree with. Use concessive subordinators to join contrasting opinions, placing a concessive word in front of the point you want to de-emphasize.

Be sure to start each body paragraph with a topic sentence that states what the paragraph will cover. For example, you might start a body paragraph with a sentence like this: "In 1862 and 1863, during the middle of the Civil War, Lincoln's attitude toward slavery seems to have changed." The paragraph would then discuss what was new about Lincoln's position on slavery from 1862 through 1864.

In your conclusion, you can sum up the main points that convinced you that the high school should, or should not, celebrate Lincoln's Birthday.

### Step Three: Write a Rough Draft
At home, using your list outline as your basis, write a rough draft of your essay. Try to get all of your information on paper in a logical order without worrying about spelling or mechanics.

Use the following checklist to see whether your own draft meets the requirements for this assignment, and use it also in class in peer review.

Make two copies of your draft so that you have three copies to bring to class.

---

### CHECKLIST FOR EVALUATING ROUGH DRAFTS

1. Does the introduction indicate what the essay will be about and why the subject is important?
2. Is the essay divided into body paragraphs that cover single subjects?
3. Does each body paragraph start with a topic sentence, a sentence that tells what the paragraph will discuss?
4. Are all the sentences in each body paragraph related to the point expressed in the topic sentence? Are there any places where unrelated ideas seem to come into any body paragraphs?
5. Are Lincoln's different positions on African-Americans and on slavery at different points in his life all considered?
6. Does the order of the points covered seem logical, or does anything seem out of place?
7. Is there a conclusion explaining what the high school should do and why?
8. Has the writer used the words *but, while, whereas, although, even though,* and *though* to show contrast and concession?
9. Has the writer used appositives to identify or describe nouns? Review exercises 6D and 6E in the Getting Your Writing Right section at the end of this chapter, where you practiced writing appositives about the Abraham Lincoln controversy.

---

### Step Four: Peer Review

In class, in groups of three, exchange your rough drafts and take turns reading your own drafts aloud. If you spot any errors as you read, correct them. Using the checklist, go over each paper to identify both strengths and weaknesses. It is just as important to tell when something works really well as when it doesn't work. Call in your teacher if you need help or advice.

### Step Five: Write a Final Draft

At home, using your peers' and teacher's advice for guidance, write the final version of your paper.

Check to make sure that you have used the joining words *but, while, whereas, although, even though,* and *though* to show contrast and concession.

Now that you have practiced using appositives in the Getting Your Writing Right section of this chapter, you should use them to identify or describe nouns in your sentences. Look over your paper for places that you can use appositives. Review exercises 6D and 6E for hints about places where you can use them.

Finally, review the proofreading tips in Chapter 1 and the following Special Proofreading guidelines, and proofread a printed copy of your paper.

## Special Proofreading

- As you did in previous papers, proofread for subject verb agreement and plural -*s* endings on nouns.
- This assignment asks you to discuss actions that took place in the past, so it is especially important to check that you've used the past tense in describing them and that your past-tense verbs have -*ed* endings.
- Check for possessive apostrophes. Every time you've used Abraham Lincoln's name, check to see whether it is a possessive, that is, whether you are discussing *Lincoln's opinion*, *Lincoln's decision*, or *Lincoln's letter*.
- If pronouns have been a problem for you, check to see that you've used subject and object pronouns correctly.

**CASE STUDY TWO:**
**WHAT DOES THE SECOND AMENDMENT MEAN?**

Read the following case involving conflicting interpretations of the Second Amendment, and read the assignment and discussion sections. Then go back over the case carefully, underlining or highlighting the most important points. Don't try to find these points on your first reading.

## What Does the Second Amendment Mean?

The Bill of Rights—the first ten amendments, which guarantee individual freedoms—was originally not part of the U.S. Constitution. When the U.S. Constitution was ratified by 1788, many people feared that it gave the federal government too many powers previously exercised by state governments, and that a strong central government would not honor the individual liberties fought for in the Revolutionary War. Although they approved the Constitution, several states proposed amendments to protect individual rights. After reviewing the states' proposals and each state government's bill of rights, James Madison, who played a major role in the framing of the Constitution, drafted amendments for consideration by Congress, and in 1791, the Bill of Rights was ratified to prevent the federal government from violating individual rights.

Easily the most controversial section of the Constitution of the United States is the Second Amendment, part of our Bill of Rights. The Second Amendment reads as follows:

> A well regulated militia being necessary to the security of a free state,
> the right of the people to keep and bear arms shall not be infringed.

With a tradition, founded on this amendment, of gun ownership by individuals, the United States imposes fewer restrictions on guns than any other developed nation and has by far the highest death rate by guns. In 1990, according to Handgun Control, Inc., while 22 people were killed with handguns in Great Britain, 68 in Canada, and 87 in Japan, 10,567 were killed in the United States.

Periodically, both in the United States and in other countries, seriously disturbed persons will find a way to arm themselves, and a major disaster will result. It is interesting, then, to see how the nation reacts. In March 1996, such a person in Great Britain went to a schoolyard in a small town in Scotland and killed 16 first-graders and their teacher. The British government reacted by banning private ownership of all handguns over .22-caliber. Those owning such guns were required to turn them in to the police by October 1, 1997.

In 1989 in the United States, a young man named Patrick Purdy bought an assault rifle for $350 and went to a schoolyard in Stockton, California, where he opened fire, killing 5 children, aged between six and nine, and wounding 31 others and a teacher. This was the fifth schoolyard attack in the United States in less than a year. Two years later, in 1991, a man named George Jo Hennard drove his truck through the window of a cafeteria in Killeen, Texas, and then shot and killed 22 people. He used one 17-shot and two 15-shot handguns.

As a result of these incidents, the U.S. Congress has passed a weak law banning a few kinds of assault rifles and another law requiring a 15-day waiting period before one can buy a gun. Another law outlawing ammunition clips for guns that hold more than seven bullets was defeated.

Both those who defend and those who attack the right of Americans to own guns with few restrictions usually cite the Second Amendment to support their claims. Your problem here will not be to decide whether guns should be freely owned or severely restricted in the United States. Instead, you are going to become a constitutional lawyer and, using the evidence that follows, decide what you think the Second Amendment really means.

## The British Background of the Second Amendment

One of the things that makes comparing the British and American reactions to massacres like those that took place in California, Texas, and Scotland interesting is that the right to bear arms that we find in the Second Amendment had its origin in Britain itself. As you know, the American colonists in the eighteenth century saw themselves, prior to the Revolution, as Englishmen. They or their ancestors had mostly come from Britain, and they naturally brought with them British customs and laws. If Britain had not made the mistake of treating them as colonists and had instead treated them as citizens, there would have been no American Revolution.

The first time the English expressed in writing the right to own guns was in 1689, 87 years before the American Revolution, when the English Parliament wrote a document entitled "Declaration of Rights." There were two reasons why Parliament might want to safeguard the individual's right to own guns. One was, simply, that police as we know them had not yet been invented, and it was usually up to the individual to defend him- or herself from robbers or worse. Although the British police did come into being in the eighteenth century, police forces as we know them were not very effective until the very end of the eighteenth or early in the nineteenth century, some time after the "Declaration of Rights" and after the American Constitution.

The second reason is that the English, separated from other European countries by the English Channel, did not have to worry much about being attacked by neighboring countries, and so they did not like the idea of maintaining a professional army—a standing army, as it was called. They did not trust their kings to have a large military power that they might use to establish a dictatorship, and so they felt that in the event of attack from outside or rebellion within the country, the government should rely upon a citizen militia to defend itself.

### BRITAIN: 1689 "DECLARATION OF RIGHTS"

Like one of your papers, the "Declaration of Rights" exists in a first draft and a final draft. The first draft reads as follows:

> That the raising or keeping of a standing army within the kingdom in time of Peace, unless it be with consent of Parliament, is against the law.

> That the subjects [citizens] may provide and keep arms, for their com-
> mon defence.

In the final draft, the second sentence was changed, as follows:

> That the subjects may have arms for their defence . . . as allowed by
> law.

Notice that the words "for their common defence," which means for defense
of society, have been changed to simply "for their defence," which means
defense as individuals, and that "as allowed by law" has been added.

### BRITAIN: 1697

A very popular writer of the time, John Trenchard, who was the equivalent of
one of today's newspaper columnists, wrote essays on subjects of common
interest. He was as widely read in the American colonies as he was in Britain.
In two of his essays, he addressed the issue of standing armies versus militias:

> It is certain that all parts of Europe which are enslaved have been
> enslaved by armies; and it is absolutely impossible that any nation which
> keeps them amongst themselves can long preserve their liberties; nor
> can any nation perfectly lose their liberties who are without such
> guests. . . . Dare any man lay his hand upon his heart and say that his
> majesty will find greater security in a few thousand more men already
> regimented than in the steady affections of so many hundred thousands
> who will be always ready to be regimented. When the people are easy
> and satisfied, the whole kingdom is his army.

In other words, Trenchard strongly believed that standing armies were a danger to the freedom of a country and that a citizen militia would always better
serve the king for the nation's defense.

### BRITAIN: 1765

In 1765 a work appeared that had more influence on both English and American law over the next century than any other, *Blackstone's Commentaries on
the Laws of England*. Blackstone was by far the most important writer on the
law, and his work was studied thoroughly by American judges and lawyers
both before and long after the American Revolution. In a chapter entitled

"Absolute Rights of Individuals," Blackstone includes the "Right to bear arms."

> The fifth and last auxiliary right of the subject [citizen] . . . is that of having arms for their defense . . . and it is indeed a public allowance, under due restrictions, of the natural right of resistance [to attack] and self-preservation, when the (2)sanctions of society and laws are found insufficient to restrain the violence of oppression.

In short, Blackstone believed that citizens needed arms to defend themselves, not the country, and in the summary of this chapter, he again refers to "the right of having and using arms for self-preservation and defense."

### BRITAIN: 1780

While the British were fighting the Americans overseas, a series of violent riots erupted in London in which about 450 people were killed, and the British army of over 100,000 men, while putting down the riots, disarmed a large number of the poor. The English militia had, by this time, practically disappeared as an institution, and there was as yet no police force strong enough to handle large public disturbances. The city of London's legal advisor, William Blizard, was asked to give his opinion on the issue of who might own arms:

> The right of his majesty's . . . subjects to have arms for their own defence, and to use them for lawful purposes is most clear and undeniable. It seems, indeed, to be considered by the ancient laws of this kingdom not only as a *right* but as a *duty;* for all the subjects of the realm who are able to bear arms are bound to be ready at all times to assist the sheriff and other civil magistrates in the execution of the laws and the preservation of the public peace. And that right, which every [citizen] most unquestionably possesses *individually,* may, and in many cases *must,* be exercised collectively . . .

Blizard believed that citizens had both an individual and a (3)collective right to own arms. It is important to note that nowhere in British law or history was it ever argued that citizens had the right to bear arms as protection from their own government. In any case, with a strong professional army, an increasingly capable police force, and the steadily increasing power of Parliament and decreasing power of the king, most British citizens saw no need to own arms, and the practice dwindled away.

## The American Background of the Second Amendment
### AMERICA BEFORE THE REVOLUTION: 1623–1776

The early American colonies, [4]living precariously on the edge of a wilderness, required their male citizens to carry arms, and all males between the ages of 16 and 60 were required to serve, if called, in the local militia. A law passed in Virginia in 1640 was typical; it required "all masters of families" to supply "all those of their families which shall be capable of arms . . . with arms both offensive and defensive." The seventeenth-century laws were primarily aimed at protecting the individual and community from hostile Indians and predatory animals. In the eighteenth century, not long before the Revolution, a Connecticut law ordered all citizens to "always be provided with and have in continual readiness, a well-fixed firelock [rifle] . . . or other good fire-arms . . . a good sword or cutlass . . . one pound of good powder, four pounds of bullets fit for his gun, and twelve flints." This law was aimed specifically not at individual defense but at providing a citizen militia for the common defense.

Like their British brothers, the early Americans distrusted standing armies and relied on militias for their defense. This dislike and distrust of armies was made worse by the fact that as relations with Britain worsened, the British were sending larger and larger numbers of troops to America and trying to get the Americans to pay for them. One of the charges of the Declaration of Independence was that King George III "kept among us in times of peace standing armies (and ships of war) without the consent of our legislatures. He has affected to render the military independent of and superior to the Civil power. He has combined with others to subject us to a jurisdiction foreign to our constitution, and unacknowledged by our laws; for [5]quartering large bodies of armed troops among us. . . . "

### AMERICA: 1787–89

After the American colonies won their independence, their first task was to form a more effective government than the clumsy and inefficient one that was in power when America won the war. The convention that produced the Constitution did not also provide a Bill of Rights, and although most states eventually ratified the new constitution, there was a strong demand that the first Congress write amendments to it that would ensure the basic rights of American citizens.

One of the problems was that of an army. Even though the Americans did not have to worry about giving a king too much power, they had inherited the old British distrust of standing armies. On the other hand, the delegates to the convention had seen that during the Revolutionary War, the American militias had performed very poorly against the British professionals while the Continental Army had done well. One delegate wrote as follows:

> The danger we meant chiefly to provide against was the hazarding of the national safety by reliance on [a militia]. An [6]overweening vanity leads the fond many, each man against the conviction of his own heart, to believe or affect to believe, that militia can beat veteran troops in the open field . . . of battle. . . . To rely on undisciplined, ill-officered men, though each were individually as brave as Caesar, to resist the well-directed impulse of veterans, is to act in defiance of reason and experience.

Although, as a result, the Constitution provides for an army and gives the national government ultimate authority over state militias, the delegates were as concerned as their English ancestors that such an army could be misused to establish a dictatorship. Several of the states proposed that a bill of rights be added to the Constitution, and some of these included sections on standing armies and the right to bear arms.

When the new U.S. Congress first convened in March 1789, James Madison, the person most responsible for the new Constitution, presented a draft of a bill of rights that included the following:

> The right of the people to keep and bear arms shall not be infringed; a well armed, and well regulated militia being the best security of a free country: but no person [7]religiously scrupulous of *bearing arms* shall be compelled to render military service in person.

Here, Madison expresses the old prejudice in favor of militias, calling them "the *best* security" of the nation. But in writing the final form of the Second Amendment, Congress made several changes in Madison's proposal and rejected one other proposed change. While Madison wrote that a "well armed and well regulated" militia was "the best security of a free country," the Second Amendment now says that the militia should only be "well regulated" and that it is "necessary to the security of a free state." Madison's last sentence, allowing for religious exemptions, was dropped. A motion was made to add the phrase "for the common defense" after the words "to keep and bear arms," but this phrase was rejected.

The question that has been handed down to us, then, is what did the people of the new United States really understand when they read the final version that Congress passed and that the 13 states ratified? Did they believe that the right to own weapons was unconditional—that everyone was entitled to them under any circumstances? Did they believe that owning weapons was primarily for national defense? Did they believe that they could own weapons for personal defense? Was the right to own weapons a guard against a government's abuse of their freedoms through the use of a standing army? Historians and legal scholars have been arguing about these questions for years.

What does the evidence from the American discussions and their English background indicate to you?

## ASSIGNMENT

Write an essay in which you examine the historical evidence leading up to the writing of the Second Amendment to the U.S. Constitution and argue

a. that those who wrote this amendment wanted all Americans to be able to own guns,

b. that they wanted Americans to own guns only in order to protect the nation, *or*

c. that the evidence of what they wanted isn't clear.

To do this assignment successfully, you will need to address three questions:

1. Was the right to bear arms supposed to be a total and permanent right, like the right of freedom of speech or freedom of religion, or not?

2. Was the Second Amendment aimed at providing a militia for the defense of the country, or not?

3. Was the Second Amendment intended for the personal defense of the individual, or not?

## Discussion

In doing this assignment, you are cautioned not to be led by your own prejudices or opinions about gun ownership. This is an area in which experts on the law and on the Constitution disagree sharply. There is no one view that all scholars consider correct. A report in 1975 by the American Bar Association, the national professional organization of American lawyers, stated that there is more disagreement and more misinformation about the Second Amendment than about any other constitutional issue.

To indicate what the problems here are, the leading American authority on the Second Amendment, Joyce Lee Malcolm, has written a summary of some of the confusions in her book *To Keep and Bear Arms: The Origins of an Anglo-American Right* (Cambridge: Harvard University Press). The word "militia" in the Second Amendment refers to a group of citizen-soldiers who would gather together when called upon by their government to go to the defense of their country. A large part of the American Revolution and our second war against Britain, the War of 1812, was fought by state militias. The National Guard is the closest thing we have today to a militia. Professor Malcolm writes,

> Although the amendment's drafters presumably believed it quite clear, the shared understandings upon which it was based have vanished and this single sentence has proven capable of an amazing range of inter-pretations. Its most troublesome aspect is the purpose of its pronounce-ment "a well regulated militia being necessary to the security of a free state." Two hundred years after its passage there is no agreement why it is there or what it means. Was it meant to restrict the right to have arms to militia members; to indicate *the* most pressing reason for an armed citizenry; or simply to proclaim the need for a free people to have a conscript, rather than a professional, army? And what sort of militia did the framers have in mind—a select group of citizen-soldiers, every able-bodied male citizen, or didn't it matter?

The arguments come down to two basic views of the Second Amendment. In one view, the words "A well regulated militia being necessary to the security of a free state" mean that the right to bear arms is only a *collective*, not an individual right. It means that one is entitled to bear arms only in order to defend the nation. In the other view, the words "the right of the people to keep and bear arms shall not be infringed" means that each American has an *individual* right to own guns.

***Step One: Make Notes and Compare Them with Others***
Underline or highlight the most important points in the readings. Then make three separate groups of notes. One group should cover the issue of whether the right to bear arms seems to have been subject to other laws—or not; that is, was it a permanent and total right, like the right to free speech or to choose

one's own religion, or wasn't it? A second group should cover whether the Second Amendment was aimed at providing a militia for defense of the country—or not. A third group should cover whether the Second Amendment was intended to provide personal defense for the individual—or not.

In class, work with two other students to compare your notes. If you find disagreements or omissions, try to come to a consensus on the important points.

Each group should now report on the points the group members consider most important so that the teacher can write them on the board for class discussion. Now the class as a whole can come to a consensus on the most important points. Write these points down since your notes will form the basis for the next step in the assignment.

### Step Two: Make an Outline and Compare It with Others
Read the following guidelines for organizing "What Does the Second Amendment Mean?" At home, go over your notes and decide how you think you might organize them into an essay. Make a rough list outline as you did for your first assignment, and bring your outline to class for discussion of ways to organize this paper.

## Organizing "What Does the Second Amendment Mean?"

In your introduction, you should inform your reader about what your essay will do—examine the historical evidence leading up to the writing of the Second Amendment and come to a conclusion about what the Second Amendment was intended to mean.

It is possible to organize this essay chronologically—that is, by following this issue from year to year—but that will probably turn out to be fairly difficult. Since the question is actually three questions—whether or not the Second Amendment was meant to be a permanent right, whether it was directed toward the militia for defense of the country, and whether it was intended for personal defense of the individual—it might be easier to organize your essay on that basis, taking up one question at a time and then writing a conclusion in which you sum up what you think the evidence means. Be sure to start each body paragraph with a topic sentence that tells what you are going to be discussing there.

### Step Three: Write a Rough Draft
At home, using your list outline as your basis, write a rough draft of your essay. Try to get all of your information on paper in a logical order without worrying about spelling and other mechanics.

Use the following checklist to see whether your draft meets the requirements for this assignment, and use it also in class in peer review.

Make two copies of your draft so that you have three copies to bring to class.

---

### CHECKLIST FOR EVALUATING ROUGH DRAFTS

1. Does the introduction indicate what the essay will be about and why the subject is important?
2. Is the essay divided into body paragraphs that cover single subjects?
3. Does each body paragraph start with a topic sentence, a sentence that tells what the paragraph will discuss?
4. Are all the sentences in each paragraph related to the point expressed in the topic sentence? Are there any places where unrelated ideas seem to come into any body paragraphs?
5. Are all the central questions covered—whether the right to own weapons was absolute or whether it was subject to other laws; whether it was intended for the defense of the country or community or not; whether it was intended for personal defense or not?
6. Does the order of the points covered seem logical, or does anything seem out of place?
7. Is there a conclusion in which the writer sums up what the evidence means?
8. Has the writer used the joining words *but, while, whereas, although, even though,* and *though* to show contrast and concession?
9. Has the writer used appositives to identify and describe nouns? (Review exercises 6F and 6G in the Getting Your Writing Right section at the end of this chapter, where you practiced writing appositives about the Second Amendment controversy.)

---

### *Step Four: Peer Review*

In class, in groups of three, exchange your rough drafts and take turns reading your own drafts aloud. If you spot any errors as you read, correct them. Using the checklist, go over each paper to identify both strengths and weaknesses. It is just as important to tell when something works really well as when it doesn't work. Call in your teacher if you need help or advice.

*Step Five: Write a Final Draft*

At home, write the final version of your paper, using your peers' and teacher's suggestions for guidance.

Check for places to use the joining words *but, while, whereas, although, even though*, and *though* to show contrast and concession.

Check to make sure that you have used appositives to identify and describe nouns. Review exercises 6F and 6G for hints about using appositives in this assignment.

Proofread a printed copy of your paper. Review the proofreading tips in Chapter 1 and the following Special Proofreading section.

## Special Proofreading

- Proofread for subject-verb agreement and plural -*s* endings on nouns.
- Since in much of your paper you will be telling about things that happened or were said in the past, be sure that all sentences about those past events are in the past tense. Check your verbs for past-tense -*ed* endings.
- Check for possessive apostrophes. Every time you've used someone's name check to see whether it is a possessive—that is, whether you are discussing something he or she had (such as his opinion, his decision, his problem, his position on something). For instance, you may use an expression like "In James Madison's opinion.")
- If pronouns have been a problem for you, check to make sure that you have used subject and object pronouns correctly.

## CASE STUDY THREE: THE OTHER BATTLE OF THE LITTLE BIG HORN

Read the following case and the assignment and discussion sections following it. Then go back over the case, underlining or highlighting the most important points, the ones you will want to consider in your essay. Don't try to do this on your first reading.

## The Other Battle of the Little Big Horn

In 1876, eleven years after the end of the Civil War, the Indian wars in the American west were heating up. In one of these, the American government wanted to open for settlement most of the land in what are now the states of

Wyoming, Montana, and North and South Dakota. These lands had traditionally been the hunting grounds of the Sioux and Cheyenne Indians. The government repeatedly tried to get the Indians to accept financial assistance and guaranteed land reservations if they would give up their traditional nomadic life on the Great Plains. But the Indians just as repeatedly refused these offers. Now the army was ordered to defeat the Indians and force them onto government reservations.

As part of the army's effort, General George A. Custer led about 600 men of the U.S. 7th Cavalry to attack an Indian camp, or village as it was sometimes called, in the valley of the Little Big Horn River, containing, he believed, perhaps 1,000 warriors. In fact, the camp held between 2,000 and 4,000 Sioux and Cheyenne warriors who were united and determined to win under the leadership of the great Indian chiefs Crazy Horse and Sitting Bull.

In the hills above the Little Big Horn River, Custer divided his command into four groups. First, he sent 125 soldiers under Captain Benteen south to see whether there was an Indian encampment behind him. Then, having learned of the large village in the valley in front of him, he left 130 soldiers under Captain McDougall to guard his supply train of mules and sent Major Marcus A. Reno with about 120 soldiers into the valley of the Little Big Horn to attack the southern end of the Indian village while he took his remaining 225 men along the hills above the valley, apparently planning to attack the middle or northern end of the village from there.

When Reno rode down from the hills, across the Little Big Horn into the valley, and spotted the Indian village, he dismounted his troops and prepared to attack from the woods near the river. Instead, he was attacked by the Indians, who quickly surrounded his force. Reno ordered a retreat back across the Little Big Horn River into the hills from which he had come. In the testimony given after the battle, this retreat was often referred to as a "charge." In fact, since Reno was surrounded, he did order his troops to charge because that was the only way he could see to get them out of an encirclement. They charged in order to retreat. In the hills above the Little Big Horn, Reno was joined first by Benteen and later by McDougall, and was able to hold out for two days until the Indians withdrew. In his official report, Major Reno wrote that three of his officers and 29 enlisted men were killed, and seven wounded, by the time his forces reached the hills.

As Major Reno was attempting to attack the Indians at the southern end of the village, Custer's force was being surrounded by the Sioux and Cheyenne. Custer sent messages to Benteen and McDougall telling them to hurry forward to join him, but Benteen and McDougall did not arrive in time to help him. Custer's battle has come to be known as the Battle of the Little Big Horn or, sometimes, "Custer's Last Stand." Custer and the entire force with him were killed.

On the following page is a map showing the area in which Reno's battle with the Indians took place.

Because of the shock of the Custer disaster to the nation and to the army, a military court was convened to look into the operation. As part of its inquiry, the court was ordered to examine whether Major Reno's actions with his troops were proper. The court ordered testimony from some of the men under Reno's command.

To understand the testimony of these men, it is necessary to know a few things about the nature of war in general, and the ways in which the U.S. Army [8]cavalry and the Plains Indians fought in particular.

The essence of war is confusion. Every man in combat sees only through his own eyes, and he sees things differently from even the man standing next to him. As you will see when you read the testimony of the men fighting at the Little Big Horn River, the perceptions of men who were all in the same place can differ widely. No one, necessarily, is lying, though some might be. Each man usually tells what he believes he saw. Of course, commanding officers have the same difficulty evaluating a situation in combat as the men under them. The trouble is that in the general confusion, and with bullets whistling about their ears, they have to make crucial decisions involving the effectiveness and safety of their commands. And sometimes they have to make these decisions within seconds, not minutes. Soldiers fighting desperately when their lives are at stake also make decisions about what they will do and how they will do it. Not surprisingly, veterans, those who have been in combat before, will make better decisions than will recruits, those completely new to combat. New recruits usually make wrong decisions, and they suffer more casualties than veterans do.

During the Civil War, the U.S. Army discovered that trying to fight from horseback was ineffective. Accordingly, when the American cavalry came into a situation in which a fight was likely, they dismounted and fought on foot. Of every four men, three would fight and one would hold the four horses.

The Plains Indians, on the other hand, did not like to fight on foot. Their traditional method of warfare was to fight from horseback, and they were probably the best in the world at this form of combat. They did not fight in organized formations like the cavalry, with everyone taking orders from an officer or a chief. The Sioux, Cheyenne, and other Plains Indian tribes were

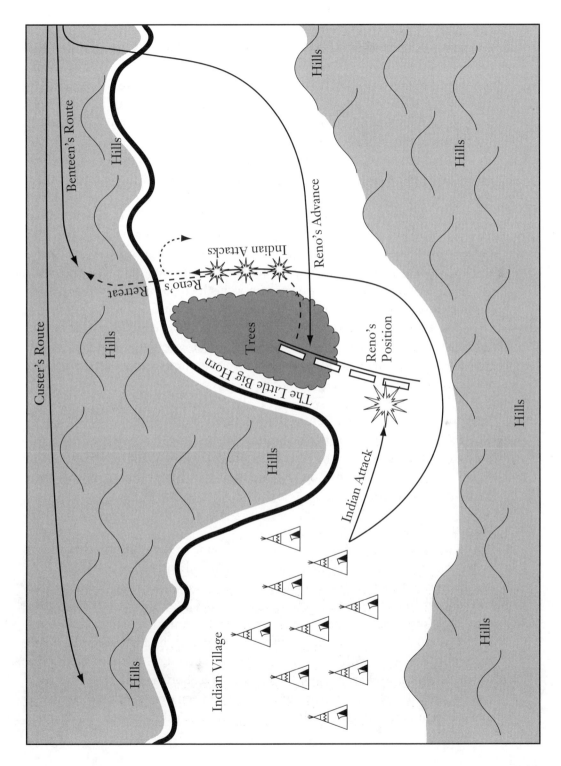

Benteen's Route

Custer's Route

Hills

Hills

Hills

Hills

Hills

Hills

Hills

Hills

Hills

Reno's Advance

Indian Attacks

Reno's Retreat

Trees

The Little Big Horn

Reno's Position

Indian Attack

Indian Village

extremely democratic. Even great chiefs like Crazy Horse and Sitting Bull could only suggest what others should do. They could not command. For that reason, the U.S. Army did not hesitate to enter a fight with Indians who out-numbered them. They knew that the Indians would often, to a great extent, waste their strength through their extreme individualism. As an organized body, the U.S. soldiers could charge the Indians, but it was almost unheard of for the Indians to do the same.

At the same time, it was difficult for the Plains Indians to organize them-selves into groups larger than about a hundred because of the nature of their life. As nomads, groups moving from place to place in search of food and water, and as hunter-gatherers, tribes dependent on local sources of animal food and wild grains, they had to keep their numbers fairly small. No one area could provide food for very large numbers of people and horses. A group of a thousand Indians would quickly exhaust an area's food supply. Of course, Custer knew this, and it was one of the reasons he did not suspect that he was about to attack an overwhelming number of his enemies.

Even after the great victory of the Sioux and Cheyenne over Custer, the Indians could not follow up their success by sticking together and going after the rest of the army. Instead, they split up into hundreds of their traditional small groups, and each group went its own way.

## Testimony of Reno's Men Before the Military Court

The following excerpts of the testimony of some of Reno's men before the military court begins with the testimony of Lieutenant Wallace, who gave the court necessary background on the situation that Major Reno and his men found themselves in.

### LIEUTENANT GEORGE D. WALLACE

About 2:15, Cook, the regimental [(9)]adjutant, came to Reno and transmitted an order from Custer: "The Indians are about two and one half miles ahead. Fol-low them as fast as you can and charge them wherever you find them, and we will support you." We moved forward at a gallop. Custer followed at a slow trot for a short distance, and then moved to our right. This was the last time I saw him. I supposed that he was following us. We forded the Little Big Horn and then moved forward with Companies A and M abreast, G to the rear, and the Indian scouts under Varnum and Hare ahead. The bottom land along the river was flat and mostly covered with grass that had been grazed off and cut up by many Indian pony hoofs. The Indian village was a little more than two miles from the ford, but there was so much dust in the air that I did not see it until we had dismounted. At first the Indians seemed to be running away, but later they ran toward us. Company G was brought up to the right side of our line. We dismounted at a place where the river made a big loop to the left, and a stand of trees lined the bank. We formed a line in the trees and out to the left.

There were then 200 or 300 Indians engaging us at that time and many more began to appear. The firing was brisk, but the Indians did not make much of an attack on our front. Instead, many passed around our left and began to encircle us. The whole space to our rear, for a mile or two, was filled with Indians—not a solid mass, but individuals riding around, yelling and hooting, and those within range were shooting. We fell back into the timber and mounted, and I heard Reno order a charge.

When I got out of the woods, the troops were moving at a gallop in a column of fours, and Indians were all over the landscape. Some were riding alongside the troops with Winchester repeating rifles set across the [10]pommels of the saddles, pumping shots into the column. It was half or three-quarters of a mile to the hill where we retreated, and it took about 15 minutes, including three to five minutes to cross the river. After getting to the top of the hill, we halted, preparing to stand off the Indians. Benteen soon joined us. The pack train came up later.

Each soldier was armed with two revolvers and a [11]carbine. They carried two additional revolver loadings and 50 carbine cartridges in their belts, as well as 50 more carbine cartridges in their saddlebags. [Each man, then, had a total of 24 revolver cartridges and 100 rifle cartridges—50 in their saddlebags on their horses.] While some of the men had been in the service for two to four years, a great many were recruits who used up most of their 50 rounds, and one company had to get ammunition from their saddlebags. Most of the recruits had never been on a horse until that campaign, and they lost control of their horses when galloping in line.

### F. F. GIRARD

I was assigned to the 7th Cavalry Regiment as a civilian scout and interpreter. About a mile and a quarter from the river, I could see the Indian village. Reno was ordered forward almost at once. Custer told him to bring the Indians to battle, and he would support him. We lost sight of Custer at about the time we reached the river.

When Reno's column got to the woods along the river, they dismounted and went into line. The Indians were coming toward us. They were about

1,000 yards away from the left end of the line. The Indians were firing at our scouts and the scouts at them. They advanced to within 200 yards. There were only about 50 or 75 of them. The village was then a mile and a half away.

The timber was about 75 yards at the widest portion, narrowing to about thirty yards. We stayed in the timber four or five minutes and fired about seven shots. Somebody gave the order, "Men, to your horses. The Indians are in our rear." Charlie Reynolds looked at me, and I said, "What damn fool move is this?" He said, "I don't know. We will have to go. We will have to get out of this."

The troops were mounted and going by very fast, [12]pell-mell. They were in a great hurry to get out and were completely disorderly. Every man was for himself. There were no Indians in the timber. I asked an officer, "What are you going to do?" and he said, "Charge the Indians." I thought they were going to charge out onto the plain and then return to the timber, so I stayed there. Reynolds galloped after the troops, trying to catch up with them, but the Indians surrounded and killed him. De Rudio, O'Neill, and Jackson were left in the woods with me. We stayed in the timber until about 9 P.M., when it became dark, and then made our way to Reno's position across the river.

All the Indians I saw go to Reno's left and rear numbered about two hundred. The party I was firing at numbered only 20 or 30. I think that if Reno had been determined and resolute, he could have held out against all the Indians as long as his ammunition and provisions held out.

I asked, "What is this damn move?" because I thought that to move out of the timber onto the prairie was like running into certain death.

Before this action, Reno had dismissed me from my position as interpreter and Custer reinstated me, but I have no unkind feelings toward Reno.

### LIEUTENANT CHARLES A. VARNUM

I was in command of the Indian scouts and I rode with them down the valley 50 or 75 yards ahead of the column. There was a large body of Indians some distance off, running around on the prairie in every direction, kicking up all the dust they could, so that it was impossible to tell their number. The troops dismounted in the woods and to their left, at a right angle to the river. There was light firing between the troops and the Indians. There was a lot of confusion. Everybody was mounted. I heard no orders.

Captain Moylan called to me that Indians were circling to the left into the timber. He said something must be done or our horses and ammunition would be cut off. I had dismounted and returned to the line when I heard Moylan say that he was out of ammunition and had ordered every alternate man back to get ammunition from the saddlebags. Then we heard cries of, "Charge, charge, we are going to charge!" There was a lot of confusion. Everybody was mounted. I heard no orders.

When I came out of the timber, there were a great many Indians with Winchester rifles across their saddles, riding next to the column and firing into it. As the column rode out and across the river, the men were using revolvers. The crossing was not covered by troops to hold off the Indians. The retreat from the woods was hasty, and the rear of the column disorganized.

When we got on the hill, the command was [13]demoralized to a certain degree. They had left a great many behind; the organization was not as good as when it went in; a great many men were missing. I don't know how the command felt when we got to the hill, but I personally thought we had been licked badly.

The position in the timber was as good as any place on the left bank of the river, but I don't think we had enough men to hold it and keep the Indians out. Of course, the position threatened the village to some extent and kept a containing force of Indians there, but it was not a very safe place.

Many [14]casualties must have occurred at the rear of the column as it left the timber. The majority of ours were killed and wounded in the retreat from the woods to the hill. I do not consider Reno's retreat a disorganized rout insofar as the head of the column was concerned, but the rear I think was.

As to Reno's conduct, I have nothing to say against him and nothing in particular for him, either one way or another. If Reno thought he could not hold the timber and saw no troops coming to his aid, it was for him to use his own judgment and leave it for a place he could better defend.

### DR. H. R. PORTER

I was assistant surgeon under Custer. I heard the adjutant give an order to Reno. The adjutant told Reno that Indians were just ahead, and Custer directed him to charge them. Reno asked whether Custer was going to support him, and the adjutant answered that Custer would support him.

I saw a few Indians and a great many ponies. They seemed to be driving the ponies down the river. When we got to the woods, the men dismounted and formed a skirmish line. I watched the fight a few minutes and then led my horse into the woods, looking for my orderly who had the bandages and medicines. I had been there only a few minutes when the men on the left and right came in, and I heard Reno say that we would have to get out of there and charge the Indians. He rode out. One man had been wounded up to that time. Only about 50 Indians were engaging Reno when he halted. They increased to 75 or 100. There were many more down the river, but I could not see how many.

When Reno moved out, the men followed from all directions. They had a great deal of trouble finding their horses, but as soon as they mounted, they went out. I went out expecting to see the command charging the Indians, but instead the Indians were charging the command. There was a great deal of dust, hallooing, and confusion.

There was no order in the rear of the column. The river was 40 to 50 feet wide, and the water was up to the saddle pockets. When I got there everybody was rushing in, trying to get across as fast as possible, and the Indians were firing at them. It was every man for himself.

The first officer I saw on the hills was Varnum. He had his hat off and was saying, "For God's sake, men, don't run. There are a good many officers and men killed and wounded, and we've got to go back and get them." When I saw Reno, I said to him, "Major, the men were pretty well demoralized, weren't they?" He replied, "No, that was a charge, sir." The command was demoralized. They seemed to think they had been whipped. In a few minutes I saw some troops coming, and some of the men shouted, "Here comes Custer," but it was Benteen and his battalion.

I saw nothing in the conduct of Reno particularly heroic or the reverse. I think he was a little embarrassed and (15)flurried. The bullets were coming thick and fast, and he did not know whether it was best to stay there or leave. That was my impression at the time. During the run to the river I think there were two hundred or three hundred Indians mixed in with the troops to the right and rear. Reno knew as well as I did that there were officers and men killed in that stampede. Everybody knew it.

## CAPTAIN MYLES MOYLAN

I believe that Reno's column was discovered before it crossed the Little Big Horn. The village was lower than the place where the troops crossed the river, and if the Indians didn't see the command, they saw the dust it raised.

I think it took us about 10 minutes to ride into the valley to where the trees were. I think that when we dismounted, enough Indians were within 500 yards to warrant Reno's halting. About 400 Indians were from 200 to 400 yards away. The Indian fire was scattered, and the companies commenced firing as soon as they were (16)deployed. Some of the men were new, and it was impossible to regulate their fire, but the fire of the majority was well regulated. We remained there from 25 to 30 minutes under heavy fire until the Indians seemed to be withdrawing from our front and working around to the left. Reno was on his horse overlooking the formation. He asked my opinion as to the point to which we should retreat. He designated a high point on the opposite side of the river where we could go to establish ourselves and await developments. The command moved forward at the trot and then at the gallop.

The Indians closed in on both flanks and fired into the column. None were at the front of the column but a good many were on our right and rear, and the firing on the rear of the column was severe. The Indians passed along the banks of the stream, and 30 or 40 fired on us as we crossed. I do not know how many Indians were in the timber. I saw 40 or 50, but there may have been several times that many. I saw only 600 or 700 Indians while in the valley.

If we had stayed 30 minutes longer in the timber, unsupported, I doubt whether we would have gotten out with as many as we did. If we reached the other bank, there was a possibility of aid coming up. We could not have successfully resisted the force of Indians if they had followed us across the river because we did not have sufficient ammunition. The command was not actually driven from the timber, but virtually so, and would have been actually, in a very short time.

The men were not demoralized or [17]despondent when they reached the hill. Neither were they exultant with success. Reno gave his orders during the advance into the valley as coolly as any man could under the circumstances. He was in front of the command during the retreat all the time. I saw nothing during the afternoon that indicated cowardice. I do not know whether any officer was charged with looking after the rear of the column.

In my judgment, if Reno had continued to charge down the valley, we would all have died there. The purpose of leaving the timber was to save the command, which, in my judgment, would have been [18]annihilated there unless it had been reinforced. If the Indians had followed and closed in on the retreat to the hills, the same result would have followed.

### GEORGE HERENDEEN

I was a civilian scout assigned to the 7th Cavalry Regiment. About a mile and a half from the river, I heard Custer tell Reno to lead out and he would be with him. When we got to the timber along the river, the scouts sat down and watched the fire of the troops for a few minutes. The troops fired rapidly. At that time I could not see any Indians close to the line. A little while after, the Indians in the valley came up to within 300 or 400 yards.

After watching for a few minutes, we scouts took our horses into the timber and tied them there. I saw Indians circling around through the hills and coming closer to us. Presently the soldiers ceased firing, and the Indians came to within 40 or 50 steps of me. As there was no firing on the line, they came closer and ran into the timber. I fired at 20 or 25, and more were coming. I was there six or seven minutes and fired seven or eight shots.

Reno was sitting on his horse. I heard him order, "Dismount." Then a volley was fired by the Indians. An Indian scout called Bloody Knife was standing about eight feet in front of Reno, and he and another soldier were hit. The soldiers had just touched the ground when Reno gave the order to mount, and then everybody left the timber on the run. I followed and got to the edge of the timber. I got about 150 yards when my horse went down, and I fell off. Men were passing me all the time, and everybody was running for his life. I got up and ran back into the timber. I found 11 enlisted men in the timber, 3 of them wounded. We stayed there about two hours and were not troubled by the Indians. Then we rejoined Reno's command on the hill across the river.

In my judgment, 100 men with 6,000 or 7,000 rounds of ammunition could have held that timber against the Indians. If they had water and provisions, the Indians couldn't have gotten them out of there at all.

### Lieutenant L. R. Hare

I was on duty with the scouts. After we got to the timber and the command dismounted, 400 or 500 Indians appeared in front of us and moved to our left and rear. Reno could not have seen the Indians until he halted and deployed his men. I was in a better position than he, and I saw nothing until we had dismounted and formed a line. During the time we were in the valley, there were always Indians in our front, downstream, 200 consistently, maybe more. There were probably a total of 1,000 Indians opposing Reno in that valley.

During the retreat, all the Indians were on our right, 50 to 100 yards away and firing into the column. I did not think the movement from the timber was a run, but it was a pretty fast retreat. After I got on the hill, I looked back. Not a great many Indians—perhaps 100—remained in the valley. The command was scattered but not demoralized. They rallied and formed promptly.

The hill position was much better than the timber. If the Indians had charged us in the timber, we could not have stood it more than a few minutes. But Indians don't do that. We could have stood them off for perhaps 30 minutes by using our ammunition judiciously.

The men's firing was continuous from the time they dismounted until they left the timber. They probably expended 40 rounds per man. By careful use, the ammunition might have lasted an hour longer, though that would have depended on the action of the Indians.

Reno stayed in the timber until all hope of rear support from Custer had vanished. I think the reason we left was because if we had stayed much longer, say 20 minutes, we could not have gotten out at all.

### LIEUTENANT CHARLES DE RUDIO

I saw no indication of cowardice on Reno's part. When he halted and dismounted, I said to myself, "Good for you," because I thought that if we went 500 yards further we would be butchered.

Reno could have held his position in the timber three or four hours by careful use of ammunition. The men out in the open fired rapidly. Those in the woods fired slowly and deliberately. I noticed that when the men in the open fired fast, they overheated their rifles and had to use knives to extract empty shells after firing 8 or 10 rounds.

### SERGEANT F. A. CULBERTSON

I was at the extreme left of the line. We had remained on the line for a time, some of the new men firing very fast.

If the line had not been retired within three minutes from the time it was, I don't think anyone would have gotten off the line. I don't think Reno could have held the timber but a very few minutes. My estimate of the number of Indians about his position is 1,000 to 1,200. Most of the men were new and had never been under fire before. They tended to fire at random. I fired 21 shots, but one of the new men told me he had fired 60.

### ASSIGNMENT

Write an essay in which you evaluate the testimony of the nine witnesses and come to a conclusion as to whether it would have been better for Major Reno to stay in the woods along the Little Big Horn River and try to fight off the Indians, or whether he did the right thing in retreating across the valley floor and the river to the hills beyond.

Remember that it is easy afterward to decide what a person should have done in a situation where a split-second judgment must be made. Acting coolly in such cases is hard enough, but when bullets are flying and lives of one's self and more than a hundred others are at stake, it is far more difficult. Did Reno, in your judgment, do the right thing?

### Discussion and Questions to Consider

The situation that Major Reno and his soldiers found themselves in was not their fault. It was Custer's. He did not use his scouts to find out how numerous the Sioux and Cheyenne were, and he foolishly divided his command into small groups that even a force of Indians smaller than the one he faced could have overwhelmed. Further, his orders to Reno were unclear. He simply ordered Reno to attack a force of unknown size, saying that he would support him. He didn't say how he would do that, and as it turned out, he was in no position to support anyone. There were perhaps as many as four thousand warriors in the Indian camp, and although Reno had to face only a fraction of them, we don't know how large a fraction it was.

In any case, Reno had orders to obey. His problem then became how to deal with a situation that was totally unexpected. Far from being about to attack a small Indian village, he found himself attacked by a force much larger than his own. The question then became, what to do? Although some historians claim that Reno could have helped Custer by keeping some of the Indians engaged in a fight near the woods, Reno had no way of knowing that Custer was under attack by a great number of Indians, and he couldn't have known whether he would be a bigger threat to the Indians in the timber or in the hills. The question in his mind had to be, "Will I save more of my men by staying here or by retreating to the nearby hills?" Although he could not be sure where Benteen or McDougall was at this time, he knew that if he retreated into the hills above the Little Big Horn River, he could at least be closer to them.

Every competent commander knows what the quality of his troops is, and the turnover among white soldiers in the frontier cavalry was enormous. The desertion rate was high, and the reenlistment rate was low. (On the contrary, in the 9th and 10th U.S. Cavalry Regiments, all-Black units, the desertion rate was very low and the reenlistment rate very high.) So at any given time, a white regiment like the 7th Cavalry would have a high percentage of inexperienced soldiers. Would Reno have saved the lives of more of these soldiers if he had stayed in the woods?

Like the members of the military court evaluating Major Reno's conduct, you must evaluate contradictory testimonies. You will have to try to decide which evidence seems the most convincing. In doing so, you must ask—and answer from the testimonies given—the following questions:

1. How many Indians, more or less, seem to have been attacking Reno's command? Why do you think your number is probably the right one?

2. Reno had a little over a hundred men under his command, many of them recruits. Did he have enough ammunition to hold out in the woods by the river? If so, for how long? Why do you think so?

In answering these questions, you need to consider whether you think Benteen could have come to Reno's aid in the woods. If Benteen could have come to Reno's aid, would he have had enough soldiers and supplies to make a difference?

You also need to consider the ways in which the Indian warriors fought. Do you think that if Reno had stayed in the valley, they would have overwhelmed him (and possibly Benteen) as they did Custer?

3. Reno knew that many of his troops were inexperienced horsemen and probably would not be able to survive a gallop through several hundred Indians, who were expert riders and equipped with repeating rifles. To what extent should this knowledge have influenced his decision to retreat?
4. Consider *how* Reno's forces retreated. How did Reno's men describe the retreat? After studying questions one through three, do you see any connections between the reasons for Reno's retreat and the way it happened?

### Step One: Make Notes and Compare Them with Others

After you have underlined or highlighted the most important points in the case, make four separate groups of notes. One group of notes should cover the question of the number of Indian warriors Reno's men faced; a second group of notes should cover whether Reno's men had the ammunition and the skill to use it carefully; a third group should cover Reno's men's experience with horses; and a fourth group should cover how the retreat was done. If you think that more issues should be considered, make a note of them.

Since the men who testified differ in their reports of the battle, and in their opinions about it, you will want to be able to compare their conflicting reports and opinions as you take notes on the four issues raised above. You may find it helpful to make a chart in which you write the four main issues across the top, enter the information we now have from historians who have studied the battle, and list the names of the men who testified in a column on the left side of the paper, allowing space to record the men's information and opinions.

You can begin your chart like this:

|  | Number of Indian warriors | Ammunition | Soldiers' Experience | The Retreat |
|---|---|---|---|---|
| Information from historians | Probably 2,000 to 4,000 warriors in the village | Each man had a total of 24 revolver cartridges and 100 rifle cartridges. | Many were new recruits. | Most of Reno's men retreated from the woods to the hills across the river. |
| 1. Wallace | 200 or 300 when the men dismounted | Many used up most of their rounds; one company had to get ammo from saddlebags. | Men used their ammo quickly. Many hadn't ridden a horse before and lost control when galloping. | Indians were riding next to Reno's men, shooting at them. |
| 2. Girard |  |  |  |  |

Beginning with Girard's testimony, you will continue recording information from the remaining men who testified; be sure to allow space to record any new information you may learn during work in class. And if you feel that more than the above four issues should be considered, be sure to take notes and present them in class.

As you take notes, consider the reliability of each man's testimony and his opinion about the battle and the retreat. To do so, you will need to consider the role he played in the battle, his position during the battle, and any possible biases he may have had. Which men's testimony seems most reliable to you? Why?

In class, work with two other students to compare your notes. If you find disagreements or omissions, try to come to an agreement on the important points.

Each group should now report on the points the group members consider most important so that the teacher can write them on the board for class discussion. The class can come to a consensus on the most important points. Write down these points since your notes will form the basis for the next step in the assignment.

*Step Two: Make an Outline and Compare It with Others*

At home, read the following guidelines for organizing "The Other Battle of the Little Big Horn." Make a rough list outline as you did for your previous assignments, and bring the list to class for discussion of ways to organize this paper.

## Organizing "The Other Battle of the Little Big Horn"

Your introduction should briefly describe the predicament and retreat of Major Reno and his men. You can state your opinion about Major Reno's actions in a thesis in your introduction, or you can save your opinion for your conclusion.

As you plan the organization of your essay, you will want to present the issues point by point, so that your reader can see how you compared the testimony of Reno's men as you evaluated his retreat. Since you began this assignment with four issues to consider, and the class has discussed and come to a consensus on the most important points, you will want to be sure to cover them in your essay. Your chart will provide you with the basis of a good outline for the body of your essay. Be sure to write a topic sentence to make the main point of each body paragraph clear.

Be sure to avoid "sack" paragraphs. If you put all of the arguments showing how Reno did the right thing in one body paragraph, and all of the arguments showing how Reno did *not* do the right thing in another, your readers won't be able to see how you compared related points and arrived at your judgment of Reno's actions. And if you try to organize chronologically, by following the battle from the beginning to the end, your readers will have the same problem.

In your conclusion, you should explain why you think Reno did the right thing, or why he did not. You may find that you think he did some things right, but not others; if so, you can explain why in your conclusion.

*Step Three: Write a Rough Draft*

At home, using your outline as a basis, write a rough draft of your essay. Do not worry about mechanics while you are trying to get all of your information on paper in a logical order. Use the following checklist to make sure that you have covered the requirements of the assignment, and use it in class for peer review.

Make two copies of your draft so that you have three copies to bring to class.

## CHECKLIST FOR EVALUATING ROUGH DRAFTS

1. Does the introduction indicate what the essay will be about and why the subject is important?
2. Is the essay divided into body paragraphs that cover single subjects?
3. Does each body paragraph start with a topic sentence, a sentence that tells what the paragraph will discuss?
4. Are all the sentences in each body paragraph related to the point expressed in the topic sentence? Are there any places where unrelated ideas seem to come into any paragraphs?
5. Are the most important issues covered—the size of the Indian force, the supply of ammunition, the experience of the soldiers under Reno's command, and the way the retreat was carried out?
6. Does the order of the points covered seem logical, or does anything seem out of place?
7. Has the writer used the words *but, while, whereas, although, even though*, and *though* to show contrast and concession?
8. Has the writer used appositives to identify or describe people or places in the essay? See exercises 6H and 6I for help using appositives.

### Step Four: Peer Review

In class, in groups of three, exchange your rough drafts and take turns reading your own drafts aloud. If you spot any errors as you read, correct them. Using the checklist, go over each paper question by question to identify both strengths and weaknesses. Call in your teacher if you need help or advice.

### Step Five: Write a Final Draft

Write the final draft of your essay, using your peers' and teacher's advice for guidance.

Check to see that you have used the words *but, while, whereas, although, even though*, and *though* to show contrast and concession.

Look for places to use appositives to identify and describe nouns for your readers. See exercises 6H and 6I in this chapter.

Finally, proofread a printed copy of your paper. Review the proofreading tips in Chapter 1 and in the following Special Proofreading section.

### Special Proofreading

- Proofread for subject-verb agreement and plural *-s* endings on nouns.
- In your essay, you discussed many past actions; check to make sure that you've used the past-tense verbs in describing them, and that your past-tense verbs have *-ed* endings.
- Check for possessive apostrophes; you will need them in expressions like "Reno's men" or "the soldiers' experience."
- If pronouns have been a problem for you, check to make sure you've used subject pronouns before verbs and object pronouns after them.

## Getting Your Writing Right

### Paraphrasing

Paraphrasing—expressing an author's ideas in your own words—is an important skill to have. Most college writing assignments require you to analyze and synthesize information and ideas from readings. You may want to quote some of the information you get from published writers, but often you'll need to paraphrase. You cannot copy a published author's work word for word unless you quote it, and you do not want quotations to dominate your essays.

### To Paraphrase Successfully

1. Read the original text, and make sure you understand its meaning, so that you can explain it in your own words to a friend. Write brief notes for yourself so that you can work from your notes when you paraphrase.
2. Don't try to paraphrase word by word or line by line. Instead, paraphrase each idea or point. It's fine to use authors' key words or brief phrases, but you cannot copy the published text.
3. Don't rely on a thesaurus. Writers sometimes try to paraphrase by substituting a word they find in a thesaurus to avoid using the same word the author used. But words given as synonyms in a thesaurus are often not truly synonyms, or some synonyms may not fit grammatically into sentences in the same way as the words we're trying to replace. If you follow guideline #2, you can avoid this problem.
4. Once you have paraphrased an idea or point, check to make sure that your paraphrase accurately states the author's meaning.
5. Proofread your paraphrasing, just as you would your own original work.

**Example from Case Study One:** The following is a paragraph from Case Study One that attempts to explain why many Americans didn't see anything wrong with the Supreme Court's ruling (in the Dred Scott decision) that Blacks were inferior, undeserving of the rights of white Americans.

> ORIGINAL:  Most citizens of the northern states were opposed to slavery, but they had little idea of what it really involved. The average farmer in the north had never even seen a Black person and had no idea of what kind of treatment African-Americans were receiving on the plantations in the South. The whole idea of there even being Black people was, to most Northerners, like the idea of there being Martians.

If you want to paraphrase this information in your essay, work with the whole paragraph—the whole idea—instead of trying to paraphrase word by word or sentence by sentence. The first sentence states the main idea—that citizens of the northern states had little idea of what slavery involved, and the following two sentences explain why.

So you can shape your paraphrase to show this cause-result relationship:

> PARAPHRASE:  Most Americans in the northern states had never had any contact with African-Americans, so they didn't know what slavery was like or how slaves were treated on the southern plantations.

> or        Because most Northerners had no experience with African-Americans, they didn't know what slavery was like or how slaves were treated on the southern plantations.

## Exercise for Case Study One

On a separate sheet of paper paraphrase the following passage written about Lincoln by the History Team, following the steps listed under To Paraphrase Successfully; then, in class, compare your paraphrase with a classmate's.

> ORIGINAL: When the U.S. Constitution was adopted in 1789, one of the compromises that made it possible was an understanding that Congress would not even discuss the issue of slavery. Slavery was such a touchy issue in both the north, which was against it, and the South, which was for it, that the southern states would not even agree to the

Constitution unless the northern states would agree that slavery could not even be discussed in Congress.

**Example from Case Study Two:** The following is a passage from Case Study Two that shows the status of individual gun ownership in Britain in 1780.

> ORIGINAL: . . . with a strong professional army, an increasingly capable police force, and the steadily increasing power of Parliament and decreasing power of the king, most British citizens saw no need to own arms, and the practice dwindled away.

The first part of the sentence, ending with the word *king*, identifies the factors that caused gun ownership to decline in Britain. So you can paraphrase this passage by stating the cause-effect relationship:

> PARAPHRASE: By 1780, most British citizens felt they did not need to own guns because Britain had a strong army, an effective police force, and a strong Parliament that could limit the power of the king.

> *or*    By 1780, Britain had a strong army, an effective police force, and a strong Parliament that could limit the power of the king, so most British citizens felt they did not need to own guns.

## Exercise for Case Study Two

On a separate sheet of paper, paraphrase the following passage, following the steps listed under To Paraphrase Successfully; then, in class, compare your paraphrase with a classmate's.

> ORIGINAL: The early American colonies, living precariously on the edge of a wilderness, required their male citizens to carry arms, and all males between the ages of 16 and 60 were required to serve, if called, in the local militia.

**Example from Case Study Three:** The following passage describes the opinion of Lieutenant Charles A. Varnum, one of Reno's officers who testified before the military court.

> ORIGINAL: As to Reno's conduct, I have nothing to say against him and nothing in particular for him, either one way or another. If Reno

thought he could not hold the timber and saw no troops coming to his aid, it was for him to use his own judgment and leave it for a place he could better defend.

Identify the speaker, and paraphrase his opinion:

PARAPHRASE: Lieutenant Charles A. Varnum did not judge Major Reno's behavior. He simply said that Reno had to consider whether his men could defend themselves better in the woods or somewhere else.

*or*        Without judging Major Reno's behavior, Lieutenant Charles A. Varnum said that Reno had to consider whether his men could defend themselves better in the woods or somewhere else.

## Exercise for Case Study Three

After reviewing the tips for paraphrasing successfully, paraphrase the following passage from Captain Myles Moylan's testimony on a separate sheet of paper. Be sure to identify the speaker.

ORIGINAL: In my judgment, if Reno had continued to charge down the valley, we would all have died there. The purpose of leaving the timber was to save the command, which, in my judgment, would have been annihilated there unless it had been reinforced.

## Using Quotations: Review

Sometimes you will need to quote from your original source, to make a point or to support a point you have made. In the case studies in this chapter, you have many statements about historical events that you will want to quote. Use the two common ways to introduce quotations that you practiced in Chapter 5.

## Examples from Case Studies

1. *According to* author's name, + quotation:

Case Study One: According to the History Team, "Lincoln was the first to bring Blacks into the White House to discuss important issues and the first to take the advice of a Black leader."

Case Study Two: According to William Blizard, "The right of his majesty's . . . subjects to have arms for their own defence, and to use them for lawful purposes is most clear and undeniable."

Case Study Three: According to Dr. H. R. Porter, assistant surgeon under Custer, "There was no order in the rear of the column. Every man seemed to be running under his own hook."

2. Author's name *wrote / said / claimed that / argued that*, + quotation:

Case Study One: In 1857, Lincoln said, "All the powers of earth seem rapidly combining against [the Negro]."

Case Study Two: Joyce Lee Malcolm claims that "although the amendment's drafters presumably believed it quite clear, the shared understandings upon which it is based have vanished and this single sentence has proven capable of an amazing range of interpretations."

Case Study Three: In his testimony, Captain Myles Moylan argued that "we could not have successfully resisted the force of Indians if they had followed us across the river because we did not have sufficient ammunition."

## Using Appositives

Appositives are used extensively by writers to get more information into their sentences.

An appositive is a very simple thing. It is a noun along with any words attached to it used to refer to another noun. The underlined words here are appositives:

My friend, <u>the King of England</u>, dropped by yesterday.

My favorite hockey team, <u>the Blackhawks</u>, will not win the championship again this year.

She took the most attractive cookie, <u>the biggest one</u>.

He was considering a used car, <u>a piece of junk that consisted mainly of rust held together with tape</u>.

As you can see, each of those appositives is set off by a comma and each one has a noun that refers to a noun preceding it: *king* refers to *friend*, *Blackhawks* refers to *team*, *one* refers to *cookie*, and *piece* refers to *car*. Notice that appositives can be very short, one word, or they can be very long, even longer than the sentence they're attached to. No matter how long they are, they are never sentences by themselves; they are phrases, or parts of sentences, attached to complete sentences.

Notice also that appositive phrases almost always begin with the words *a*, *an*, or *the*. That's because they are noun phrases, and *a*, *an*, and *the* are words we often use before nouns. Of course, other noun phrases, names of things, don't always begin with those words. Here are a few more appositives:

> Denzel Washington and Gene Hackman made a terrific adventure movie a few years ago, *Crimson Tide*.

> The longest-serving president of the United States, *Franklin Delano Roosevelt*, was disabled by polio.

## Exercise 6A

Try your hand at writing some appositives. Unless you are going to use a name of something as your appositive, remember that it should begin with *a*, *an*, or *the*.

> EXAMPLE:  I watch my favorite movie,_____,
> at least once a month.
> [Name your favorite movie.]

> I watch my favorite movie, *The Thomas Crown Affair*, at least once a month.

1.  I enjoy watching my favorite TV show, _____.
    [Name your favorite show.]

2.  I'd like to have my favorite food, _____, right now.
    [Name your favorite food or describe it, as, "chicken roasted with garlic."]

3.  When I was a little kid, I was afraid there was a monster under the bed, _____.
    [Describe the monster.]

4. I'd like to buy a brand new car, _____.
   [Name the car, but also include color and other features you'd like to have.]

5. I wish I had a great place of my own, _____.
   [Describe an apartment or a house you'd like to have.]

## Exercise 6B

Combine the following groups of sentences to make one sentence; make the second sentence into an appositive following the underlined noun in the first sentence.

EXAMPLE: <u>John</u> got into a lot of trouble.
John was my best friend.
John, my best friend, got into a lot of trouble.

1. <u>Becky Tam and Carlita Rodriguez</u> got inspired by their astronomy class. They were two freshmen at Mountainview State College.

   _____

2. They decided to explore the heavens with a new <u>telescope</u>. The telescope was one they would buy together.

   _____

3. Becky was in favor of looking for <u>comets</u>. Comets are chunks of ice hurtling around through space.

   _____

4. They had learned that many amateur <u>astronomers</u> had discovered new comets. The astronomers were people just like them.

   _____

5. <u>Carlita</u> was more interested in discovering some new galaxies. Carlita was an extremely ambitious young woman.

   _____

6. They felt that if they could discover <u>anything new</u>, they might become famous, or at least get an A in astronomy. Anything new was a comet, a galaxy, or even an asteroid.

   _____

7. They went shopping for a good <u>telescope</u>. A telescope was the instrument they needed to achieve fame and fortune.

   _____

8. Unfortunately, they found out that to get a really good telescope they needed a <u>fortune</u>.
A fortune was a lot more money than they could scrape together.

_____

9. They finally settled for a very modest <u>instrument</u>.
The instrument was a small handheld telescope.

_____

10. They didn't find any new heavenly bodies with it, but they did spot some other <u>bodies</u>.
The other bodies were the guys in the dormitory wing across from their room.

_____

## Exercise 6C

Write an appositive of your own for the underlined nouns in the following sentences. Sometimes writers will repeat the noun they want to write an appositive for:

It was the best <u>plan</u> they could come up with, *a plan* they thought would surely work.

Often, an appositive will be a word that has no content of its own, a word like *one* or *kind* that the writer just uses to hang his or her real meaning on:

It was the best <u>plan</u> they could come up with, *one* they thought would surely work.

He went on a new <u>diet</u>, *the kind* where you mostly take in liquids.

1. I have to spend the afternoon studying for my toughest <u>class</u>.
[Name the class.]

_____

2. This semester, I've studied a <u>subject</u> that's new to me.
[Name the subject.]

_____

3. This semester, I've studied a <u>subject</u> that's new to me.
[Start your appositive with *one* and tell something about it.]

_____

4. Once I had an opportunity to go on a terrific trip.
   [Start your appositive with *one* and tell something about it.]

   _____

5. In high school I didn't have to work half as hard as I do here.
   [Say something either positive or negative about your high school.
   You could start this appositive with words like *a place*.]

   _____

6. I do not fondly remember the worst person I ever dated.
   [Use an appositive to describe him or her briefly; you could start this
   appositive with words like *a guy who* or *a girl who*.]

   _____

7. I do fondly remember one of the best persons I ever dated.
   [Use an appositive to describe him or her briefly.]

   _____

8. When I was in elementary school/middle school/high school [choose
   one], there was a boy/girl [choose one] I had a big crush on but was
   afraid to approach.
   [Use an appositive to describe him or her briefly, or instead of that,
   write an appositive referring to the word *crush* and say something
   about it.]

   _____

9. I'd really like to get a computer that would put me on the Internet.
   [Put your appositive at the end of this sentence and start it by repeating the word *computer* and saying something about it.]

   _____

10. There was one writing assignment that gave me a lot of trouble.
    [Put your appositive at the end of this sentence and start it by repeat-
    ing the word *assignment* and saying something about it.]

    _____

### Exercise 6D: Exercise Based on Case Study One

Following are sentences based on Case Study One in this chapter—the Abraham Lincoln writing assignment. To do these, you will have to read that
assignment if you haven't already. Follow the directions beneath each sentence
to make an appositive referring to the underlined words in the sentence.

1. The most important event in American history after the Revolution was the <u>Civil War</u>.
   [Use an appositive to say something about why the Civil War was so important; you could start the appositive with words like *a war that* or *an event* or *a turning point*.]

   _____

2. At the beginning of the Civil War, there were <u>four border states</u> that both the Union and the Confederacy hoped would join their sides.
   [List the names of these four states.]

   _____

3. A prewar <u>law</u> required that slaves who escaped to the north had to be returned to their owners.
   [Give the name of this law.]

   _____

4. In 1861, Lincoln took his <u>first two steps</u> in actively opposing slavery.
   [Name the two steps.]

   _____

5. In 1862, Lincoln issued an <u>order</u> freeing only those slaves in territory held by the Confederacy.
   [Give the name of that order.]

   _____

6. In a famous <u>speech</u> in 1863, Lincoln stressed that "all men are created equal."
   [Give the name of that speech.]

   _____

7. In 1864, Lincoln became the first American president to invite an <u>African-American</u> to the White House.
   [Name the person he invited.]

   _____

8. In 1864, Lincoln was instrumental in getting passed <u>the law</u> that ended slavery in the United States.
   [Name that law.]

   _____

## Exercise 6E (for Case Study One)

In the Abraham Lincoln writing assignment, a number of people are named: Horace Greeley, Dred Scott, Roger B. Taney, Abolitionists, Frederick Douglass. On a separate sheet of paper, write a sentence about each of these people or groups and use an appositive to tell who exactly they were. For instance, if you were writing about Lincoln, you might write a sentence like this:

> Abraham Lincoln, *the president who saved the Union and ended slavery,* did not at first consider slavery the main issue in the Civil War.

*Note:* Be sure that your appositives do not begin with *who.* The word *who* begins another kind of modifier that describes nouns, not an appositive.

### Exercise 6F: Exercise Based on Case Study Two

This exercise contains sentences based on the Second Amendment case study. Follow the directions beneath each sentence to make an appositive referring to the underlined word(s) in the first sentence.

1. The most important event in American history was the <u>Revolutionary War</u>.
   [Use an appositive to say something about the Revolutionary War; you could start the appositive with words like *a war that,* or *an event,* or *the beginning of.*]

   _____

2. After the Constitution was completed and ratified by the states, most people wanted a <u>Bill of Rights</u> added to it.
   [Use an appositive to say what a Bill of Rights is; you could start the appositive with words like *a document that,* or *a list of,* or *rights that.*]

   _____

3. The <u>American colonists</u> decided they had to form an independent nation.
   [Use an appositive to say who the American colonists were or something important about them; you could start the appositive with the words *a people.*]

   _____

4. A great many English and Americans believed that a <u>militia</u> was the best defense of their country.
   [Use an appositive to say what a militia is.]

   _____

5. They feared that a <u>standing army</u> could lead to a dictatorship by the country's leader.
   [Use an appositive to say what a standing army is.]

   _____

6. Our <u>second war against Britain</u> demonstrated again the ineffectiveness of militias when fighting professional armies.
   [Use an appositive to name our second war against Britain.]

7. The <u>King of England during the American Revolution</u> had a very bad reputation among British kings.
   [Use an appositive to name the Kind of England during the American Revolution.]

8. The <u>American Bar Association</u> has acknowledged that the Second Amendment is the most controversial one in the Bill of Rights.
   [Use an appositive to identify the American Bar Association.]

## Exercise 6G (for Case Study Two)

In the Second Amendment case study, there are a number of people named: Joyce Lee Malcolm, John Trenchard, William Blizard, William Blackstone, and James Madison. On a separate sheet of paper write a sentence about each of these people and use an appositive to tell exactly who the person was. For instance, if you were writing about King George III, you might write a sentence like this:

King George III, *the British king who ruled when the Americans defeated the British,* was not popular in America.

*Note:* Be sure that your appositives do not begin with the word *who* because the word *who* after a noun starts another kind of descriptive modifier—not an appositive.

## Exercise 6H: Exercise Based on Case Study Three

The following exercise contains sentences based on Case Study Three—"The Other Battle of the Little Big Horn." Follow the directions beneath each sentence to make an appositive referring to the underlined words in the sentence.

1. The U.S. government wanted to open for settlement the <u>traditional hunting lands of the Sioux and Cheyenne Indians</u>.
   [Write an appositive that tells what states now occupy these former hunting grounds; you can repeat the noun *lands* in your appositive.]

2.  The Cheyenne and Sioux tribes were <u>nomads</u>.
    [Write an appositive that defines the word *nomads*.]

    _____

3.  To convince the Indians to give up their nomadic life, the U.S. government offered <u>concessions</u>.
    [Write an appositive naming the two things the U.S. government offered the Indians.]

    _____

4.  The Sioux and Cheyenne Indians fought under the leadership of <u>two great Indian chiefs</u>.
    [Write an appositive to identify the two Indian chiefs.]

    _____

5.  Six hundred American soldiers were under the command of a controversial <u>officer</u>.
    [Write an appositive that identifies the officer.]

    _____

6.  General Custer kept 225 soldiers with him and divided the remaining soldiers into groups led by <u>four officers</u>.
    [Use an appositive to identify the four officers.]

    _____

7.  Custer wanted to destroy <u>the Indian camp</u>.
    [Write an appositive telling how many warriors the camp contained. You can begin with " a camp containing" or use another word meaning "camp."]

    _____

8.  The Battle of Little Big Horn has <u>another name</u>.
    [Write an appositive to state what the name is.]

    _____

## Exercise 6I (for Case Study Three)

In Case Study Three, a number of people are named: Major Reno, F. F. Girard, Charles A. Varnum, Dr. H. R. Porter, and George Herendeen. On a separate sheet of paper write a sentence about each of these people and use an appositive to tell who each one was.

> EXAMPLE:  Robert Utley, *one of the leading historians of the American west,* claimed that forty of Reno's men died and thirteen were wounded.

*Note:* Be sure that your appositives do not begin with *who,* because *who* following a noun begins another kind of descriptive modifier, not an appositive.

## Summary and Review of Chapter 6

### Paraphrasing

Often you will need to paraphrase, or state in your own words, the statements of published authors because you can't use the exact words of an author without quoting them. Paraphrasing is a good way to balance your use of quotations. Follow the steps to paraphrasing successfully.

### Quotations

In this chapter, you read a great deal of historical information and quoted much of it to make or support a point. Two commonly used ways to introduce quotations are:

1. *According to* author's name, + quotation.

2. Author's name *writes / says / said / claimed / argued that,* + quotation.

### Appositives

Appositives are noun phrases that modify other nouns preceding them. They are set off by commas.

My hardest subject this semester, *math,* is also the one I put in the most time on, *the one I have to study when I'd rather be doing other things.*

Appositives are effective ways to identify, define, or describe nouns.
Appositives are not complete sentences by themselves; rather, they are additions to complete sentences.

### Chapter 6: Glossary

1. **to be conciliatory**     to try to pacify
2. **sanctions**              rules

 3. **collective**            group
 4. **living precariously**   living dangerously
 5. **quartering**            providing housing for
 6. **overweening**           arrogant
 7. **religiously scrupulous** objecting for religious reasons
 8. **cavalry**               soldiers who went to battle on horseback
 9. **adjutant**              assistant to a commanding officer
10. **pommels**               front parts of saddles
11. **carbine**               rifle
12. **pell-mell**             disorderly
13. **demoralized**           discouraged
14. **casualties**            deaths
15. **flurried**              bewildered
16. **deployed**              spread out in position for battle
17. **despondent**            depressed
18. **annihilated**           destroyed

# CHAPTER SEVEN
## Debating Issues

**CASE STUDY ONE: MEDIA VIOLENCE AND CHILDREN**

Read the following three articles and the assignment. Then go back over the articles, reading closely and underlining or highlighting the most important information. Don't try to identify this information on your first reading.

### MANY RESEARCHERS SAY LINK IS ALREADY CLEAR ON MEDIA AND YOUTH VIOLENCE
#### by Lawrie Mifflin

Both the White House and Congress are considering asking the Surgeon General to conduct a comprehensive study of the effects of media violence on American youths. But most academic researchers say they believe the evidence is already at the . . . Surgeon General's fingertips. Hundreds of studies done at the nation's top universities in the last three decades have come to the same conclusion: That there is at least some demonstrable link between watching violent acts in movies and TV shows and acting aggressively in life.

Proving such links [1]irrefutably is almost impossible, and many studies have been criticized for methodological or other flaws. It is not one individual study, however, but the entire range of studies, taken as a whole, that has convinced most social scientists of the probability of a link. "The evidence is overwhelming," said Jeffrey McIntyre, legislative and federal affairs officer for the American Psychological Association. "To argue against it is like arguing against gravity." Indeed, the Surgeon General's office has already done two comprehensive overviews of existing studies, the first published in 1972, and the second a 1982 update. Both called television violence a contributing factor to increases in violent crime and antisocial behavior. The research does not demonstrate that watching violent acts in films or television shows directly and immediately causes people to commit violent acts. Rather, the scholarly evidence cited by McIntyre either demonstrates [2]cumulative effects of violent entertainment or establishes it as a "risk factor" that contributes to increasing a person's aggressiveness.

A few scholars object to this research, saying the links do not prove cause and effect and are therefore relatively unimportant. "There's no question there's a correlational link, that children who watch television violence tend to be more aggressive," said Jonathan L. Freedman, a professor of psychology at the University of Toronto. "It's a very small correlation, but it's there." But Freedman said links could come from many factors, including the likelihood that children who watch a lot of violent television shows are often children who are least supervised by responsible adults. "My reading of the research is it's pathetic in terms of showing the link to be causal," he said.

Still, from 1990 to 1996, major reviews of scientific studies on the subject were separately conducted by the American Medical Association, the American Psychological Association, the American Academy of Pediatrics, the American Academy of Child and Adolescent Psychiatry, and the National Institute of Mental Health. "All of them said that television violence contributes to real-world violence," said Dale Kunkel, a UCLA professor of communications who led a three-year study—financed by the National Cable Television Association—documenting the amount of television violence and its contexts.

One of the most academically reputable researchers, L. Rowell Huesmann of the University of Michigan at Ann Arbor, told a Senate hearing [recently]: "Not every child who watches a lot of violence or plays a lot of violent games will grow up to be violent. Other forces must converge. . . . But just as every cigarette increases the chance that someday you will get lung cancer, every exposure to violence increases the chances that some day a child will behave more violently than they otherwise would."

Far less research exists on the effects of popular music—the snarling hostility of rock performers like Marilyn Manson or the group Rammstein, for example, or some rap music lyrics that seem to glorify violence against women—or of violent video games, some of which allow a player to [3]simulate murder. Both video games and explicitly violent lyrics are relatively recent phenomena and have not been widely studied.

*Other media factors that may contribute but haven't been studied*

Professor Kunkel estimates that more than 1,000 studies on the effects of media violence—in televised entertainment, television news, or movies—have been done in the last 40 years, in academic departments ranging from sociology to [4]epidemiology. Some are experiments in which different groups of children were shown different television shows and their playground behavior monitored immediately afterward, for example, or in which college students were given buzzers and told they could "zap" someone who had offended them and were found more likely to do so after having watched violent movies. Some are surveys, where parents recorded what their children watched and were interviewed at various stages about their children's behavior. Some are statistical analyses, showing the increase in crime rates in certain geographic areas after the introduction of television. So these studies must inevitably vary in reliability. But the general findings are consistent, and several meta-analyses—which collate the findings of all known studies on a subject, calculating compensations for the different methods—have found a definite link between watching violent entertainment and behaving aggressively.

Professor Huesmann, the University of Michigan researcher, has done two [5]longitudinal studies of the effects of television violence, one begun in 1960 that examined about 600 people at age 8, age 18, and age 30, and one he is finishing now that has tracked 750 Chicago-area elementary schoolchildren for three years. "Boys at age 8 who had been watching more television violence than other boys grew up to be more aggressive than other boys," Huesmann said, describing his first study. "They also grew up to be more aggressive and violent than you'd have

*longitudinal studies*

expected them to be on the basis of how aggressive they were as 8-year-olds."

In his more recent study, Professor Huesmann has found that children who watched more violence behaved more aggressively the next year than those who watched less violence on television, and more aggressively than would have been expected based on how they had behaved the previous year. In both cases, he said, this was true even after statistically canceling out all known effects for social class, educational level of the parents, quality of the parenting, and intelligence quotient of the child. In the later study, it was true of girls as well as boys.

Network executives have been reluctant to talk about the subject, either fearing to appear insensitive in the wake of the Colorado shooting on April 20 [1999] or fearing high-profile attacks on the day of the White House meeting. But network and movie studio executives, as well as producers and writers, have repeatedly [6]bristled at the academic findings, arguing that the link found is far too small to warrant the attention paid to them. The executives also accuse social scientists of looking for easy solutions—censoring or restricting entertainment media—to avoid confronting more difficult solutions, like reducing poverty, improving child-rearing skills and child care services, or restricting the availability of guns.

Like Professor Huesmann, mainstream researchers agree that media violence cannot be singled out as influencing a person's aggressiveness more than any other factor. "Media and cultural influences," Professor Kunkel said, "are not necessarily the most potent, but they are one of the most [7]pervasive influences on children." And Kathryn C. Montgomery, president of the Center for Media Education, a Washington research and advocacy group, said: "The accumulation over time is the concern, not a single incident or a single viewing. A steady diet of violent content over time creates a culture that tells kids that violence is the accepted way we solve our problems."

Nobody argues that the teenage gunmen in Littleton, Colorado, for example, were inspired by watching violent movies or playing violent video games, even though they were known to enjoy the game Doom, in which players simulate killing. "There have always been kids drawn toward extreme behavior, but what qualifies as extreme depends on what is normal behavior," said David Walsh, a psychologist who heads the National Institute on Media and the Family, a Minneapolis group that educates families on how to cope with media influences. "It's not

*establishing TV violence as the critical difference in behavior*

*industry reaction*

as direct as 'Oh, they played Doom and then they went and got their guns,' " Dr. Walsh said. "It's a redefining of our [8]repertoire of responses. If the norm is respect, an extreme response might be a punch in the nose, but if the norm is 'in your face' hostility then the extreme is something more extreme."

Dr. Walsh, Ms. Montgomery, and many of the public-health groups would like to see society adopt more warning systems about the potential effects of media violence, with public education campaigns similar to those on smoking, drunken driving, or seat belts. "All we want is to be able to tell parents that watching violence is an unhealthy influence, just the way eating candy is unhealthy if it's done in excess," said Joanne Cantor, a professor of communication arts at the University of Wisconsin at Madison and the author of *Mommy, I'm Scared: How TV and Movies Frighten Children and What We Can Do to Protect Them* (Harcourt, Brace & Company, 1998). Rather than call for censorship, Professor Cantor and others call for better labeling, like the rating systems for movies and television programs, and for more intensive parental education efforts.

*[handwritten margin note: norms determine extremes. If violence becomes the norm, the extreme will be extreme violence (i.e. Littleton)]*

## KIDS LESS VIOLENT AFTER CUTTING BACK ON TV
### by Ulysses Torassa

Aggressive tendencies fostered in children by violent television shows and video games can be tempered if they cut back their viewing and playing, a new Stanford University study shows. Researchers found a decrease in the level of aggression at a San Jose elementary school after an effort to get pupils to watch less television. The effect was greatest for children who were already showing signs of hostility.

The study, being published in today's edition of the *Archives of Pediatrics and Adolescent Medicine,* is the latest in a string of studies linking violence with television and video games. But it is the first to show that those tendencies can be reversed. "When kids reduced their exposure to videotapes, TV, and video games, they became less aggressive," said Thomas N. Robinson, an assistant professor of medicine at Stanford and the study's lead author. "What this says is there is something you can do in a practical way, in a real-world setting, and see the effects."

Robinson also was author of a 1999 study based on the same research that found that children who cut down on television watching gained less weight than their peers. Both studies relied on data gathered at two similar San Jose elementary schools, where researchers asked 192 third- and fourth-graders about aggressive classmates and made playground observations of both verbal and physical aggression. The researchers declined to identify the schools, citing promises of confidentiality.

Among their initial findings, 43 percent of the children in both schools had television sets in their rooms. Boys were seen being physically aggressive (punching, hitting, pushing, pulling, or throwing objects) once every two minutes. For girls, it was once every five minutes.

After getting baseline measurements, the researchers introduced a curriculum at one school meant to encourage children to cut back on video games and to watch less TV. Two-thirds of the pupils participated in an initial, 10-day effort to turn off television altogether, which was monitored by slips signed by parents. Just over half continued to limit their television watching to under seven hours per week at least once during the next 20 weeks.

When researchers went back, they found a 50 percent reduction in the level of verbal aggression seen on the playground at the experimental school compared with the one that did not follow the curriculum. They also noted 40 percent fewer instances of physical aggression, although that finding was not considered statistically significant. Children who were the most aggressive at the outset of the study showed the greatest benefit. "They have the most room to improve," Robinson said. "Our goal was to reduce aggression in the population as a whole. In doing that, it may have had a greater impact on those kids who tended to be more aggressive."

Besides the declines in aggression and obesity, Robinson said, there were [9]anecdotal reports from teachers and parents of other benefits, including more effort spent on after-school projects. "We had parents who said, 'This is the best thing that's happened to our family—we talk to our kids at dinnertime now,' " he said. "One mother called and said her daughter used to sit at home and watch TV, and now she's found a friend down the block and they play outside every afternoon."

Dennis Wharton, a spokesman for the National Association of Broadcasters, said he had not seen the study and could not comment on it. But he said the industry believes that there is "conflicting evidence" on the link between television and real-world violence. The television and film industry has consistently fought government attempts to control the content of programming. Instead, Wharton said, they support ratings systems and technologies like the V-chip that allow parents to control what their children watch.

According to James Garbarino, a professor at Cornell University and author of *Lost Boys: Why Our Sons Turn Violent and How We Can Save Them,* there is clearly a link between television violence and aggression in children. However, in an editorial he wrote accompanying the Stanford study, Garbarino said it probably accounts for only about 10 percent of children's aggression—a link that is comparable to the one between smoking and cancer. Other contributing factors, he said, include guns, child abuse, bad schools, inadequate mental health services—even spiritual emptiness. "Most people who smoke don't get cancer," Garbarino wrote. "Most kids who watch television do not act violently."

Robinson, who has two televisions in his own home, said he doesn't think television is "evil." But he does think the study shows that cutting back can have real benefits for children. "Parents can set budgets in the households" for television viewing, he said. "That way they and their kids are watching what they really want to watch, rather than just whatever is on."

## Why a Little Violence Is Good for Kids
by James Spencer

While I deplore violent films and television shows as much as, if not more than, the next person, I think some critics are getting a little carried away in their crusade against violence in the media. By oversimplifying the issue, they would ban children from exposure to some of the most delightful and healthy programs television has to offer.

I really don't like truly violent movies, and I don't think they're good for us. One critic has argued that slasher films actually portray women as heroes rather than victims since the slasher is always killed or at least thwarted in the end by a young woman he has been pursuing. But this rosy view tends to ignore all the other young women, and men, murdered along the way, usually, at least in the women's cases, while nude or at least topless. I don't think that this equation of female sexuality with victimhood is healthy.

Similarly, I truly despise the kinds of violent movies made by Clint Eastwood and his imitators. The steely eyed avenger who flouts the law in order to kill those he dislikes is a disastrously bad model for anyone. How healthy is it for us to admire someone who asks only that his victim "make my day" by making a move that will justify murdering him?

But there are other kinds of violence in the media, and these kinds aren't like the slasher films or the Eastwood films at all. When Stan Laurel smacks Oliver Hardy in the face with a custard pie, that's violent. When Charlie Chaplin ducks so that the big guy who is going to hit him winds up hitting an innocent bystander, that's also violent. When James Bond blows a bunch of bad guys away with a rocket launched from the tailpipe of his car, that's violent. When the cat, Tom, is trying to flatten the mouse, Jerry, with a cast iron frying pan and winds up hitting a dog over the head repeatedly, that's violent. But are these all bad?

Well, I was a child once, and I had a child once, and I have a granddaughter now, and I've known and played with lots of children, and so I'm a child expert of sorts, and I disagree. I've never seen a kid take a Tom and Jerry cartoon seriously or do anything but laugh at Charlie Chaplin.

We need to make some distinctions. First, there are two different kinds of violence, comic and serious. There is the violence that makes us laugh and the violence that makes us cringe. Outlaw comic violence, and you outlaw slapstick—all those great silent movies of the '20s, Abbot and Costello, Martin and Lewis, Tom and Jerry, Bugs Bunny, the Roadrunner, and on and on. And, yes, James Bond. It's entirely possible that small children might not understand the difference between *Dirty Harry* violence and James Bond violence, and I wouldn't take a small child to a Bond movie. Any normal child, however, clearly understands what's going on in a Tom and Jerry movie. My granddaughter did when she was four and we watched a tape of those cartoons together. When I was a teenager, we had some neighbors with a little boy of about six or so, and I'd take him to the Saturday matinee movies sometimes. The antics of Tom and Jerry or Bugs Bunny or any of those "violent" cartoons would have him so convulsed with laughter that he'd literally fall off his seat onto the floor. People laughing like that aren't planning mayhem, either then or in the future.

"Violent" programs aimed at kids play another function as well. They completely exclude adults, and they operate according to an ethos all their own. The characters whap each other around just the way kids do and with just as much effect. Or you get a series like the *Teenage*

*Mutant Ninja Turtles* (even the title gives it away), which portrays teenagers as heroic on behalf of the good. They're a lot better models for all of us than the adult heroes portrayed by Eastwood and Stallone and the rest.

Essentially, I think that parents ought to use some common sense about what they let their kids see, and not leave their child rearing to professors.

**ASSIGNMENT**

Write an essay in which you analyze the information and opinions in the articles, consider your own experiences and observations, and explain your views on the dangers of violence in electronic media to children.

## Discussion

The assignment above does *not* ask you to take an all-or-nothing stand—to say that all children should be allowed to view all types of media violence or that no children should be allowed to view any type media violence. Instead, you are to consider the opinions and information that you have read as well as your own experiences and present a discussion of the issue. You may decide that some kinds of media violence are not harmful to children who watch it, and that some kinds are. You may decide that some children are too young to view some kinds of violence, and some children are not. Whatever you decide, you should present both positive and negative sides of the issue so that your readers see a balanced discussion.

### Step One: Make Notes and Compare Them with Others

Write notes on the points in the three articles that you think are most important. Don't worry about being "wrong." It is perfectly natural for different persons to disagree to some extent on the importance of particular points; there isn't necessarily one right answer.

In class, work with two other students, comparing your notes on the most important points. If you find some disagreements, as you should, discuss them with each other. Try to see whether you can come to a consensus on which points are most important. If you can't entirely agree, don't worry about it.

Each group should now report on the points the group members consider most important so that the teacher can write them on the board for class discussion. Now the class as a whole can come to a consensus on the most important points from each article. Write these points down since your notes will form the basis for the next step in the assignment.

When these points are written on the board, you will be able to see that many of them contradict each other. For example, one negative point may be that the violence in animated cartoons is bad for children, while a positive point might be that cartoon violence is harmless because it is so unrealistic and exaggerated. It is important to identify all such pairs of positive and negative points because doing so will help you organize your essay.

### Step Two: Make an Outline and Compare It with Others

Read the following guidelines for organizing "Media Violence and Children." Then go over your notes and decide how you might organize them into an essay, point by point. Make a rough list outline of your essay, and bring the outline to class for discussion of ways to organize.

## Organizing "Media Violence and Children"

In college and the professional world, you will often be asked to discuss issues on which disagreement is possible. In these cases, teachers and supervisors do *not* expect or want you to oversimplify the issue, to argue or present only one side of it, leaving the other side out. They expect a complete discussion in which *all* points are presented—bad as well as good, negative as well as positive, opposing views as well as your own. This is a process that will be helped if you remember to use the words showing contrast and concession—*but, whereas, while, although, though,* and *even though.*

As you make an organization plan for the body of your essay, you should list all pairs of points you and your classmates have found—positive and negative ones regarding electronic media violence—and make any other groupings of points that seem logical. Arrange all of these pairs of points in the order you want to write about them, and devote a body paragraph to each pair of matching opposing points. Now choose two or three quotations to use from the articles, ones that will support points you want to make or ones that express points you disagree with.

Your conclusion is your chance to sum up your position on the effects of media violence on children.

### *Step Three: Write a Rough Draft*

At home, write a rough draft of your essay. Do not worry about spelling and grammar as you try to get all of your information on paper in a logical order.

Choose two or three quotations from the readings, ones that will support points you want to make or ones that express points you disagree with.

Look for places that you can use contrast and concession words to join ideas. Check for places that you can use *appositives* or *verbal phrases*.

*Appositives* can come in handy in identifying authors:

James Garbarino, *a professor at Cornell University,* wrote that "Most kids who watch television do not act violently."

*Verbal phrases* can be used like this:

*After reviewing several scientific studies on the effects of media violence,* Dale Kunkel, a UCLA professor of communications, found that "All of them said that television violence contributes to real-world violence."

Use the following Checklist for Evaluating Rough Drafts to see whether your draft meets the assignment requirements, and use it in peer review.

Make two copies of your draft so that you have three copies to bring to class.

---

**CHECKLIST FOR EVALUATING ROUGH DRAFTS**

1. Does the introduction indicate what the essay will be about and why the subject is important?
2. Is the rest of the essay divided into body paragraphs that cover the main points involved in discussing this issue?
3. Does each body paragraph start with a topic sentence, a sentence that tells what the paragraph will discuss?
4. Are all the sentences in each body paragraph related to the point expressed in the topic sentence? Are there any places where unrelated ideas seem to come into any body paragraphs?

> 5. Are all the most important points involved covered, or is anything missing?
> 6. Does the order of the points seem logical, or does anything seem out of place?
> 7. Is there a conclusion explaining the writer's position?
> 8. Has the writer used two or three quotations from the articles?
> 9. Are there at least three sentences using the concession or contrast words in the paper?
> 10. Are there at least three sentences using appositives?
> 11. Are there at least two sentences using verbal phrases?

### Step Four: Peer Review

In class, in groups of three, exchange your rough drafts, and take turns reading your own drafts aloud. Correct any mistakes you find as you read. Refer to the Checklist for Evaluating Rough Drafts, answering each question about the essays written by your group members. Call in the teacher if you need help or advice.

### Step Five: Write a Final Draft

At home, write the final version of your paper, using the advice you received during peer review to strengthen your essay.

Have you used two or three quotations from the readings?

Have you used contrast and concession words—*but, while, whereas, even though, though,* and *although*—to join logically related ideas?

Have you used appositives and verbal phrases?

Proofread a printed copy of your paper after reviewing the proofreading tips in Chapter 1 and the following Special Proofreading section.

## Special Proofreading

- As you did in your previous papers, proofread for subject-verb agreement and plural *-s* endings on nouns.
- Check to make sure that you have *-ed* endings on past-tense verbs. You will need to use past-tense verbs in referring to the many studies of media violence done before this year.
- Check for possessive apostrophes. Watch out especially for places where you might mention Stanford University's study or use a possessive form of one of the authors' names, for example, Lawrie Mifflin's article.

- If pronouns have been a problem for you, check to make sure you've used subject pronouns in front of your verbs and object pronouns after them, and check to make sure that you've used *they* and *them* to refer to plural nouns.

---

**CASE STUDY TWO: DOES ABUSE EVER JUSTIFY MURDER?**

Read the following case, the articles, and the assignment and discussion sections. Then go back over the readings, carefully underlining or highlighting the most important points, the ones you will want to consider in your essay. Don't try to identify these points on your first reading.

---

### Does Abuse Ever Justify Murder?

In 1994, a series of events suddenly brought to public consciousness a problem that had long been ignored, what one writer has called "the abuse excuse." While it isn't always clear who starts a domestic fight, when such a fight starts to become violent, it is far more often the woman who is likely to get physically hurt than the man. When angry, some women tend to express themselves verbally while some men are more likely to use their fists. By the same token, some men raised in families in which male dominance is accepted as natural casually use their fists to keep their wives "in line." When physical abuse begins to reach the danger point, some of these wives resort to killing their husbands to head off what they see as threats to their own lives.

Similarly, husbands have murdered wives who have been unfaithful, and people have killed other people because they have felt provoked by their behavior. Deaths resulting from being cut off on a city street or having one's car dinged by someone else or simply having been given "the finger" by another driver are certainly not unknown.

When are such acts justified and when are they not? Following are three articles on this subject.

#### 'TIL DEATH DO US PART
##### by Nancy Gibbs

. . . Last year the American Medical Association, backed by the Surgeon General, declared that violent men constitute a major threat to women's health. The National League of Cities estimates that as many as half of all women will experience violence at some time in their marriage. Between 22 percent and 35 percent of all visits by females to emergency rooms are for injuries from domestic assaults. Though some studies have found that women are just as likely to start a fight as men, others indicate they are six times as likely to be seriously injured in one. Especially grotesque is the brutality reserved for pregnant women: The March of Dimes has concluded that the battering of women during pregnancy causes more birth defects than all the diseases put together for which children are usually immunized. Anywhere from one-third to as many as half of all female murder victims are killed by their spouses or lovers, compared with 4 percent of male victims.

"Male violence against women is at least as old an institution as marriage," says clinical psychologist Gus Kaufman Jr., cofounder of Men Stopping Violence, an Atlanta clinic established to help men face their battering problems. So long as a woman was considered her husband's legal property, police and the courts were unable to prevent—and unwilling to punish—domestic assaults. . . .

Out of that old reluctance grew the modern double standard. Until the first wave of legal reform in the 1970s, an aggravated assault against a stranger was a felony, but assaulting a spouse was considered a misdemeanor, which rarely landed the attacker in court, much less in jail. That distinction, which still exists in most states, does not reflect the danger involved; a study by the Boston Bar Association found that the domestic attacks were at least as dangerous as 90 percent of felony assaults. "Police seldom arrest, even when there are injuries serious enough to require hospitalization of the victim," declared the Florida Supreme Court in a 1990 gender-bias study, which also noted the tendency of prosecutors to drop domestic-violence cases.

Researcher and author Angela Browne points out that a woman is much more likely to be killed by her partner than to kill him. In 1991, when some 4 million women were beaten and 1,320 murdered in domestic attacks, 622 women killed their husbands or boyfriends. Yet the women have become the lightning rods for debate, since their circumstances, and their response, were most extreme.

"There is an appropriate means to deal with one's marital problems—[10]legal recourse. Not a .357 Magnum," argues former Florida prosecutor Bill Catto. "If you choose to use a gun to end a problem, then you must suffer the consequences of your act." Defense lawyers call it legitimate self-protection when a victim of abuse fights back—even if she shoots her husband in his sleep. Prosecutors call it an act of vengeance, and in the past, juries have usually agreed and sent the killer to jail. Michael Dowd, director of the Pace University Battered Women's Justice Center, has found that the average sentence for a woman who kills her mate is 15 to 20 years; for a man, 2 to 6.

The punishment is not surprising, since many judges insist that evidence of past abuse, even if it went on for years, is not relevant in court unless it occurred around the time of the killing. It is not the dead husband who is on trial, they note, but the wife who pulled the trigger. "Frankly, I feel changing the law would be authorizing preventive murder," argued Los Angeles Superior Court Judge Lillian Stevens in the Los Angeles *Times*. "The only thing that really matters is, Was there an immediate danger? There can't be an old grievance." And even if a woman is allowed to testify about past violence, the jury may still condemn her response to it. If he was really so savage, the prosecutor typically asks, why didn't she leave, seek shelter, call the police, file a complaint?

"The question presumes she has good options," says Julie Blackman, a New Jersey-based social psychologist who has testified as an expert witness in abuse and murder cases. "Sometimes, they don't leave because they have young children and no other way to support them, or because they grow up in cultures that are so immersed in violence that they don't figure there's any place better to go, or because they can't get apartments." The shelter facilities around the country are uniformly inadequate; New York has about 1,300 beds for a state with 18 million people. In 1990 the Baltimore Zoo spent twice as much money to care for animals as the state of Maryland spent on shelters for victims of domestic violence.

The other reason women don't flee is because, ironically, they are afraid for their life. Law-enforcement experts agree that running away greatly increases the danger a woman faces. Angered at the loss of power and control, violent men often try to track down their wives and threaten them, or their children, if they don't come home. James Cox III, an unemployed dishwasher in Jacksonville, Florida, was determined to find his ex-girlfriend, despite a court order to stay away from her. Two weeks ago, he forced her mother at gunpoint to tell him the location of the battered women's shelter where her daughter had fled, and stormed

the building, firing a shotgun. Police shot him dead. "This case illus-
trates the extent to which men go to pursue their victims," said executive director Rita DeYoung. "It creates a [11]catch-22 for all battered
women. Some will choose to return to their abusers, thinking they can
control their behavior. . . . "

It is hard for juries to understand why [some women] do not turn to
the courts for orders of protection. But these are a makeshift shield at
best, often violated and hard to enforce. Olympic skier Patricia Kastle
had a restraining order when her former husband shot her. Lisa Bianco
in Indiana remained terrified of her husband even after he was sent to
jail for eight years. When prison officials granted Alan Matheney an
eight-hour pass in March 1989, he drove directly to Bianco's home,
broke in and beat her to death with the butt of a shotgun. Last March,
Shirley Lowery, a grandmother of 11, was stabbed 19 times with a
butcher knife by her former boyfriend in the hallway of the courthouse
where she had gone to get an order of protection.

### The Mind of the Victim

Defense lawyers have a hard time explaining to juries the shame, isola-
tion and emotional dependency that bind victims to their abusers. Many
women are too proud to admit to their family or friends that their marriage is not working and blame themselves for its failure even as they
cling to the faith that their violent lover will change. "People confuse
the woman's love for the man with love of abuse," says Pace's Dowd.
"It's not the same thing. . . . "

Many lawyers say it is virtually impossible to defend a battered
woman without some expert testimony about the effect of that [12]syn-
drome over time. Such testimony allows attorneys to stretch the rules
governing self-defense, which were designed to deal with two men
caught in a bar fight, not a woman caught in a violent relationship with
a stronger man.

In a traditional case of self-defense, a jury is presented a "snapshot"
of a crime: The mugger threatens a subway rider with a knife; the rider
pulls a gun and shoots the attacker. It is up to the jurors to decide whether
the danger was real and immediate and whether the response was reasonable. A woman who shoots her husband while he lunges at her with a
knife should have little trouble claiming that she acted in self-defense. Yet
lawyers still find jurors to be very uncomfortable with female violence

under any circumstances, especially violence directed at a man she may have lived with for years.

Given that bias, it is even harder for a lawyer to call it self-defense when a woman shoots a sleeping husband. The danger is hardly immediate, prosecutors argue, nor was the lethal response reasonable. Evidence about battered-woman syndrome may be the only way to persuade a jury to identify with a killer. "Battered women are extraordinarily sensitive to cues of danger, and that's how they survive," says Walker. "That is why many battered women kill, not during what looks like the middle of a fight, but when the man is more vulnerable or the violence is just beginning."

A classic self-defense plea also demands a fair fight. A person who is punched can punch back, but if he shoots, he runs the risk of being charged with murder or manslaughter. This leaves women and children, who are almost always smaller and weaker than their attackers, in a bind. They often see no way to escape an assault without using a weapon and the element of surprise—arguing, in essence, that their best hope of self-defense was a [13]preemptive strike. "Morally and legally a woman should not be expected to wait until his hands are around her neck," argues Los Angeles defense attorney Leslie Abramson. "Say a husband says, 'When I get up tomorrow morning, I'm going to beat the living daylights out of you,' " says Joshua Dressler, a law professor at Wayne State University who specializes in criminal procedures. "If you use the word [14]imminent, the woman would have to wait until the next morning and, just as he's about to kill her, then use self-defense."

That argument, prosecutors retort, is an invitation to anarchy. If a woman has survived past beatings, what persuaded her that this time was different, that she had no choice but to kill or be killed? The real [15]catalyst, they suggest, was not her fear, but her fury. Prosecutors often turn a woman's history of abuse into a motive for murder. "What some clemency advocates are really saying is that that s.o.b. deserved to die and why should she be punished for what she did," argues Dressler. Unless the killing came in the midst of a violent attack, it amounts to a personal death-penalty sentence. "I find it very hard to say that killing the most rotten human being in the world when he's not currently threatening the individual is the right thing to do."

Those who oppose changes in the laws point out that many domestic disputes are much more complicated than the clemency movement would suggest. "We've got to stop perpetuating the myth that men are all vicious and that women are all Snow White," says Sonny Burmeister, a divorced father of three children who, as president of the Georgia Council for Children's Rights in Marietta, lobbies for equal treatment of men involved in custody battles. He recently sheltered a husband whose wife had pulled a gun on him. When police were called, their response was "So?" Says Burmeister: "We perpetuate this macho, chauvinistic, paternalistic, attitude for men. We are taught to be protective of the weaker sex. We encourage women to report domestic violence. We believe men are guilty. But women are just as guilty. . . . "

[As of January 1993] only nine states have passed laws permitting expert testimony on battered-woman syndrome and spousal violence. In most cases it remains a matter of judicial discretion. One Pennsylvania judge ruled that testimony presented by a prosecutor showed that the defendant had not been beaten badly enough to qualify as a battered woman and therefore could not have that standard applied to her case. President Bush [the senior George Bush, U.S. president 1989–1992] signed legislation in October [1992] urging states to accept expert testimony in criminal cases involving battered women. The law calls for development of training materials to assist defendants and their attorneys in using such testimony in appropriate cases.

In a sense, a society's priorities can be measured by whom it punishes. A survey of the population of a typical prison suggests that violent husbands and fathers are still not viewed as criminals. In New York State, about half the inmates are drug offenders, the result of a decade-long War on Drugs that demanded mandatory sentences. A War on Violence would send the same message, that society genuinely [16]abhors parents who beat children and spouses who batter each other, and is willing to punish the behavior rather than dismiss it.

Minnesota serves as a model for other states. In 1981 Duluth was the first U.S. city to institute mandatory arrests in domestic disputes. Since then about half the states have done the same, which means that even if a victim does not wish to press charges, the police are obliged to make an arrest if they see evidence of abuse.

Better training of police officers, judges, emergency-room personnel, and other professionals is having an impact in many cities. . . . In Jacksonville, Florida, new procedures helped raise the arrest rate from 25 percent to 40 percent. "Arrests send a message to the woman that help is available and to men that abuse is not accepted," says shelter executive director DeYoung, who also serves as president of the Florida Coalition Against Domestic Violence. "Children too see that it's not accepted and are more likely to grow up not accepting abuse in the home."

Since 1990 at least 28 states have passed "stalking laws" that make it a crime to threaten, follow or harass someone. Congress this month may take up the Violence Against Women bill, which would increase penalties for federal sex crimes; provide $300 million to police, prosecutors, and courts to combat violent crimes against women; and reinforce state domestic-violence laws. Most women, of course, are not looking to put their partners in jail; they just want the violence to stop.

## Making Excuses
### by Stanton Peele

What do you call it when a woman kills her spouse? If the husband had a history of abusing and intimidating her, the homicide may be considered an expression of "battered-woman syndrome." Because of repeated abuse, the theory goes, the battered woman has low self-esteem. Depressed and unmotivated, she is unable to leave her husband. She comes to believe that the only way of [17]extricating herself is to [18]maim or kill him. Even though she is not in immediate danger at the time she strikes back (if she were, she could plead self-defense), promoters of battered-woman syndrome argue that she should be treated leniently.

Now what do you call it when a man kills his spouse? For Kenneth Peacock, a trucker in Towson, Maryland, the answer was "manslaughter." Mr. Peacock, who shot his wife in the head after he came home at night to find her in bed with another man, received an 18-month sentence. . . . Judge Robert E. Cahill sympathized with the [19]perpetrator. "I seriously wonder how many men married five, four years would have the strength to walk away without inflicting some [20]corporal punishment," he remarked. Judge Cahill couldn't think of a situation that would provoke "an uncontrollable rage greater than this: for someone who is happily married to be betrayed in your personal life, when you're out working to support the spouse." The judge almost apologized for sentencing Mr. Peacock: "I am forced to impose a sentence . . . only because I think I must do it to make the system honest."

Law students at the University of Maryland immediately organized protests. Patricia Ireland, director of the National Organization for Women, promised a national campaign to make sentences tougher for men who kill their wives. "This judge is excusing this behavior by giving this lenient sentence," said Maryland attorney Judith A. Wolfer. "Until judges start treating a homicide of a spouse as any other homicide, men are going to continue to kill their wives with [21]impunity for reasons of jealousy, control, or rage. You name it, they'll use it.

## Double Standards

Ironically, Miss Wolfer has been a prominent advocate of the battered-woman defense, which hardly "treat[s] a homicide of a spouse as any other homicide." In 1991 she and the group she represents, the House of Ruth, successfully lobbied Maryland Governor William Schaefer to pardon eight women who were serving long sentences for assaulting or killing their husbands (following a similar move by Ohio Governor Richard F. Celeste in December 1990). She and her colleagues presented the governor with [22]dossiers that described abuse allegedly committed by the women's husbands.

Although a woman who kills an abusive husband may seem more sympathetic than a man who kills an unfaithful wife, there are striking parallels between the leniency Miss Wolfer condemns and the leniency she advocates. Both hinge on a spouse's misbehavior and its impact on the defendant's state of mind. Neither is based on an argument of self-defense. Indeed, the homicide often does not immediately follow the provocation. Mr. Peacock shot his wife four hours after chasing away her lover; in the [23]interim, he drank and argued with her. Francine Hughes, whose story inspired the film *The Burning Bed,* set her husband on fire as he slept.

Both the battered woman and the betrayed man have an alternative: They can leave. (Mrs. Hughes, like many battered women, had separated from her husband several times, only to return to him voluntarily.) When the wronged spouse does not simply leave, we are told it is because he or she has been incapacitated by the circumstances; the battered-woman defense emphasizes the female stereotype of passivity, while the betrayed-man defense emphasizes the male stereotype of jealous rage. Given these similarities, it's not surprising that the attorney who got Mr. Peacock such a light sentence, David B. Irwin, has been equally successful in representing women who killed their husbands.

## One-Time Killers?

Critics of both the Maryland and the Ohio pardons argued that the governors heard only information favorable to the prisoners and did not examine the trial transcripts. The *Baltimore Sun* noted that one of the women released in Maryland had hired a hit man and collected on her dead husband's insurance. Governor Schaefer responded by describing the emotional testimony of the prisoners he had interviewed, most of whom were not likely to commit additional crimes. But jailed assailants often seem [24]contrite. Judge Cahill had the same impression of Mr. Peacock: "I have no question in my mind that no judge . . . will ever see Kenneth Peacock again," he said. Mr. Peacock had no criminal record, and the prosecutor noted that Mrs. Peacock's mother sympathized with her son-in-law.

Maryland Attorney General J. Joseph Curran Jr. criticized the prosecutor, Assistant State's Attorney Michael G. DeHaven, for agreeing to the manslaughter plea. Mr. Curran rejected the notion that men who have found their wives [25]in flagrante delicto are justified in killing them. The appropriate response, he said, is divorce. Of course, the same could be said for battered women, but Mr. Curran did not publicly object to Governor Schaefer's pardons in 1991.

Curran argued that Peacock's sentence was based on [26]retrograde thinking. Yet manslaughter pleas are still typical in cases like this one. Stephen Schulhofer, a criminologist at the University of Chicago, says juries "tend to think it is reasonable for men to lose it when they hear about adultery." Modern courts have consistently accepted a wife's adultery as a [27]mitigating factor in homicide cases.

Critics of this practice note that it may invite husbands who kill in cold blood to claim that they lost their heads after learning of their wives' infidelity. The battered-woman defense poses a similar danger. In some cases the women have indeed suffered a long history of [28]egregious abuse. In 1985, for example, New Jersey Governor Tom Kean pardoned Joyce Bunch, who had been sentenced to seven years in prison for the nonfatal shooting of her husband. Over the years her husband's attacks had left her unconscious, disfigured, and in one instance temporarily paralyzed. But Mrs. Bunch's case does not appear to be typical. The *Columbus Dispatch* reported that 15 of the 25 women pardoned by Governor Celeste in 1990 said they had not been physically abused. Six had discussed killing their husbands beforehand, and two had tracked down men from whom they were separated.

Since men are much more likely to kill women than vice versa, feminists should hesitate before broadening the excuses available to murderers. It is tempting to say that a man's outrageous conduct justifies lenient treatment of his wife when she kills him. But the Peacock case shows that such logic cuts both ways.

## ASSIGNMENT

Write an essay in which you analyze the information and opinions in the articles and explain your views about when provocation or abuse justifies killing and when it doesn't.

## Discussion

Notice that the assignment above doesn't ask *whether* provocation or abuse justifies killing but *when* provocation or abuse justifies it. Of course, you may wish to argue that provocation or abuse *never* justifies killing, but it probably would be hard to argue that it *always* does. Most people, however, would probably tend to agree that sometimes, in extreme cases, abuse of certain kinds does justify killing. In any case, you will need to make a list of the arguments both against abuse justifying killing and for abuse justifying killing, and in the latter case, you will certainly need to list the specific situations in which you feel that it does. Then you will need to examine these arguments to see how you feel about them.

### Step One: Make Notes and Compare Them with Others

On paper, write notes on the points in the three articles that you think are most important. Don't worry about being "wrong." It is perfectly natural for different persons to disagree to some extent on the importance of particular points; there isn't necessarily one right answer.

In class, work with two other students, comparing your notes on the most important points. Your teacher may ask you to compare notes on all three articles or on only one of them. If you find some disagreements, as you should, discuss them with each other. Try to see whether you can come to a consensus on which points are most important. If you can't entirely agree, don't worry about it.

Each group should now report to the teacher on the points the group considers most important so that the teacher can write them on the board for class discussion. Now the class as a whole can come to a consensus on the most important points from each article. Write these down since these notes will form the basis for your outlines.

*Step Two: Write an Outline and Compare It with Others*
Read the following guidelines on organizing "Does Abuse Ever Justify Murder?" Then write a rough list outline for your essay, and bring a copy of your outline to class for discussion of ways to organize.

## Organizing "Does Abuse Ever Justify Murder?"

As in the essays you have written so far, your introduction should briefly provide background information on the issue. You can state your opinion in a thesis in your introduction, or you can save it for your conclusion.

In college and the professional world, you will often be asked to discuss issues on which disagreement is possible. In these cases, teachers and supervisors do *not* expect or want you to oversimplify the issue, to argue or present only one side of it, leaving the other side out. They expect a complete discussion, one in which *all* points are presented—bad as well as good, negative as well as positive, opposing views as well as your own. This is a process that will be helped if you remember to use the words showing contrast and concession—*but, whereas, while, although,* and *even though.*

Accordingly, you should list all pairs of points you and your classmates have found—positive and negative ones—and make any other groupings of points that seems logical. Arrange all of these materials in the order you want to write about them and plan the organization of your essay point by point. Be sure that each of your body paragraphs will have a topic sentence.

Your conclusion is your chance to sum up your position on when abuse or provocation justifies murder.

*Step Three: Write a Rough Draft*
At home, using your outline as a basis, write a rough draft of your essay. Do not worry about spelling and mechanics as you try to get all of your information on paper in a logical order.

Look for places you can join ideas with contrast and concession words.

Now choose two or three quotations to use from the articles, ones that will support points you want to make or ones that express points you disagree with.

Check for places you can use appositives. Appositives are very useful for identifying authors:

Nancy Gibbs, *author of* " *'Til Death Do Us Part,"* wrote that some battered women don't leave their husbands because they are "afraid for their life."

Check also for places you can use verbal phrases. Verbal phrases can be used in sentences like this:

*Comparing battered women and betrayed men,* Stanton Peele, author of "Making Excuses," points out that both groups can leave their marriages.

Use the following Checklist for Evaluating Rough Drafts to see whether your essay meets the assignment's requirements, and use it in peer review.

Make two copies of your draft so that you have three copies to bring to class.

---

**CHECKLIST FOR EVALUATING ROUGH DRAFTS**

1. Does the introduction indicate what the essay will be about and why the subject is important?
2. Is the essay divided into body paragraphs that cover the main points involved in discussing this issue?
3. Does each body paragraph start with a topic sentence, a sentence that tells what the paragraph will discuss?
4. Are all the sentences in each paragraph related to the point expressed in the topic sentence? Are there any places where unrelated ideas seem to come into any body paragraphs?
5. Are all the most important points involved in the issue covered, or is anything missing?
6. Does the order of the points seem logical, or does anything seem out of place?
7. Does the essay have a conclusion explaining the writer's position on the issue?
8. Has the writer used two or three quotations from the articles?
9. Are there at least three sentences using the concession or contrast words?
10. Are there at least two sentences using verbal phrases?
11. Are there at least three sentences using appositives?

---

### Step Four: Peer Review

In class, in groups of three, exchange your rough drafts and take turns reading your own drafts aloud. Correct any mistakes you find as you read. Go over the Checklist for Evaluating Rough Drafts, and discuss with your partners the strengths and weaknesses you notice in the drafts. Call in your teacher if you need help or advice.

### Step Five: Write a Final Draft

At home, write the final version of your paper, using the advice you received during peer review to strengthen your essay. Print your essay, then check for the following:

> Have you used two or three quotations from the readings?
> Have you used contrast and concession words—*but, while, whereas, although, even though,* or *though*—to join sentences?
> Have you used appositives to identify or describe nouns?
> Have you used verbal phrases?

Finally, proofread your paper after reviewing the proofreading tips in Chapter 1 and the following Special Proofreading guidelines.

## Special Proofreading

- Proofread for subject-verb agreement and plural -*s* endings on nouns.
- In this assignment, you probably needed to discuss actions that took place in the past, so be sure to check for past-tense verbs and make sure they have -*ed* endings. Check also to make sure that verb forms following forms of *be, have, become,* and *get* have -*ed* endings.
- Check for possessive apostrophes. Watch out especially for places where you might use a possessive form of one of the authors' names, for example, Stanton Peele's article.
- If pronouns have been a problem for you, check to make sure you've used subject pronouns in front of your verbs and object pronouns after them. Check also to make sure that you've used *they* and *them* to refer to plural nouns.

### CASE STUDY THREE:
### THE "ZERO-TOLERANCE" ISSUE IN PUBLIC SCHOOLS

Read the following articles and the assignment and discussion sections following them. Then go back over the case, reading carefully and underlining or highlighting important points. Don't try to identify these points on your first reading.

### The "Zero-Tolerance" Issue in Public Schools

As you probably know, in 1999, two students at Columbine High School in Littleton, Colorado, a suburb of Denver, armed themselves with an array of weapons, made some bombs, and attacked the students and teachers in their school, killing 11 students and 1 teacher before they committed suicide. In other incidents within a few years of the Columbine one, a 16-year-old student in Mississippi killed his mother and shot 9 fellow students, killing 2 of them. In Arkansas, two high school students shot and killed 4 students and a teacher. In Oregon, a 5-year-old boy killed 4 and wounded 26. And in 2001, in California, a 15-year-old boy brought a gun to school and killed 2 teenagers and injured 13 others. Naturally, attacks like these have caused most schools to tighten security and try to identify potential problem students.

But even before any of these disasters, in 1994 Congress passed a bill entitled the Safe and Drug-Free School Act, which said that any student found with drugs or a weapon had to be expelled, or the school would lose its federal aid. As Debra Nussbaum has written in the *New York Times*, school policies "have now gone well beyond drugs and weapons, with many schools having adopted a comprehensive set of standards that apply even to dress and speech as well as personal conduct." Schools across the country have adopted what is often called a "zero-tolerance" policy for student behavior. This means, for instance, that even pushing and shoving may be considered a fight and result in expulsion, even possession of Tylenol or Advil may be considered possession of a drug and result in expulsion, even nail clippers or a pocketknife may be considered a weapon and result in expulsion for its owner.

As you can imagine, such policies have resulted in a lot more expulsions and suspensions than there used to be, but they seem also to have resulted in schools with fewer problems of violence, criminality, and sexual harassment than previously

Following are two newspaper articles about these issues.

#### SCHOOLS' NEW WATCHWORD: ZERO TOLERANCE
by Dirk Johnson

Just as two 16-year-old girls began quarreling over a magazine in the lunchroom at Curie High School here, an assistant principal stepped in to lay down the law. No punches had been thrown, no hair pulled. But the incident became a part of the girls' official record. They were "written up" for the [29]infraction, banished to a detention room for the rest of the day, and told that their parents would be notified. "You have disrupted the lunchroom," the assistant principal, Rochelle Wade, told the girls.

Their punishment reflects a widespread crackdown on misconduct in American schools. A zero-tolerance approach—much of it directed at behavior that administrators would once have dealt with solely by issuing a rebuke on the spot—has been brought on by school shootings from coast to coast and by officials' fear of bias lawsuits arising from policies that provide for [30]discretion in punishment and its severity.

While precise national figures on school punishment are sketchy, experts agree that as a result of the new approach, the country is witnessing a vast increase in detentions, suspensions, and even expulsions, in which the ousted offenders are typically made to attend alternative schools. In Chicago, the expulsion rate has jumped nearly tenfold in the last three years.

Beyond a crackdown on weapons and drugs—zero tolerance for which typically means automatic expulsion—the new school-conduct [31]ethos has profoundly changed views about what was once deemed usual, if annoying, behavior by adolescents. No longer is the playground scrap or the kickball tussle deemed a rite of passage best settled by a teacher who orders the combatants to their corners, hears out the two sides and demands apologies and a handshake.

Under the new get-tough policies, aggressive behavior like pushing, shoving, or general roughhousing is typically viewed as violence, and teachers are often forbidden to resolve any physical confrontation with a lecture. Instead, they must file a report with administrators, so that a uniform policy can run its course: Punishments for specific offenses are themselves very specific, and rare is the student who is granted leniency. A recent report by the Juvenile Justice and Delinquency Program of the U.S. Justice Department found that the vast majority of schools now had zero-tolerance policies, not only for crimes like gun possession but also for infractions like using tobacco. Proponents say a tough, uniform approach to even these lesser infractions is necessary to create an atmosphere of discipline in the schoolhouse. "The issues are different today," said Gerald Tirozzi, executive director of the National Association of Secondary School Principals. "Years ago we didn't have hundreds of knives and guns in schools."

Evidence in support of the proponents' argument comes from Baltimore, where a new policy requires that disruptive behavior bring suspension or expulsion, with assignment to an alternative school. Officials there say the hard-line approach has brought a 31 percent drop in criminal activity in the city's high schools.

Zero tolerance for weapons possession and other crime aside, some educators and psychologists maintain that rigid discipline sometimes treats youthful [(32)]rambunctiousness as [criminal behavior]. They condemn the absence of discretion in the disciplinary process. Gil Noam, a professor of education at Harvard University, has criticized what he calls a "heavily bureaucratized, cookbook approach" to resolving individual cases with blanket policies. "It's understandable where this is coming from," Professor Noam said of pressure that has been mounting on schools to stem violence, especially after the spate of school shootings over the last two years. "People are very concerned about safety. Parents demand these stricter codes. And it sells well." But the loss of discretion, and of on-the-spot resolution, can mean "a lost moment to teach children about respect," he said, and a missed chance to inspire their trust of authority figures.

In New York City, school safety officers have been under the supervision of the Police Department since last year, and now offenses on school premises there more frequently lead to arrests. That has raised the eyebrows of William C. Thompson Jr., president of the city's Board of Education, who said at a recent board meeting: "For the kind of thing like a fistfight on the school grounds, I don't understand why it would trigger an arrest. But there does appear to be an increase in arrests for things like fistfights. That's a concern."

In Chicago, the get-tough policy is largely the creation of Paul Vallas, the chief executive of the school system, who has won praise for improving test scores and bringing order to classrooms. Punishments range from detention to two-year expulsion, and the disciplinary code applies to students 24 hours a day, 7 days a week; if a student gets into trouble with the police on Saturday, the school will take action on Monday.

The zero-tolerance policies largely grew out of the Safe and Drug-Free School Act of 1994, which stipulates that schools must expel any student found with a weapon, or lose federal aid. Those policies have now gone well beyond drugs and weapons, with many schools having adopted a comprehensive set of standards that apply even to dress codes.

The policies' uniform approach, which mostly removes discretion, is intended to ensure fairness and protect schools from lawsuits maintaining that a student was treated with bias. Mr. Tirozzi, of the school principals' group, said the number of such suits had soared in recent years. "If you treat Johnny one way, and he's Black" Mr. Tirozzi said, "and you treat Joey another way, and he's white, you've got a problem."

The tougher approach has won praise from many experts on adolescence, who say youths must learn that unacceptable behavior means certain punishment. One school safety consultant, Charles Ewing, a professor of law and psychology at the State University of New York at Buffalo, urges educators to suspend any student who even threatens to engage in violence. "You must look at kids as potential violent actors," Professor Ewing said. "You must develop an absolute zero-tolerance policy. Unacceptable acts must be met swiftly and harshly. It's the only hope we have" of [33]subduing school violence. Another backer of the new approach is William Damon, director of the Center on Adolescence at Stanford University, who says students are hungering for the clarity of tough, consistent rules. "You need a consistent policy that is firm," he said, "and you need follow-through."

But Professor Noam, of Harvard, said schools bent on discipline should not forget about justice. Not every mistake, he said, must necessarily mean severe punishment. "Surely there are consequences for actions," he said. "But when a police officer stops someone for speeding, he doesn't write a ticket every time."

And some experts on child development say the new prevailing attitude tries to instill unnatural [34]docile behavior in normal, spirited adolescents. Michael Gurian, a family therapist who is author of *The Good Son* (Putnam, 1999), argues that rigid disciplinary policies have "essentially criminalized" the sort of aggressive behavior that is normal for young people, especially boys. "We have confused aggression and violence," Mr. Gurian said. "Every primate is aggressive. There is nothing wrong with being aggressive. There is something wrong with being violent."

Joan First, executive director of the National Coalition of Advocates for Students, a Boston-based group that focuses on children at risk of dropping out of school, said the new policies reflected a broader antiyouth sentiment [35]prevalent in America. She noted the practice of sending many juvenile criminal defendants to adult courts. "Raising a child is about patience," Ms. First said. "It seems to me that zero-tolerance policies are the ultimate impatience."

Further, Donald Moore, executive director of Designs for Change, a private group that studies education, said most expulsions had nothing to do with drugs or violence. Mr. Moore said some schools were dropping truants from the rolls, in part out of a desire to rid themselves of marginal students and so improve test-score averages. Some critics of the tougher policy, including Mr. Moore, say troubled students are simply being set adrift, destined to cause problems that will exact a much greater toll later. Precisely that view has been advanced by the Rev. Jesse Jackson in his protest over the expulsion of six students after a brawl among football spectators in Decatur, Illinois.

But, as Mr. Vallas points out, in Chicago (and many other districts) expelled students are quickly enrolled in alternative schools rather than being "expelled to the streets." For infractions that fall short of expulsion, the offenders are generally held in school and put through a rigorous academic and physical boot camp, where they are given plenty of book work and sometimes required to scrub floors, clean windows, and mow grass.

The Chicago school system makes the rules clear to parents and teachers. They are discussed at assemblies. They are posted on the walls of schools. They are printed inside notebooks given to students. Mr. Vallas says he gets few complaints. At Curie High School the other day, some students said they were grateful for the strict approach. "I feel safer at school than I do at home," said Chameka Cole, a 16-year-old junior. But Salvador Farias, a 17-year-old star football player who had missed a big game for his involvement in a graffiti prank, said the policies were written by people who had forgotten the ways of the young. "Isn't it natural to have fights in school?" he said. "I mean, I'm not saying it's right, but why is it so surprising that teenagers would act a certain way?"

## "ZERO TOLERANCE" IN SCHOOLS ADDS UP TO DEBATE
### by Jesse Katz

Mrs. Ellingsen, the French teacher, was Cosmo's favorite. "She was the funniest," the 13-year-old honors student said. "She was the nicest." On his A-average report card in December, she reciprocated. "A pleasure to have in class," she wrote.

Every Christmas, Cosmo gives his favorite teachers a present. He sits down with his parents and they decide on gifts tailored to the special tastes of each instructor. For his French teacher, Cosmo put a bottle of French wine in a box and wrapped it in elf-spotted paper. "She opened it up and said, 'Merci beaucoup'," the eighth-grader recalled. "I thought it was a great gift. I mean, she told us she had lived in France. I assumed she would at least drink a little wine."

When it comes to drugs and alcohol, however, the Cobb County School District in suburban Atlanta is guided by a policy of "zero toler-ance," not (36)"joie de vivre." As she is required, Betsey Ellingsen turned over the (37)contraband to the Griffin Middle School principal, Shirley Bachus. Bachus summoned the offender to her office. Cosmo Zinkow found himself in the deepest trouble of his young academic life, slapped with a two-week suspension. "Zero tolerance means zero tolerance," explained Jay Dillon, the district's director of communications. "In mat-ters of student safety, we can't take chances."

All across America, educators are embracing that absolutist philoso-phy—no slipups, no exceptions, no excuses. In a growing number of celebrated cases, no common sense also might be added to the litany. The rules are seductively simple. Every weapon is a weapon, whether it's an AK-47 or a Boy Scout camping knife. Every drug is a drug, whether it's a rock of cocaine or a Tylenol tablet. Every violation is met by a pre-determined punishment—ranging from suspension to expulsion—whether the violator's heart is malevolent or benign.

"Too much is at stake," said Gary Marx, spokesman for the Ameri-can Association of School Administrators, which represents about 15,000 superintendents and other top officials. "If the rules appear strict, well, that's just the price we pay for maintaining the sanctity of the learning environment." The impulse to stand firm, to reduce all choices to right or wrong, permeates more than just school campuses these days. Zero tolerance has become a mantra for the '90s—a call for order, for discipline, for a society that punishes bad behavior, instead of rewarding it with a movie deal.

As a rallying cry, this is a no-lose proposition; nobody, after all, wants to tolerate (38)repugnant or criminal conduct. But as a practical matter, zero tolerance sometimes means zero options, a one-size-fits-all punishment for offenses that are not always equally offensive. It is one thing to say that guns and drugs have no place in schools. It is quite another to use those rules against students like these, all suspended for violating zero-tolerance policies in recent years:

- A 13-year-old Oregon boy, for taking a swig of Scope after lunch.
- A 13-year-old Texas girl, for carrying a bottle of Advil, detected in her backpack by a drug-sniffing dog.
- A seventh-grader in West Virginia, for sharing a zinc cough lozenge with a friend.
- An eighth-grader in Pennsylvania, for trying to get laughs by sucking on an Alka-Seltzer tablet.
- A 17-year-old Georgia girl, for bringing an African tribal knife to her world history class.
- A 5-year-old Virginia boy, for taking his mother's beeper on a kindergarten trip to the pumpkin patch.
- An 11-year-old North Carolina boy, for passing around a home-grown chili pepper that caused another child's face to swell up.
- And another North Carolina boy, 6-year-old Jonathan Prevette, who made headlines for planting an unwelcome kiss on the cheek of a first-grade classmate.

"If this is how we treat our kids, we might as well be communists," said Gina Coslett, a social worker from Longmont, Colorado, a suburb of Denver. Last month, Coslett's 10-year-old daughter, Shanon, became the latest child to call the [39]righteousness of zero tolerance into question. An A-student at a rigorous charter academy that emphasizes "character education," Shanon was preparing her lunch one morning only to discover that she had forgotten to bring her lunch box home from school. So the fifth-grader threw her pasta salad and crackers into her mother's lunch box, a soft nylon pack with a mesh pocket under the top flap.

At lunchtime, Shanon opened it up and began to eat. Only after she was finished did she notice that the wooden handle of an old steak knife was sticking out of the pouch. "I eat a green apple every day," explained her mother, who uses the knife to slice the fruit. "Shanon didn't even recognize the knife. She didn't know that I carried one in my lunch box. She didn't have any idea where it came from." But Shanon did know what to do. She raised her hand, expressed her surprise to the cafeteria attendant and handed over the utensil.

"At a quarter to 3, they called me," Coslett said. "They said that Shanon had brought a deadly weapon to school and was being expelled. I could hear her crying in the background. It was just unimaginable to me. Then I realized it was my knife and I was so relieved. I was thinking, this is ridiculous, I'm going to fix this and it's going to be over tomorrow."

But Twin Peaks Charter Academy—a private school that opened last fall under the domain of the public St. Vrain Valley School District— really did mean to kick out Shanon. Under the Colorado Safe Schools Act of 1993, any student possessing a knife with a blade of three inches or longer must be expelled.

Shanon is back in class now, reinstated by the St. Vrain Valley School Board after missing two days.

"Zero tolerance is a simplistic political response to an incredibly complicated social issue," said Peter Blauvelt, president of the Maryland-based National Alliance for Safe Schools, a nonprofit consulting group run by former school security directors. "It sells well. But, God, we've already got rules upon rules upon rules. We're paying our educators to be decision-makers. Make the goddamn decisions that have to be made!"

Even when school districts try to be stern, things can still end up a mess. Consider the lessons of the Fairborn School District, near Dayton, Ohio, where two middle-school girls were busted in the fall of 1996 for sharing a packet of Midol, a nonprescription pain reliever that is usually taken to ease menstrual cramps. The 10-day suspensions imposed on Erica Taylor, 13, and Kimberly Smartt, 14, triggered a barrage of national publicity—much of which referred mockingly to the case as "MidolGate."

After nine days, the district agreed to reinstate Erica, who cooperated by attending a drug-and-alcohol counseling program. But when the superintendent decided to add an 80-day expulsion to Kimberly's sentence—because she had snatched the medicine from the school infirmary and offered it to Erica—her family hit the district with a federal lawsuit on the grounds of racial discrimination.

Kimberly is black, Erica is white, and the Smartt family argued that no other factor could adequately explain the [40]disparity in their punishments. A day after the suit was filed, the school board relented and let Kimberly back in class. She arrived in a limousine. Suddenly, the outrage shifted. "The girl is being treated like a hero for being a thief," the president of the Fairborn Education Association complained to the *Dayton Daily News.*

A U.S. District Court judge eventually dismissed Kimberly's claim of bias, ruling that a school's need to provide a safe environment outweighed a student's right to possess even a relatively harmless medication. But the question remained: Did the district overreact in the first place/? Or was it cowed at the end?

The answer, for many educators, is to err on the side of caution.

In addition to the information from the articles, you are also informed about what your own school experience was like and what the policies of your schools were. Make notes about the following questions so that you can use your answers in the paper you write:

Did any school you attended have a "zero-tolerance" policy?

If it did, did this policy result in students being expelled or suspended when you thought they should not have been?

Did it result in violent or difficult students being expelled or suspended? Everything considered, did it have a positive or negative effect on your school as a good place for learning?

If your school did not have a "zero-tolerance" policy, do you think it should have?

Give specific reasons why you think it should or shouldn't have.

## ASSIGNMENT

Write an essay in which you analyze the information and opinions in the articles, consider your own experiences in public high schools, and explain your views on zero-tolerance policies in schools.

## Discussion

As you read the articles written about zero-tolerance policies, you probably noticed that while school districts are justifiably concerned about the potential for serious acts of violence in public schools, some of the cases involving punishment for breaking rules seem extreme, even silly. Are cases such as these unavoidable in schools that have zero-tolerance policies? Or is there a way to write such policies so that cases like Shanon Coslett's do not occur? Can the problems addressed by these policies be handled in other ways? As you consider this issue, be sure to acknowledge its complexities.

### *Step One: Make Notes and Compare Them with Others*

After you have made lists of the positive and negative points of zero-tolerance policies, compare your notes in class with those of two other students and try to come to a consensus on what the most important points are. If you disagree, that's normal. The point is to listen to and consider other points of view.

Each group should report on the points the group members have listed so that the teacher can write them on the board for class discussion, and the class can try to come to a consensus on these points. Take notes on this discussion so that you won't forget any good ideas you hear from your classmates.

### *Step Two: Make an Outline and Compare It with Others*

Read the following guidelines on organizing "The 'Zero-Tolerance' Issue in Public Schools." Then go over your notes and decide how you might organize them into an essay. Make a rough list outline and bring it to class for discussion of ways to organize the essay.

## Organizing "The 'Zero-Tolerance' Issue in Public Schools"

As you did in previous papers, you will want to introduce the issue to your reader in your introduction. You can state your opinion in a thesis in your introduction, or you can save it for your conclusion.

In college and the professional world, you will often be asked to discuss issues on which disagreement is possible. In these cases, teachers and supervisors do not expect or want you to oversimplify the issue, to argue or present only one side of it, leaving the other side out. They expect a complete discussion, one in which all points are presented—bad as well as good, negative as well as positive, opposing views as well as your own. This process can be helped if you remember to use the words showing contrast and concession—*but, whereas, while, although,* and *even though.*

Accordingly, you should list all pairs of points you and your classmates have found—positive and negative ones—and make any other groupings of points that seems logical. Arrange all of these materials in the order you want to write about them, and in the body of your essay, address each set of matching opposing points. Be sure to write a topic sentence so that the point of each body paragraph is clear.

In your conclusion, you can explain your position on zero-tolerance policies, making clear which arguments you found to be the most convincing.

*Step Three: Write a Rough Draft*

At home, using your outline as a basis, write a rough draft of your essay. Do not worry about spelling and mechanics as you try to get all of your information on paper in a logical order.

Choose two or three quotations to use from the readings, ones that will support points you want to make, or ones that express points you disagree with.

Look for places to use contrast and concession words to join logically related ideas.

Look for ideas you can join using contrast and concessive words *but*, *while*, *whereas*, *even though*, *though*, and *although*. Be sure to acknowledge, and at the same time, de-emphasize points you do not agree with by placing concessive subordinators *although*, *even though*, or *though* in front of them.

Look for places to use *appositives* or verbal phrases.

Appositives can come in handy in identifying authors:

According to Joan First, *executive director of the National Coalition of Advocates for Students,* "Raising a child is about patience. It seems to me that zero-tolerance policies are the ultimate impatience."

Verbal phrases can be used in sentences like this:

*Arguing for zero-tolerance policies,* Charles Ewing says, "You must look at kids as potential violent actors."

Use the following Checklist for Evaluating Rough Drafts to see whether your draft meets the assignment requirements, and use it during peer review.

Make two copies of your draft so that you have three copies to bring to class.

---

### CHECKLIST FOR EVALUATING ROUGH DRAFTS

1. Does the introduction indicate what the essay will be about and why the subject is important?
2. Is the essay divided into body paragraphs that cover the main points involved in discussing this issue?
3. Does each body paragraph start with a topic sentence, a sentence that tells what the paragraph will discuss?
4. Are all of the sentences in each body paragraph related to the point expressed in the topic sentence? Are there any places where unrelated ideas seem to come into any body paragraphs?

5. Are all of the most important points involved in the issue covered, or is anything missing?
6. Does the order of the points seem logical, or does anything seem out of place?
7. Does the essay have a conclusion explaining the writer's position on the issue?
8. Are there at least three sentences using the concession or contrast words?
9. Has the writer used two or three quotations from the articles?
10. Are there at least two sentences using appositives?
11. Are there at least three sentences using verbal phrases?

### Step Four: Peer Review

In class, in groups of three, exchange your rough drafts and take turns reading your own drafts aloud. Correct any mistakes you find as you read. Refer to the Checklist for Evaluating Rough Drafts as you evaluate each rough draft and discuss the strengths and weaknesses you notice.

### Step Five: Write a Final Draft

At home, write the final version of your paper, using the advice you received during peer review to strengthen your essay. Then check for the following:

Have you used two or three quotations from the readings?
Have you used contrast and concession words—*but, while, whereas, although, even though,* or *though*—to join logically related ideas?
Have you used appositives to identify or describe nouns?
Have you used verbal phrases?

Then after reviewing the proofreading tips in Chapter 1 and the following Special Proofreading guidelines, proofread a printed copy of your paper.

### Special Proofreading

- Proofread for subject-verb agreement and plural *-s* endings on nouns.
- In this assignment, you probably needed to discuss actions that took place in the past, so be sure to check for past-tense verbs and make sure they have *-ed* endings. Check also for *-ed* ending verb forms after the verbs *be, have, become,* and *get.*

- Check for possessive apostrophes. Watch out especially for places where you might mention Chicago's zero-tolerance policy or use a possessive form of one of the authors' names, for example, Dirk Johnson's article.
- If pronouns have been a problem for you, check to make sure you've used subject pronouns in front of verbs and object pronouns after them. Also check to make sure that you have used *they* and *them* to refer to plural nouns.

## Getting Your Writing Right

### Using Quotations

Sometimes when we are making a point, or opposing a point we disagree with, we need to quote from the original source. A quotation from another writer can help us back up our own position or even express it. The most common way of quoting is to introduce the quotation with words like "she said," or "he wrote," putting a comma after the introductory phrase and capitalizing the first word in the quotation. A quotation introduced in this way must be a complete sentence.

> Ulysses Torassa writes, "The television and film industry has consistently fought government attempts to control the content of programming."

You can do also introduce a quotation with *according to:*

> According to Thomas Robinson, "When kids reduced their exposure to videotapes, TV, and video games, they became less aggressive.

You can also incorporate the quotation right into your own sentence. In this case, you don't use a comma in front of the quotation—you use the word *that* instead—and you don't capitalize the first word:

> L. Rowell Huesmann claimed that "boys at age 8 who had been watching more television violence than other boys grew up to be more aggressive than other boys."

You can put phrases written by someone else into your own sentences, but you must tell who wrote them and they must be grammatical in your sentence just as though you wrote them yourself:

I agree with James Spencer because I see both "comic and serious" violence on TV.

*A Final Note:* The first time you give the name of an author you are referring to or quoting, you should use the author's whole name, as it appears on the article. After that, use the author's *last* name only.

## Using Verbal Phrases

Look at the following short passages about a writing assignment in Chapter 6:

Lincoln's feelings about African-Americans changed drastically during the course of the Civil War. He had at first known only uneducated slaves. He thought of Blacks as being essentially inferior to whites. He saw them only in subordinate positions. He thought they would make inferior soldiers. But he met Black men like Frederick Douglass, who were his intellectual equal. He realized that he had been wrong about the mental capacity of African-Americans. He saw the bravery of Black soldiers in battle. He realized that African-Americans deserved the same rights as all American citizens.

Lincoln's feelings about African-Americans changed drastically during the course of the Civil War. Having at first known only uneducated slaves, he thought of Blacks as being mentally inferior to whites. Seeing them only in subordinate positions, he thought they would make inferior soldiers. But after meeting Black men like Frederick Douglass who were his intellectual equal, he realized that he had been wrong about the mental capacity of African-Americans, and after seeing the bravery of Black soldiers in battle, he realized that African-Americans deserved the same rights as all American citizens.

Which passage reads better?

## Exercise 7A

Compare the above two passages. It is clear that the sentences in the second one are longer than the sentences in the first one. What makes them longer? Underline the parts of sentences in the second passage that are whole sentences in the first passage.

What do your underlined sentence parts have in common? That is, what is the same in all of them?

You know that there are words called verbs. There are also words called *verbals*. The verbals we are going to look at now all have one characteristic: They end in *-ing*. Every English verb has an *-ing* form, and in every case, it is the base form of the verb with *-ing* added, like these:

run     running
ask     asking
be      being

While we use these verbals in lots of ways, particularly as parts of regular verbs ("She *was running* the company very efficiently"), we are going to examine them now as ways of joining ideas, like the coordinators and subordinators. For instance, here is an idea broken up into two sentences. Since it is only one idea, it should be only one sentence:

Lincoln had seen Blacks only in subordinate positions.
He thought they would make poor soldiers.

We could join these two sentences with a *coordinator:*

Lincoln had seen Blacks only in subordinate positions, *so* he thought they would make poor soldiers.

Or we could join them with a *subordinator:*

*Because* Lincoln had seen Blacks only in subordinate positions, he thought they would make poor soldiers.

Or we could join them with a *verbal:*

*Having seen Blacks only in subordinate positions,* Lincoln thought they would make poor soldiers.

While all three ways of joining these sentences are good, and in your writing you should use them all, they really represent three stages of writing development. The original version, with two separate sentences, and the version joined with a coordinator are the kind of writing young children typically do. They write a lot of very short sentences and use a lot of coordinators.

The second version with the subordinator *because* is typical of writing at the high-school level of development. By that time, children have matured somewhat and are using a lot more subordinators than grade-school kids.

At the highest level of development, writers still use coordinators and subordinators and still write short sentences sometimes, but they tend much more frequently to use phrases to join and expand on their ideas, with appositives, for example. Verbal phrases are another kind they often use.

### Constructing Verbals

Verbal phrases are easy to create. For example:

> She wrote the report.
> *Writing* the report
> He took a new approach to the problem.
> *Taking* a new approach to the problem

All you have to do is drop the subject and change the verb into its *-ing* form. Presto! A verbal phrase.

### Using Verbal Phrases in Sentences

So once you've got a verbal phrase, what do you do with it? As in the Lincoln passage above, we attach them to sentences, sometimes at the beginning of the sentence, sometimes at the end:

> *Writing the report herself,* she impressed her boss enormously.
> *Taking a new approach to the problem,* he saw that we had been wasting our resources.
> Lincoln eventually changed his mind about slavery, *deciding that it should be made an issue in the Civil War.*

Sometimes, as in the first two examples, the verbal phrase gives background information to what's in the main part of the sentence. Sometimes, as in the last example, the verbal phrase develops or expands on what is in the main part of the sentence.

> *Important Point:* Notice that the subject of these sentences tells who is doing the action of the verbal. This is a basic rule for using verbal phrases.

### Exercise 7B

Rewrite the following sets of sentences to create verbal phrases. Change the underlined verb in one of the sentences into a verbal. If the sentence with the underlined verb comes first, it should become a verbal phrase beginning your combined sentence. If the sentence with the underlined verb comes second, it should become a verbal phrase at the end of your new sentence.

EXAMPLES: a. Joan <u>made</u> her decision.
   She acted quickly.
   <u>Making</u> her decision, Joan acted quickly.

b. Alisha took a major step.
   She <u>applied</u> for the job.
   Alisha took a major step, <u>applying</u> for the job.

1. Carlos <u>realized</u> that student government was sandbox stuff.
   He decided to change all that.

   _____

2. He decided to run for president.
   He <u>thought</u> he would bring some new ideas to the school.

   _____

3. He <u>hoped</u> to get elected and maybe to date her as well.
   He got Brenda Lu, the most popular girl in school, to be his running
      mate.

   _____

4. Carlos and Brenda <u>got</u> all their friends to help them.
   They ran an effective campaign.

   _____

5. They <u>expected</u> to make a number of meaningful changes in the school.
   They started a school newspaper with real news.
   They tried to set up internships with local businesses.
   They encouraged cooperation instead of conflict among the racial
      groups on campus.

   _____

6. The students <u>realized</u> Carlos and Brenda were serious.
   They elected them easily.

   _____

7. The newspaper <u>published</u> an article on pregnancies in the school.
   The newspaper got censored by the principal and superintendent.

   _____

8. Carlos and Brenda <u>tried</u> to set up their first internships.
   They were told the program would have to buy insurance.

   _____

9. They <u>worked</u> for greater interracial cooperation.
   They were thwarted by ethnic clubs whose identity was threatened.

   _____

10. Carlos and Brenda <u>turned</u> student government over to the cheerlead-
    ers' club.
    They resigned and started studying seriously for college.

    _____

## Using Verbals with Subordinators

Writers often start verbal phrases with subordinators. It's the same as changing sentences into verbal phrases:

> While they were running for office
> While running for office
> After they got elected
> After getting elected
> When they tried to make changes
> When trying to make changes

Notice that in all three cases, the subject is dropped completely and the verb is
changed into a verbal.

## Exercise 7C

Rewrite the following sentences or groups of sentences to make verbal
phrases. The underlined verb should become the verbal. Note that you should
use subordinators that show time before some of the verbal phrases.

> EXAMPLE: After they <u>decided</u> to become movie stars, many students
> signed up for a drama class.
> After *deciding* to become movie starts, many students signed
> up for a drama class.

1. When they <u>were planning</u> to put on a play, the drama class ran into
   the usual unexpected problems.

   _____

2.  Everyone wanted the leading roles. They secretly <u>felt</u> that this could be the first step in a Hollywood career.

_____

3.  After the teacher <u>held</u> extensive auditions, she threatened to quit teaching.

_____

4.  After they were rejected for starring roles, eight of the students threatened to quit school. [Change <u>were</u> to <u>being</u>.]

_____

5.  The new leading actor became extremely obnoxious. He <u>strutted</u> around the place and <u>bragged</u> about how talented he was.

_____

6.  The new leading actress became extremely obnoxious. She <u>insisted</u> that she had to have a private dressing room and <u>demanded</u> that she make her own costume selections.

_____

7.  While she <u>tried</u> to get decent work out of these divas, the teacher started to lose her hair.

_____

8.  Although they <u>worked</u> hard, the set designers, Susan and Keith, caused another problem.

_____

9.  They were sent to the principal's office after they <u>spilled</u> liquid nitrogen all over the stage.

_____

10.  When you <u>put</u> on a play, try to avoid having any people in it.

_____

## Exercise 7D

To do the following exercise, you will need to refer to the description of Luis Cardenas's problem in Chapter 3.

1.  The first paragraph explains how Luis got interested in teaching and how he lost interest in law and business.

    a.  Write a sentence using a verbal phrase to give the background reason for his deciding he wanted to teach.

    _____

b.   Write a sentence using a verbal phrase to give the background reason for his deciding he didn't want to work in either law or business or both.

2.   The second paragraph explains how dedicated the teachers were and how disillusioned they were with their jobs.

a.   Write a sentence that begins with the words "Mrs. Galbraith and the other teachers were disillusioned with their jobs" and develop it using two verbal phrases that explain why they were disillusioned.

b.   Find a sentence in this paragraph that begins with *while* and rewrite it, changing the *while* clause into a verbal phrase.

3.   The third paragraph explains Luis's current dilemma.

a.   There is a sentence in this paragraph that begins "He finds that mildly amusing . . . " Rewrite this sentence so that the rest of it following those words is a verbal phrase.

b.   Use one or more introductory verbal phrases to write a sentence telling why Sunset Bank chose Luis for the job.

## Summary and Review of Chapter 7

### Quotations

The most common way of introducing quotations is with a subject, a verb, and a comma. The first word of the quotation is then capitalized.

Hickey said, "Now we are in for it."
Jackson writes, "Now you are in for it."

One can also incorporate the quotation into one's own sentence by using the word *that* instead of the comma; in this case, the first word in the quotation is not capitalized.

Hickey said that "we are in for it."
Jackson writes that "we had better change."

Another way of introducing quotations is to use the words *according to:*

According to Jackson, "There is little likelihood that we will change."

When you refer to or quote an author the first time, use the author's full name. In subsequent references, use only the author's last name.

## Book and Article Titles

Book, newspaper, and movie titles are underlined or italicized in typed papers. Article titles are put in quotation marks. In titles of all published works, all the main words are capitalized.

## Verbal Phrases

We can make either sentences or subordinate clauses into verbal phrases by deleting their subjects and changing their verbs into *-ing* verbals.

Clarisha bought her textbooks on time.
*Buying* her textbooks on time

After Clarisha bought her textbooks on time
*After* buying her textbooks on time

These phrases must be attached to complete sentences that have the same subject as the verbal.

*Buying* her textbooks on time, *Clarisha* was ready for her first classes.
After *buying* her textbooks on time, *Clarisha* was ready for her first classes.

Verbal phrases come at the beginnings of sentences when they give background information for the main part of the sentence:

After volunteering in his little brother's classroom, Henry decided to make teaching his career.

They come at the ends of sentences when they develop the idea in the main part of the sentence:

The new leading actress became extremely obnoxious, insisting that she had to have a private dressing room and demanding that she make her own costume selections.

## Chapter 7: Glossary

| | | |
|---|---|---|
| 1. | **irrefutably** | without a doubt |
| 2. | **cumulative** | accumulating over time |
| 3. | **simulate** | imitate |
| 4. | **epidemiology** | study of epidemics |
| 5. | **longitudinal studies** | research studying subjects over time |
| 6. | **bristled** | became irritated |
| 7. | **pervasive** | far reaching |
| 8. | **repertoire** | range, collection |
| 9. | **anecdotal reports** | stories |
| 10. | **legal recourse** | legal help, lawful solutions |
| 11. | **catch-22** | a problematic situation in which a solution causes another problem; from Joseph Heller's novel *Catch-22*, published in 1955 |
| 12. | **syndrome** | pattern of characteristics or behavior |
| 13. | **preemptive strike** | self-protective action taken before someone attacks |
| 14. | **imminent** | about to happen |
| 15. | **catalyst** | stimulus, cause |
| 16. | **abhors** | hates |
| 17. | **extricating** | removing |
| 18. | **maim** | physically injure |
| 19. | **perpetrator** | person committing an offense |
| 20. | **corporal** | physical |
| 21. | **impunity** | immunity from punishment |
| 22. | **dossiers** | files of documents about a subject |
| 23. | **interim** | meantime |
| 24. | **contrite** | sorry, remorseful |
| 25. | **in flagrante delicto** | in the act |
| 26. | **retrograde** | backward |
| 27. | **mitigating** | diminishing, making more tolerable |
| 28. | **egregious** | extremely bad |
| 29. | **infraction** | offense, crime |

30. **discretion**          freedom to make sensible judgments
31. **ethos**               set of values
32. **rambunctiousness**    boisterousness
33. **subduing**            controlling, overcoming
34. **docile**              obedient, submissive
35. **prevalent**           widespread
36. **joie de vivre**       joy in life
37. **contraband**          illegal substances
38. **repugnant**           offensive
39. **righteousness**       morality
40. **disparity**           difference, inequality

# EIGHT

# Designing a Research Project

## CASE STUDY: THE BEAUTY MYSTIQUE

Many writers have argued that the values women are taught in our society are the wrong ones. They feel that the message little girls receive from toys, children's television shows, and advertisements is that their main purpose in life is to be sweet and pretty.

A number of writers, including Professor Marcia Guttentag, director of the Harvard Project on Women and Mental Health, have identified women's magazines as one of the main villains in telling grown women that the way they look is the key to their success or failure in life. Guttentag conducted a study in which she identified women's magazines as being a chief source of an "epidemic" of depression among women. The problem, she believed, is that these magazines uphold an impossible ideal of beauty, one that very few women can attain. At the same time, two diseases associated with eating are common among women and almost nonexistent among men—bulimia and anorexia. The bulimic woman eats and then throws up, while the anorexic becomes fixated on slimness to the extent that she will actually starve herself to death.

Following are two articles about the beauty problem. Read them and the assignment following them, and then go back over the articles with a pen or highlighter, underlining or highlighting the most important information. Don't try to identify this information on your first reading.

### FEELING PRESSURE TO BE PRETTY
by Maureen Downey

The little girl's question usually takes her parents by surprise: "Am I pretty?" Whether reared in overalls or [(1)]organza, girls somehow pick up the message that being pretty is crucial. That's not surprising in a culture that annually spends $20 billion on cosmetics and $300 million on plastic surgery.

What is surprising is the [(2)]complicity of some parents in reinforcing the message, [(3)]albeit unintentionally. Almost from birth, parents fiddle with their daughters' appearance, adding bows to bald heads and piercing tiny ears.

Even if parents downplay beauty, the wider society and media exert tremendous influence. "I came from a feminist, supportive family and I became anorexic at 12," says Naomi Wolf of New York, author of *The Beauty Myth.*

### Pressure at a Tender Age

Although no one would deny that appearance is important for boys, social scientists say penalties for girls who fail to meet the culture's narrow standards of female beauty are far more severe. And the pressure to meet the standards begins far earlier. In a 1989 survey, 81 percent of 10-year-old girls said they had already dieted. As early as fourth grade, a girl's self-esteem relates strongly to how she feels about her body, says Judith Rodin, founder of the Yale University Eating Disorders Clinic. That is not true for boys of the same age. The closer a girl comes to the cultural ideal of thinness, Rodin says, the more likely she is to report feeling attractive, popular and successful academically. New research increasingly links depression in teenage girls with negative feelings about their weight. "Girls learn very early that their bodies and appearances are fair game for public [(4)]scrutiny," says Rodin, author of *Body Traps.* That scrutiny often is well intentioned, but it has consequences.

## Clothes Count

"A little girl who comes to the center in an adorable outfit gets so much verbal attention from other parents, from teachers," says Cheryl Smith, director of the Downtown Child Development Center in Atlanta. "That's a powerful message because it tells the child that it's the external that gets the attention." And the message is not lost on other children. Compliment one child and you will be [5]engulfed by five others showing off their new shoes, Smith says.

"You don't need a social scientist to explain why a girl dressed in bows, ribbons, and bonnets at birth and leopard-skin stretch pants at four is going to become obsessed with her appearance and might even develop an eating disorder," says David Laskin of New York, father of three daughters and coauthor of a new child-rearing guide called *The Little Girl Book*. In the back of most parents' minds, Laskin says, is the concern: What if my daughter's not attractive? That concern is not without basis. Even as early as preschool, attractive children are more popular, Rodin says.

New research suggests that many people who are teased in childhood about their appearance carry that negative body image into adulthood. J. Kevin Thompson, of the University of South Florida in Tampa, found that long-lasting effects such as eating disorders are most common among people who were teased about their appearance from ages 8 to 16.

The alternative to this obsession with appearance isn't purging a child's closet of all the frilly rompers and matching hair ribbons, says Marcia Sheinberg, senior faculty and family therapist at New York's Ackerman Institute for Family Therapy. "It is not bad in any way to dress girls up," Sheinberg says. "It becomes a problem when it is overly emphasized." The problem is that parents underestimate the degree to which they spotlight their daughters' looks.

Admitting to "oohing and ahhing" when her own little granddaughter twirls in a skirt, Georgia State University sociologist Jackie Boles says gender biases are so [6]ingrained that only a conscious effort can counter them. Even parents intent on making that effort get caught up in fussing over their little girls, says Laskin. "Many parents find themselves pulling out their hair at 8 in the morning when their 2-year-old refuses to wear anything but her white satin party dress and patent leather shoes," he says. "They forget that they were the ones who applauded every ruffle during infancy."

While the assumption is that mothers dictate their children's clothing choices, Laskin says fathers play a role. "It is very important to traditional fathers that their daughters look feminine, and they tend to be more reinforcing and more rigid in their insistence on feminine attire," he said. "I talked to one dad who bought his five-year-old her first bikini."

While parents may find it cute to deck out little girls in bikinis and other sexy clothes, child development specialists advise dressing children like children. "There is no reason on earth why a young girl should be dressed in a sexualized way," says Evan Imber-Black, director of family and group studies in the psychiatry department of Albert Einstein College of Medicine in the Bronx, N.Y. "Childhood is not supposed to be turning yourself into a little adult," Imber-Black says. "It is supposed to be about developing competencies and confidence."

## PRETEENS PARADING IN PAGEANTS
### by Gillian Judkins

Long, flowing blond hair, cascading down onto a petite body, covered in a shiny sequined dress, she turns to the left, pivots to the right and walks a little further striking her pose. Her shoulders are pushed back, her head held high with her glossy lips parted in a small smile. Her eyelashes flutter, thick with mascara. She is the [7]epitome of the male sexual fantasy—[but] she is only five years old. This describes a typical scene at a beauty pageant for young girls: parading up and down, hoping to be crowned the winner. But just how healthy is this kind of competition for a young girl's development? And what does it do to her body image?

Coordinator of Western's Women's Issues Network, Kelly Guitard feels these competitions are not at all healthy for young girls. "I think stressing competition can be damaging itself but especially dangerous when you're placing emphasis on physical appearance," she says. "All children should be valued for their individual beauty, for themselves." In a similar frame of mind is Sandra Aylward, sociologist and coordinator of the women's studies program at King's College. Aylward also points out that beauty pageants bring up issues of "racism, classism and sexism. If they don't have the money, if they have a disability or they are seen as ugly, they can't get in [to the competition]. Beauty is considered good and not fitting [society's standards] of beauty is seen as bad."

Aylward and Guitard make valid points, [but] not surprisingly, individuals involved in the modeling industry do not share the same sentiments. "I think it depends more on the individual than anything," explains Doug Carey, promotions director for Barbizon Academy of Modelling. "A lot of what pageants look at is the individual person and not strictly looks." Former Miss Canada (1974) Blair Lancaster, owner of Modelling and Fashion Agency, explains, "Whether it's pageants, hockey, baton twirling, or skating, it depends on the pressure and expectations we [as adults] put on them. Pageants can do a lot of positive things but can also do negative things if not handled properly."

Regardless of how parents may handle the pageant scene, young girls are still paraded in front of judges who will then assess them on their physical attributes, [such] things as their walk, posture, and the image they portray. What might this scrutiny do to their perception of body image? Lisa Rozak, coordinator of Western's Body Image Team, expresses extreme concern. The team's main goal is "to get people to think about body image in a positive light." The team has been busy this year visiting various residences and affiliates and speaking about body image and related health issues. Rozak expressed further [(8)]dismay once she realized that pageant contestants can be as young as three years of age. She agreed that this can definitely teach youngsters to place emphasis on their body over personality or intellect. Rozak points out [that] more and more research shows that "girls as young as five years of age are restricting their food intake. Beauty pageants just [(9)]perpetuate that kind of thinking."

Both Rozak and Guitard seem to agree that pageants will reinforce the myth that girls are to be pretty and thin and should grow into beautiful women. "[Beauty pageants] set limits for what's acceptable as beautiful and only certain people can fit into this category," Guitard explains. Lancaster disagrees, saying it would depend more on the values that parents teach their children. "My feeling is that beauty has nothing to do with body shape. It has to do with personality, frame of mind—it really has to come from inside." She also points out that parents should give their children the praise they deserve in all areas of life. "It's important that we direct our comments to our children in the right way."

The fact still remains that an average-sized woman or a slightly overweight one rarely appears on the cover of *Cosmopolitan* or *Vogue*. Due to the [(10)]stringent standards of what the media consider beautiful, those that are within that majority feel they are overweight or unattractive.

Almost any woman asked will likely [name] a part of [her] body that [she does] not like. Society continues to show young women it is all right to put value on their bodies by encouraging young girls to enter competitions where they are judged on physical attributes. "All I can see is that they're given a message that their body is for sale. It's an object separate from their personality," Aylward says. Lancaster, feels, on the other hand, that there is nothing wrong with teaching young children to carry themselves properly and allowing them to enter pageants. She does however, make the point that children should compete as children and that "taking a four-year-old and making her look like she is 21 is wrong."

So the question then becomes, just how much should parents encourage their children to enter beauty pageants? Many people will argue that spending hundreds and thousands of dollars on pageants is no different than spending that money on hockey or any other sport. But the difference between the two is that with sports, children are not using their body as the object by which they are solely judged—young girls aren't being sexualized into beautiful little women. . . .

And so she continues to walk, to turn, to pose and smile, eager to please the eyes of the judges. Due to her innocence, she is unaware that one day she may no longer fit their "standard" norm of beauty. As onlookers, contributors, parents, and concerned friends, [we] can only hope that she will escape without causing her body harm.

## ASSIGNMENT

Your job in this writing assignment is to conduct a research study on the subject of whether women are taught to pay too much attention to their appearance. There are three primary sources of information easily available to you.

One source is children's television shows. You can tell much about the messages our society is sending little girls by looking at these shows, and especially the advertisements accompanying them. What are girls being taught to want and to be like in these shows and ads?

A second source of information is women's magazines. Every supermarket checkout stand is surrounded by issues of the latest women's magazines, and these magazines sell at rates that far surpass the most popular men's magazines. Millions and millions of women buy and read them. What are the articles and the advertisements in these magazines telling women about themselves?

Finally, still another source of information about what women are being taught is women themselves. You can question women you know (and ask yourself, if you are a woman) about what they were taught by their parents, relatives, and friends about the importance of appearance, and how that compares with what boys are taught.

This research project could take a whole team of researchers years to undertake and could result in a book, and you obviously don't have time for all that. So you, your classmates, and your instructor should decide how to handle this project—what sources to use, whom to assign them to, and how to handle the writing up of the project at the end.

Accordingly, this writing assignment doesn't consist of a series of sub-assignments, as did the others you have done. Your teacher and your class will have to decide what steps to follow. You should, by this time, be well prepared to make this decision. As part of the process of deciding how to lay out the work of this assignment, the class should also decide on a Checklist for Evaluating Rough Drafts. Using the previous checklists as a guide, the class should construct its own checklist.

Finally, the class should establish a proofreading guide for the assignment. This is your opportunity to put to practical use everything you have learned this semester.

Good luck.

## Chapter 8: Glossary

1. **organza**        a dress fabric
2. **complicity**     involvement, agreement
3. **albeit**         although
4. **scrutiny**       close examination
5. **engulfed**       surrounded
6. **ingrained**      deep rooted
7. **epitome**        height, ideal
8. **dismay**         discouragement
9. **perpetuate**     cause to continue
10. **stringent**     rigid

# Workbook

## Using *A* and *An*

Normally, in writing we use *an* in front of words that begin with these letters:

a   an apple
e   an eagle
i   an incident
o   an olive
u   an upset

There is one major exception to this rule: Sometimes we pronounce words beginning with the letter *u* as though the letter *u* were actually a *y*, as in *university* or *used car*. In those cases, we use *a* in front of the *u* word. Otherwise, we use *an*.

EXAMPLES: a university    an umpire
          a used car     an ugly duckling

We use *a* in front of words that begin with all the other letters. (There are just a few exceptions: we pronounce the words *honest, honor,* and *honorable,* as though the *h* were silent, and the words began with *o*. So we use *an* in front of these words, as in *an honest man.)* Because we use *a* so much more than *an*, many people use it all the time in speech, and that's all right; but in writing it's incorrect, and most people consider it a glaring error.

## Exercise

In the following sentences, write in the correct word, *a* or *an*:

1. Mary decided to buy _____ automobile.
2. She couldn't make up her mind whether to buy _____ new one or _____ used one.
3. There was _____ old Ford that she kind of liked, but she was also looking at _____ interesting Dodge pickup.
4. _____ good friend suggested that she look for _____ ad in the newspaper for _____ car in her price range.
5. _____ interesting looking ad caught her eye, and she made _____ call to the number listed.
6. The car turned out to be _____ essentially worthless piece of junk, but it had _____ owner who was young and good looking.
7. Mary decided that _____ intelligent good-looking owner was _____ better deal than _____ old junky car, so she made _____ a date with the guy and forgot about getting _____ car.

## Using Contractions of Forms of the Verb *Be*

In some versions of speech, we can drop forms of the verb *be* in certain cases. (The verb *be*'s most common forms are *am, is, are, was,* and *were*.) For example, we can say either of the following:

| | | |
|---|---|---|
| I am going. | I'm going. | I going. |
| She is going. | She's going. | She going. |
| He is up there. | He's up there. | He up there. |
| They are awake. | They're awake. | They awake. |

Unfortunately, in writing, as opposed to speech, only the first two lists of these forms are correct; the third one, in which the verb *be* (*is, are*) is dropped entirely, is incorrect.

### Exercise

In the following exercise, write *both* correct forms of the subject and verb in the blanks.

> EXAMPLE: Today, (Leroy) *Leroy is / Leroy's* taking a bus to school.

1. (Ricky) _____ /_____ thinking about his future again.
2. (He) _____ /_____ considering either becoming a doctor or opening a nightclub.
3. He feels that both these occupations pay well, and now (he) _____/ _____ wondering which one he should get into.
4. His girlfriend thinks (he) _____ /_____ crazy.
5. She takes him seriously when he talks this way, and now (they) _____/ _____arguing about their future together.
6. In the meantime, (Ricky) _____ /_____ applying to several premed programs.
7. And as a backup, (he) _____ /_____ signing up his friends as performers in his nightclub.
8. (They) _____ /_____ quite excited at the idea of performing in a nightclub.
9. (Ricky) _____ /_____ very calm and business-like about all this.
10. And now (his girlfriend) _____ /_____ hoping she can be the lead singer in the band.

## Using Possessive Pronouns

In addition to having subject and object pronouns, English also has possessive pronouns:

| subject | object | possessive |
|---------|--------|------------|
| I | me | my |
| you | you | your |
| he | him | his |
| she | her | her |
| it | it | its |
| we | us | our |
| they | them | their |

The possessive pronouns take the place of regular noun possessives:

| | | |
|---|---|---|
| Jamal's car | = | *his* car |
| Maria's bank | = | *her* bank |
| the dog's bed | = | *its* bed |
| Jamal and Maria's relationship | = | *their* relationship |

### Exercise

Write the correct possessive pronoun in the blanks in the following sentences.

EXAMPLE: Rondelle got *her* cat from the local animal shelter.

1. Rondelle loved _____ cat.
2. Glenn, her boyfriend, hated _____ cat.
3. He didn't like cat hair on _____ pants.
4. He didn't like scratches on _____ hands.
5. The cat didn't like Glenn on _____ favorite chair.
6. The couple obviously had _____ differences about this subject.
7. They began to feel that _____ opinions on the cat were irreconcilable.
8. The cat also had _____ opinions on Rondelle and Glenn.
9. It liked to take _____ naps on Glenn's lap and leave _____ hair on _____ pants.
10. So Rondelle gave Glenn _____ cat as a present, and he left the country.

## Forming Direct Questions Beginning with *Who, What, Why, Where, When,* and *How*

In written English, unlike some forms of speech, questions beginning with the *Wh* words (see above) plus *How* have to be written in a special way. The normal word order of subject first and verb second has to be changed. How this is done depends in part on the verb being used, and in part on the tense of the verb.

### Questions with the Verb *Be*

In these questions, the *Wh* word is followed by the verb and then the subject:

| | |
|---|---|
| normal: | She is there. |
| question: | When is she there? |
| normal: | He was there. |
| question: | When was he there? |

## Questions with Verbs Other Than *Be*

In these questions, we use the verb *do* after the *Wh* word and then use regular word order; the verb *do* has to show the tense of the sentence, whether present or past.

| | |
|---|---|
| normal: | She thinks about you. |
| question: | Why does she think about you? |
| normal: | He bought a car. |
| question: | When did he buy a car? |
| normal: | She ate a burrito. |
| question: | Where did she eat a burrito? |
| normal: | He made his car payments. |
| question: | How did he make his car payments? |

## Questions in the Future Tense

Questions in the future tense, no matter what the verb, use the verb form *will* between the *Wh* word and the subject:

| | |
|---|---|
| normal: | She will think about you. |
| question: | Why will she think about you? |
| normal: | He will buy a car. |
| question: | When will he buy a car? |
| normal: | She will eat a burrito. |
| question: | Where will she eat a burrito? |
| normal: | He will make his car payments. |
| question: | How will he make his car payments? |

## Exercise 1

In the exercises below, change the sentence into a question beginning with the word indicated. Before you make the change, be sure to check:

a. to see whether the verb is *be* or some other word (to get you started, notice that the first three sentences use the verb *be*).
b. to see whether the tense is future or not.

EXAMPLE: Jorge is building a deck.
*What is Jorge building?*

1. Jason *was* employed.
   *Where* _____?

2. Arlene and Christine *are* going to New York.
   *When* _____?

3. Alonso *is* losing it.
   *What*_____?

4. LaRonda got a scholarship.
   *Where* _____?

5. Your friend got a lousy grade.
   *Why* _____?

6. Tina will handle it.
   *How* _____?

7. She is thinking of leaving town.
   *Why* _____?

8. She will look for a new career.
   *When* _____?

9. He will do it.
   *What*_____?

10. She wants a review of her case.
    *Why* _____?

## Exercise 2

1. Write three questions beginning with *where*, *what*, and *when* in which you use a form of the verb *be*.

   EXAMPLES: Where is my umbrella?
   What is she doing?
   When is the party going to be held?

   _____

   _____

   _____

2. Write three questions beginning with *where*, *what*, and *when* in which you use a verb other than *be*.

EXAMPLES: Where did he put the money?
What did he put it in?
When did he put it there?

_____

_____

_____

3. Write three questions beginning with *why, how,* and *what* in which you use a verb in the future tense.

EXAMPLES: Why will it rain?
How will you pay those bills?
What will we say to them?

_____

_____

_____

## Forming *Yes-No* Questions

Questions that require only *yes-no* answers work pretty much like the other questions.

If the verb is the verb *be,* it just flip-flops with the subject, just as in *Wh* questions.

She is a nurse.        He was at the game.
Is she a nurse?        Was he at the game?

If the verb is a single word, then we put a form of the verb *do* in front of the subject:

He bought a car.       She likes dim sum.
Did he buy a car?      Does she like dim sum?

If the verb has more than one word, the first word goes in front of the subject:

She should buy it.     He could have done it.
Should she buy it?     Could he have done it?
He is going home.      She will be here tomorrow.
Is he going home?      Will she be here tomorrow?

### Exercise 1

Change the following sentences into *yes-no* questions.

EXAMPLE: She played the piano.
*Did she play the piano?*

1. She was at the concert.

   _____

2. They will be at the party.

   _____

3. He liked the play.

   _____

4. They will attend the game.

   _____

5. They are in the living room.

   _____

6. We can do it.

   _____

7. They ate the whole pie.

   _____

8. We should move to another room.

   _____

9. She is married.

   _____

10. They haven't arrived yet.

   _____

### Exercise 2

1. Write three *yes-no* questions based on some form of the verb *be* (*is, are, was, were*).

   EXAMPLES: Is Peter awake?
   Are you from Canada?
   Was there any mail?

   _____

   _____

   _____

2. Write three *yes-no* questions based on any verb except the verb *be*.

EXAMPLES: Do you like my apartment?
Does he wear cologne?
Did you find the doctor's office?

_____

_____

3. Write six *yes-no* questions based on a two-part verb, a verb beginning with a word like *could, should, may, might, have,* or *will.*

EXAMPLES: Can you swim?
Should we go to the movies?
Have you seen Amy's new boyfriend?

_____

_____

_____

_____

_____

_____

## Forming Indirect Questions

In addition to direct questions, we can also ask what are called *indirect questions.* Here are two examples:

| | |
|---|---|
| Direct question: | How can I finish my homework? |
| Indirect question: | I wonder *how I can finish my homework.* |
| Direct question: | Can I finish this homework? |
| Indirect question: | I wonder *if* (or *whether*) I can finish this homework. |

You should notice three things about these indirect questions.

1. They do not end in question marks.
2. They keep their normal word order. The subject and verb do not change positions.
3. They always appear in sentences that start out *not* being questions, sentences that begin with words like these:

I wonder
I asked

Indirect questions always begin with the *Wh* words (plus *How*) and two other words, *whether* and *if*. In these questions be sure to use normal subject-verb word order following the question words.

### Exercise

Complete the following sentences.

1. I wonder whether _____
2. I wonder if_____
3. I wonder why _____
4. I wonder where_____
5. I wonder when _____

*Note:* When the first verb is in the past tense, normally the second verb following *whether* or *if* is also in the past tense:

EXAMPLE:  I *asked*

I *asked* my sister if she *wanted* some doughnuts.

6. I asked him whether _____
7. I asked him if_____
8. I asked her why _____
9. I asked her when _____
10. I asked them what_____

## Noncountable Nouns

English has many nouns that do not take plural -*s* endings. Generally, these are *mass nouns* and *abstract nouns*.

*Mass nouns* are the ones that refer to generic things, like *fish, coffee, iron,* and *coal.* Notice in the following phrases which nouns take -*s* plural endings and which ones don't:

cups of coffee
drops of water
grains of sand
pieces of silver
heads of lettuce

*Abstract nouns* include words like the following. Some of these words are very common in academic work, and so you should memorize them as words that *never* take *-s* plurals:

information
research
homework
knowledge
advice

Other common noncountable nouns are these:

| | |
|---|---|
| clothing | enjoyment |
| luggage | garbage |
| furniture | junk |
| equipment | help |
| housework | mail |

When you are in doubt about whether a noun can take a plural *-s* ending, you can check your dictionary. Plural forms are indicated if the noun has any.

## Exercise

Write sentences for each of the following noncountable nouns: *homework, research, information, equipment,* and *furniture.*

## Using Homophones

Homophones are words that sound alike but are spelled differently. For instance, if you were to say, "I threw the ball through the window," you would probably pronounce the words *threw* and *through* either exactly or almost exactly alike. Some people pronounce *are* and *our* the same way, while others pronounce *hour* and *our* the same. These are homophones.

The most commonly misused homophones among the ones covered here are *its* and *it's*. It may amuse you to know that Abraham Lincoln, possibly our greatest president, consistently wrote *it's* when he meant *its*. So it's not the worst error you can make. On the other hand, misspelling most of the other homophones is not so common, and so they are considered bad errors. Anyway, this is not exactly rocket science, so there's really no excuse for getting homophones wrong. Unless you're president of the United States.

### Its and It's

Read the following passage and underline *its* and *it's* every time you find them.

> It's time once again to take down the Christmas tree. The tree has now had its day, although some years it seems more to have had its month by the time we take it down. Of course, it's really dangerous to leave a tree up too long since its needles get dry and highly flammable. Then so many of them drop off that it's a pain to clean them up.

Which shows possession?
Which is a contraction of *it is?*

### Exercise 1

In the blanks below, write *its* or *it's:*

1. A cat will not permit anyone to do anything for _____ benefit.
2. If the cat is sick and has to have a pill, you cannot get the pill down _____ throat no matter how hard you try.
3. _____ a total pain to try to pill a cat, and the pain can sometimes be quite real when it sinks _____ claws into you.
4. I don't know why _____ so fashionable now to own a cat.
5. Maybe _____ actually the cat that owns the person, since the average cat gets _____ way more often than the person does.

### Exercise 2

Write two sentences of your own using *its* and two sentences using *it's.*

_____

_____

### *Your* and *You're*

Read the following passage and underline *your* and *you're* every time you find them.

> You're expecting to do well in your future career because you're developing your writing skills. Your professional growth will also depend on your reading skills, so you're working on them too. When your roommate finds out how smart you're becoming, she's going to want your help with her homework.

Which shows possession?
Which is a contraction of *you are*?

### Exercise 1

Write *your* or *you're* in the blanks in the following sentences:

1. _____ tendency is to work hard only when _____ under pressure.
2. _____ inclined to try to please your parents, and it would help if _____ grades were good.
3. I don't know how high _____ motivation is, but _____ talented enough to do well.
4. However, _____ going to succeed eventually.
5. And this is the story of _____ life.

### Exercise 2

Write two sentences of your own using *your* and two sentences using *you're*.

_____

_____

_____

_____

### *Whose* and *Who's*

Read the passage below and draw a line under *whose* and *who's* every time you find them.

> The problem comes up every evening: Who's going to walk the dog?
> The dog, whose name is Abercrombie and Fitch, is a creature whose

main pleasure in life is smelling the life around him. So the person who's trying to walk him gets dragged around from one tree to another. A person whose aim is to get a little exercise gets frustrated, but the one who's interested in wayside smells can have a good time.

Which shows possession?
Which is a contraction of *who is*?

## Exercise 1

In the blanks below, write *whose* or *who's*:

1. I think I know _____ woods these are.
2. I don't know _____ worse, me or him.
3. I know _____ going to be there, but I don't know _____ going to bring a guest.
4. The one _____ throwing the party isn't speaking to the one _____ house it will be at.
5. The person _____ dress you spilled the wine on is speaking to the person _____ a weightlifter.

## Exercise 2:

Write two sentences of your own using *whose* and two sentences using *who's*.

_____

_____

_____

_____

### *There* and *They're*

Review the previous three exercises.

What does *it's* mean?
What does *you're* mean?
What does *who's* mean?
What do you think *they're* means?

### Exercise 1

In the following sentences, write *there* or *they're:*

1. _____ is no one like you.
2. _____ are several people like me, and _____ all wonderful.
3. Now that _____ rich, they can afford a house.
4. Now that _____ is no one to oppose them, they should be happy.
5. I don't think _____ coming to the party.
6. _____ not really my kind of people.
7. _____ are others who are my kind of people.
8. I don't know who's _____ but _____ welcome anyway.
9. I don't like the way _____ looking at us.
10. But _____ is nothing I can do about it.

### Exercise 2

Write two sentences of your own using *they're* and two sentences using *there.*

_____

_____

_____

_____

### *There* and *Their*

Read the following passage and underline *there* and *their* every time you find them:

There are several different ways of dealing with visiting relatives who stay too long. The best way, of course, is to cut off their food. When they come to breakfast, they find nothing there for them. When their appetites tell them it's lunchtime, you tell them to find a restaurant. But there are subtler ways of getting their attention. When they turn back the bed covers at night and find a rattlesnake there, they usually pack their bags and leave.

Which is a way of introducing a thought or indicating a location?
Which shows possession?

### Exercise 1

In the blanks below, write *there* or *their:*

1.  _____ are basically two different kinds of tourists.
2.  One kind goes to a place and stays _____ for a while; they take _____ time and prolong _____ visit in order to get a real feeling for the place.
3.  Then _____ is the other kind, tourists who race through _____ visits, seeing the standard sights and moving on.
4.  They seem to spend most of _____ time taking pictures, as though only having pictures meant that they had spent some time _____.
5.  _____ is nothing wrong with this, I guess, but I think that if they put down _____ cameras and spent a little more time in places, they would enjoy _____ visits more.

### Exercise 2

Write two sentences using *there* to introduce an idea.

_____

_____

Write two sentences using *their.*

_____

_____

Write one sentence using *there* to indicate a place.

_____

### *To* and *Too*

Read the following paragraph and underline the words *to* and *too* every time you find them.

A relationship or a marriage ends when there are too many problems or the problems become too great. Couples always expect problems to arise. But sometimes one person can be too resistant to working them out, and in the worst cases, the other person can be resistant too, and then there is nothing to be done. While some couples decide to separate, others decide their relationship is too important to lose and begin to work on their problems.

Which form means *also* or *very?*

### Exercise 1

Write either *to* or *too* in the blanks in the following sentences. If the words *also* or *very* would fit, write *too*. Otherwise, write *to*.

1. There are _____ many tourists in my city in the summer.
2. When you try _____ drive across town on Sunday, the traffic is _____ heavy, and you need _____ allow half an hour's extra time, at least.
3. Sometimes I allow the extra time and take streets the tourists don't know about, _____, and I'm still late getting _____ a movie or whatever.
4. I'm happy _____ see that so many people want _____ visit this city, but tourists can be _____ stressful _____ those who live here.
5. We want _____ be good hosts, but we still have to live here _____.

### Exercise 2

Write three sentences using the word *too* to mean *very*.

_____

_____

_____

Write one sentence using the word *too* to mean *also*.

_____

## Sentence Fragments

A sentence fragment is a group of words written like a sentence—with a capital letter at the beginning and a period at the end—that isn't a sentence at all. Sometimes writers write fragments on purpose, perhaps to emphasize something without making it into a complete sentence. But most fragments are mistakes, and it's important to know how to correct them.

Most of the time, if you write a fragment, you can discover it yourself just by reading the fragment out loud. When we read sentences, our voices automatically do two things when we come to the end of the sentence: our tone drops slightly, and we pause.

If you read a fragment out loud, you will be momentarily confused because the "sentence" doesn't sound complete. Read the following short passage aloud:

I enjoyed our trip to Yosemite. The first camping trip of my life.

Which of these "sentences" is, in fact, not a sentence?

Reading aloud like this is the best test for fragments, but it isn't one you can normally do by yourself. If your instructor says you are writing too many fragments, you need to get him or her not to mark them on your paper but instead to have you read them aloud to him or her so you can find them yourself. Part of the problem is that a fragment like the one above doesn't stand out because it usually follows a sentence that it really works with, like this:

> I now have a clearer sense of the difficulty. A much better understanding of the problem.

This is actually quite good writing; the only thing wrong with it is the punctuation. Where there is a period after "difficulty" there should be a comma, and then it would be a correct sentence. Most fragments are of this kind.

If reading your sentences aloud doesn't help you find your fragments, there is another way of looking for them. It doesn't work for everyone, but it might work for you. When we start a sentence with the words "I think that . . . " we automatically put a complete sentence after the word *that:*

✱  I think that / she should do it.

So if you think you might have written a fragment but aren't sure, you can try saying "I think that" in front of your fragment or sentence. If it comes out sounding all right, it's not a fragment, but if it doesn't sound right, it probably is one. Here is an example, using two groups of words, one a sentence and the other a fragment:

> 1.  She considered changing jobs.
>     I think that she considered changing jobs.

Right or wrong?

> 2.  Deciding whether she should change jobs.
>     I think that deciding whether she should change jobs.

Right or wrong?

There is a second kind of fragment, one that is actually somewhat easier to find and correct—or not to write in the first place. This is the dependent clause fragment. Groups of words that begin with words like *which* and *whereas* and *because* aren't sentences all by themselves, although they are fine if they are a part of other sentences.

*[margin note: subordinate clause fragments]*

In English, it is impossible to start a sentence with the word *which* unless it is a question (like, "Which one of these do you want?"). It is possible to start a sentence with, say, *because* or *whereas,* but the *because* or *whereas* part must be attached to another complete sentence:

*[margin note: relative clause fragments]*

> She planned to go hiking. Whereas I decided to do something different.
> (not a sentence)
> He didn't do his homework. Because he was too tired.
> (not a sentence)
> He claimed that the weather was great, whereas it was actually raining.
> (a good sentence)
> She took the job because the pay was excellent.
> (a good sentence)

*Note:* There is nothing wrong with starting a complete sentence with a *because* clause; the following are both excellent sentences:

> Because her father was a doctor, she decided to become a doctor too.
> Because he had fallen in love, he decided to move to India.

## Exercise

Identify and correct the fragments you find in the sentences below. To find them, read them aloud. In most cases, the best way to correct the fragment is to attach it to the sentence preceding it, but in some cases, that won't work, and you'll have to rewrite the sentence.

Not every exercise below is incorrect.

*[margin note: verbal ph.]*

1. Juana went to work for a large corporation. Thinking that this would provide a secure future.

_____

*[margin note: appositives]*

2. She took her job seriously, and her boss considered her a definite asset. An employee who was really a model for the others.

_____

*[margin note: 3, 4, 7, 9 done in class]*

3. At first she was quite happy with her job. Because it paid well, and she liked her boss and her fellow employees.

_____

*[margin note: ✓/Th. class 2/27]*

*rel. clause*

4. The firm appreciated her hard work, and gave her a quick promotion. This confirmed to her that she had made a good choice in taking the job.

*verbal phrase*

5. Her boss came to rely on her more and more. Giving her additional responsibilities and praising her work.

*appos.*

6. Little by little, she began to discover that wonderful thing called office politics. A process that probably exists in every office of any size.

*rel. cl.*

7. She thought that staying out of the office politics was the best plan. Which was a good idea.

*appos.*

8. She had become friends with the manager who had broken up with the assistant manager. A nice man who had helped everyone.

*sub. cl.*

9. So she had become part of the manager's group. Even though she actually liked the assistant manager better.

*verbal phrase*

10. Now the assistant manager hated her because she was part of the manager's group, and the manager hated her because she liked the assistant manager, so she quit the job. Thinking that she would get a nice steady job as a bus driver.

## Run-Together Sentences

A run-together sentence is two sentences put together with a comma or with no comma at all. The following are run-together sentences:

Carmelo loved to cook, he considered becoming a professional cook.
Carmelo loved to cook he considered becoming a professional cook.

They are incorrect because the two sentences—*Carmelo loved to cook* and *he considered becoming a professional cook*—are not joined. The first example is the most common kind of run-together sentence, called a *comma splice*. A comma by itself cannot join sentences; a comma with a coordinator or subordinator is okay, as in this example:

Carmelo loved to cook, *so* he considered becoming a professional cook.

The *so* in the above sentence makes it correct.

The best way to find run-together sentences is to read your sentences out loud. When we read complete sentences, we stop and our tone drops slightly when we come to the end of the sentence. We tend to do this whether there's a period, a comma, or no punctuation at all, at the end of a sentence. Read your writing out loud, and check any places where you stop and your tone drops; does another sentence immediately follow?

There is another way of identifying run-together sentences if the read-aloud method doesn't work for you. This method is more time consuming, but it does work for some people. Since most run-together sentences are comma-splice errors, you simply go through your paper looking for commas. Every time you find a comma, you read aloud the words preceding the comma to see if they are a sentence. Then you read aloud the words following the comma to see if they are a sentence. If both the words before *and* the words after sound like sentences, you probably have a run-together sentence.

While reading your sentences aloud is the best way of finding run-together sentences, you probably won't be able to do this all by yourself at first. If you're having run-together sentence problems, ask your instructor not to mark the errors. Make an appointment to read your paper, or parts of it, out loud to your teacher so he or she can help you identify the places where you drop your voice and stop. It won't take long before you'll be able to do it by yourself.

When you find a run-together sentence, try first to see what the logical connection between the two sentences is. There will be one; otherwise you wouldn't have written them together. See if you can put a joining word where the comma is—a *because* or a *but* or an *although* or even just an *and*. If one of those words makes logical sense there, then use it.

But sometimes, although there is a close connection between the two sentences, there is no joining word that will work. In that case, just put a period where you have a comma and capitalize the second sentence.

So to find and fix run-together sentences:

1. Read your writing out loud.
2. Listen for pauses or drops in tone, and see if a sentence ends where you pause; *or* Look at every comma and read the words before and the words after the comma. If the words before and after the comma sound like complete sentences, you probably have a run-together sentence.
3. See if a word like *and, so,* or *because* will work to join the two sentences.
4. If no word can join the two sentences, separate them with a period.

### Exercise

Fix the run-together sentences. First try to fix them with a joining word, but if that doesn't work, separate the sentences with a period.

Remember: Run-together sentences can occur where there is a comma, but not every comma in the following sentences indicates a run-together sentence. Run-together sentences are *two complete sentences not joined or joined only with a comma*. Not every sentence below is incorrect.

1. George Washington High School became obsessed with one aspect of ecology, they decided that they had to try to save the whales.

2. It is difficult to understand how this happened since GWHS isn't near an ocean they got fixated on whales anyway.

3. The English classes wrote letters to the governments of the two countries that kill the most whales, Norway and Japan, pleading with them to stop.
   OK

4. The science classes studied the different species of whales, they learned that some of them are nearly extinct.

5. In the history classes, the students studied the history of whaling they learned that it was once a major New England industry.

6. One literature class studied Herman Melville's classic novel, *Moby Dick*, the story of a great white whale.
   OK

7. The students hated it, they thought it was the most boring book they'd ever read.

8. The social science and physical education classes organized a Save-the-Whales walk, they would get people to pledge money for each mile the students walked.

9. One of the students talked her mother into going on the walk to save the whales, her mother considered walking from the front door to her car an extreme amount of exercise.

10. By the end of the 10-mile walk, her mother was completely exhausted,\ she called it a "Kill-a-Mother-to-Save-a-Whale" march.

---

## Capitalization

English has too many rules for capitalizing words, but we seem to be stuck with them. Fortunately, most people who have to work with words or who read a reasonable amount gradually acquire these rules without thinking about them. The first four rules are probably the most common and easiest to remember.

1.  The first word of every sentence must be capitalized.
2.  People's names and initials and the names they give to animals are capitalized.

> Martin Luther King
> C.P.E. Bach
> Spot (a dog's name)

3.  Titles and abbreviated titles are capitalized.

> President Roosevelt
> Senator Jones
> Doctor Wong
> Jose Cruz, Ph.D.
> Eleanor Williams, Director of Student Services

But when title words are not used as actual titles, they are not capitalized.

> Our senator is ill.
> The doctor is out.

4.  Names of specific places with formal names are capitalized.

> Philadelphia
> Montana
> Death Valley
> Market Street

But words referring to places without naming them are not capitalized.

> We went into the city last night.
> I visited three states last summer.
> There is a beautiful valley farther north.
> The street that I live on is pleasant.

### Exercise 1 (Rules 1–4)

Copy out the following sentences putting capital letters where they belong.

1.  while visiting asia last summer, dr. and mrs. chew spent time in india, cambodia, and china.

    _____

2.  they saw the famous taj mahal and the great wall of china.

    _____

3.  they managed to see the president of india but not the premier of china.

    _____

*The next three rules are closely related to the first four.*

5.  Just as we capitalize names of countries, so we also capitalize names of nationalities and languages.

    | | | |
    |---|---|---|
    | Mexico | Mexican | Spanish |
    | China | Chinese | Chinese |
    | England | English | English |
    | Brazil | Brazilian | Portuguese |

But we don't capitalize these words when they don't refer to the language or the country:

> french fries
> dutch chocolate
> chinese checkers

6. Like the names of countries and nationalities, we also capitalize the names of religions:

| | |
|---|---|
| Catholic | Catholicism |
| Buddhist | Buddhism |
| Methodist | Methodism |
| Jewish | Judaism |
| Muslim | Islam |

7. As we capitalize places that have formal names, so do we also capitalize the formal names of organizations.

Mexican-American Legal Defense and Education Fund
Republican Party
African-American Business Students Association
General Electric

## Exercise 2 (Rules 1–7)

Copy out the following sentences using capital letters where appropriate.

1. the american civil liberties union is known for its advocacy of the separation of church and state.

2. because most american communities are predominately christian, they sometimes put up religious symbols on their civic property.

3. this is a common practice in countries such as spain or japan, where there is essentially only one religion.

4. but in the united states, where people of many religions live—jews and buddhists and confucians and many others—it is seen as unconstitutional.

8. We also capitalize the names of days, months, and holidays, but not seasons, and we capitalize all the words in the titles of books, movies,

newspapers, and so on except for little words like *a, the, of, in, and,* and so on, unless these words happen to be the first words in the titles.

Monday
April
Thanksgiving Day
*The Merchant of Venice*
*Catcher in the Rye*
*The Chicago Tribune*

# Index

# Literary Credits

American Civil Liberties Union. "Court Blocks Enforcement of West New York Curfew."

Downey, Maureen. "Feeling Pressure to Be Pretty." *Atlanta Journal and Consitution*

Frekins, Beth. "Curfews Curtail Crime." *Newhouse News Service*

Gibbs, Nancy. "Til Death Do Us Part." *Time*

Johnson, Dirk. "Schools' New Watchword: Zero Tolerance." *New York Times*

Judkins, Gillian. "Preteens Parading in Pageants." *The Gazette* (The University of Western Ontario)

Katz, Jesse. "Zero Tolerance in Schools." *Los Angeles Times Syndicate*

Mifflin, Lawrie. "Many Reasearchers Say Link Is Already Clear on Media and Youth Violence." *New York Times*

Peele, Stanton. "Making Excuses" *National Review*

Torassa, Ulysses. "Kids Less Violent After Cutting Back on TV." *San Francisco Chronicle*